Energy Healing for Beginners

50+ Techniques For Spiritual Awakening & Raising Your Vibration- Crystals, Third Eye & Kundalini Opening, Chakras, Guided Meditations & Hypnosis

Contents

Chapter 1: Universal Laws

Intro to Metaphysics

If you want to receive a firm grasp on energy healing, you will need to be familiar with the basics of metaphysics. This includes universal laws and the fundamental principles of spiritual energy. You can't have energy healing and the wisdom that accompanies without the recognition of spirit, or subtle spiritual energy. This is because attaining self-realization, or any type of knowledge about metaphysics and energy, inherently involves the awareness of a 'higher' reality and power. When one engages in energy healing, they do so with the purpose of balancing the whole self, which means achieving unity and harmony between mind, body, emotions, spirit, and soul. The physical, emotional, spiritual, and mental planes are all designed to function as a unity- as an interconnected system. Spiritual energy, universal energy, divine energy, Source energy, subtle energy, or superconsciousness; they are all different words to describe and understand the same energy. To heal is to 'make whole', and this is something you need to know. Thus, energy healing is all about balancing, harmonizing, and integrating the different aspects of your being, so that you can become the best version of yourself. Self-mastery is the ultimate goal.

Metaphysics signifies the abstraction of life and self. Everything abstract comes under the branch metaphysics, including concepts such as time, space, knowing, identity, being, and self-realization. Philosophy, in essence. The origins of creation and the universe are deemed metaphysics by many. But "meta" also translates as *transcendence*, we can transcend the perceived limitations of a 3-dimensional physical universe with the insights and philosophies of metaphysics. The key lies in the word 'perceived,' reality itself is an illusion; we are a range of thoughts, feelings, internal currents, emotions, beliefs, projections, and frequencies. "Reality" to one may be different to another. Metaphysics is intrinsic to energy healing (although not synonymous) as to heal oneself and transcend the limits of a purely physical reality, one must be prepared to look outside of it. One must 'go within to go without,' similar to the philosophy of 'as above so below.' Metaphysics is transcending the physical to reach heightened states of conscious, inner knowing and self-awareness. And a range of benefits, positive effects, and self-realizations can come about through this.

Universal Laws

This brings us onto the universal laws. The universal laws can be seen as fundamental focus points, or areas of insight and wisdom, for self-discovery and personal transformation. They're unchanging laws that are intuitively known and felt by many, regardless of race, sex/gender, sexuality, and other separating factors. "En*light*enment," to find the light within and around- awaken to the divine purpose (in a nutshell!). The amount of universal laws there actually are is debatable, but the clue seems to lie in numerology and patterns found in natural cycles. Some say there are 7, a number associated with light and spirituality, whilst others suggest 12; the number of star signs, constellations in the sky, and main meridians in the body. In this book we will be looking at all 12 universal laws, and how each applies to energy healing. Let's do this now.

1. The Law of Divine Oneness

This law is about the interconnectedness of all things. Everything is connected on some subtle level. You may call this "subtlety" the subconscious, angelic, spiritual, astral, ethereal, higher dimensional, or multidimensional plane, either way, subtle energy connects every living being on earth.

It also connects the trees and non-human entities, both on and within planet earth and extending to the cosmos. If we look at a human or animal eye, for example, it will look like the universe or specific galaxy. The microcosm is the macrocosm. Every thought, feeling, emotion, action, and sensation is connected to- well, everything else! In terms of energy healing this implies that we can look to the divinity that connects us to ourselves, other humans, the planet and all sentient creatures, and both our inner world and outer world (the universe, macrocosm), for healing and growth. Self-awareness is key.

Furthermore, if we're feeling *disconnected*, disempowered, or simply low and uninspired, reminding ourselves of the law of divine oneness will help us to *reconnect* to our true selves.

2. The Law of Vibration

Vibration rules everything, all life on earth and the universe itself. The sound of creation, for example; 'Om,' is believed to be a unique and specific frequency that formed the universe. Sound and silence, being and emptiness, form and formlessness... everything exists as a vibratory frequency. This is why the human language has created a term which sounds familiar and resonates with us- "vibes." We give off vibes just as we receive them. Thoughts, feelings, emotions, projections, and beliefs interact to create positive or negative experiences. Are we positively mirroring one another and treating everyone as a reflection? (Where growth, mutual respect and a sense of "oneness" are strong.) Or, are we *projecting* and allowing our unconscious fears and frustrations to ripple out and meet our mirrors, negatively?

On a subatomic level, there is 99.9% empty space within each atom. This means the universe is essentially formless! It's our thoughts, emotions, and intentions that shape and create reality as we know it.

3. The Law of Correspondence

This universal law states what was briefly shared above, that we're all mirrors of one another. But this doesn't just signify humans. It also relates to the way we mirror animals, plants, and the universe as a whole. Within is without, internal is external, and as above- so below. Patterns and cycles can be found in all of nature and within existence. In terms of energy healing, working with the various modes and channels for healing available will show you how life and being are cyclic. You may think you've learned a lesson, healed a pattern of thought or behavior, or transcended something contributing to your ill-health and imbalance, but then it will reshow itself in another time. The law of correspondence portrays the non-linear and cyclic nature of time.

4. The Law of Attraction

The most well-known law, the law of attraction portrays the power of our thoughts and intentions. Manifestation, abundance, our ability to attract positive experiences in harmony with our higher self- and our best lives- and everything related to positive manifestation are associated here. Focus on what you want, and you shall receive! (In short.) This is the basis. But, there needs to be a level of self-mastery and control in order to receive what your heart desires. And this is the key- heart and higher self, spirit. Is what you're seeking in alignment with your heart, the space of unconditional love, self-love, and compassion, and your higher self and mind; the part of self that is connected to cosmic consciousness, spiritual awareness and the divine?

Focusing every day on manifesting an expensive car or winning the lottery might not produce results, yet putting your energy and attention into manifesting perfect health, healing and recovery from addictions or limiting beliefs, may just change your life.

5. The Law of Inspired Action

Actionable steps and conscious action are what's needed next to the law of attraction. It's not enough to simply think and attract, you need to take the steps towards success and achievement. Life involves dualities and polar opposites, 'yin and yang,' for example; passivity and action, feminine and masculine, and receptivity and assertiveness. Together they create unity, balance, and wholeness, yet without both there would be missing ingredients to creation. The law of inspired action implies we need to slow down, be in stillness and silence, and create a space internally for manifestation. 'Go within to go without,' but when the intentions have been set and the space created, we must take action. Linked to this is the ability to surrender, surrender to the flow and abundance of the universe. Releasing control is important, as this allows for new opportunities and inspiration we may not have previously foresaw.

6. The Law of Perpetual Transmutation Energy

Evolution is constant. Everything is always evolving, shifting, and changing. Our own cells regenerate completely every 7 years while every aspect of creation goes through a perpetual and constant state of change. On an energetic level, things are transmuted all the time and some of it we don't even see. This law can help us understand the mind-body-spirit connection better. Every action is preceded by a thought and every thought has the power to create an action. If our physical health isn't up to par, our mental, emotional, and spiritual health will suffer too. If we have issues with the way we think, feel and attempt to connect to a spiritual reality our physical bodies will struggle to cope, which results in ill-health. Everything is interconnected and energy healers and practitioners recognize this, hence why they attempt to heal on the subtle and energetic (ethereal, astral, and spiritual) planes of being as well.

7. The Law of Cause and Effect

Every action has a consequence, quite simply. Karma is linked here. *What goes around comes around...* We often hold onto things that we are completely unconscious of. Some examples of how this manifests in the healing journey is not realizing, not being conscious of the fact, how past actions and beliefs still affect us on an energetic level. Perhaps you were once in a position of power and misused that power? At a later stage in life, someone treats you in a less than favorable way and you feel disempowered, yet you ponder why this experience is happening. The event causes stress and anxiety, mild depression and potentially even health issues like insomnia or weight loss or gain, but you still can't put your finger on why this is happening. 'I don't deserve this.' 'I'm a kind and genuine person.' 'I've already healed my karma!'

A lesson may present itself 6 months, 4 years, or 12 years down the line- time doesn't matter to karmic laws and the law of cause and effect. *Every action* has a ripple. Interconnectedness links here once more. Also, on an internal level this law relates to the feelings and emotions you experience, such as the vibration and frequency of anger or resentment. Feeling jealousy, rage or resentment at someone's successes or wins (someone who hasn't caused any harm to you!) ultimately manifests as you attracting that experience, and further closing yourself off to the same level of fame, prestige, abundance, or accomplishment. Treat others how you wish to be treated, in short. What you put or project out may not come back to you in the moment or instantly, but it will come back.

8. The Law of Compensation

At this stage, it's important to know that all the universal laws are tied in closely to one another. We can see similarities and links or bridges between many of the individual laws. This one corresponds with the laws of attraction and correspondence. *You reap what you sow*!

9. The Law of Relativity

Comparison is actually a man-made concept. In reality, the true reality of divine oneness, everything is neutral. Things exist with its polarity and opposite, yet the ultimate goal is always unity and harmony. Yang and yin, light and dark, masculine and feminine, good and bad/evil, shine and shadow, win and lose... there is a lesson and teaching in everything and a chance for unity. Relativity comes down to our perspective and perception- how we choose to perceive things and interact with our physical world. When we compare without specific intentions (such as to help us evolve or provide a framework for learning and transformation, self-betterment etc.) we create a polarity and divide within, we create the reality of lack, loss, or disappointment- never having enough or being content, or seeing the lesson and blessing in the situation. It disempowers us so we can't take control of our own lives, further leading to the disconnection from self. If you are always comparing yourself to others how are you able to connect to the law of divine oneness, vibration, or attraction?

10. The Law of Polarity

This has already been covered. (Yin and yang etc.)

11. The Law of Rhythm

Cycles and natural patterns found within our bodies, within the planet, and within the universe. Seasons are an example of this law and women have moon cycles, aka periods. Emotions and inner currents come under the law of rhythm. How we feel on a daily and cyclic basis, how we honor our emotions and need for rest, work and play; basically, balance on all levels. The earth has cycles too and everything that occurs on the microcosm can be reflected in the macrocosm, and vice versa. Music and sound are healing, so this is something you can incorporate in correspondence with this law.

12. The Law of Gender

Finally, gender is referring to the masculine and feminine energy within everything, man and woman, the universe, subtle energy etc. Being a man or woman has nothing to do with masculine and feminine energy, although it is true that men are primarily masculine in nature and women are more feminine. In the 21st Century, we've seen a rise in people identify as non-binary, transgender, or actually having sex changes. Some people say it's society and all the confusion and mixed messages coming from a consumerist global economy and society. Others may suggest a more natural and evolution-compatible theory. In truth, both are true or at least have the potential to be true, and this is a paradox in itself. Duality and polarity run through all of life!

> **"If you want to find the secrets of the universe, think in terms of energy, frequency and vibration."**
>
> ~Nikola Tesla

Vibration & Frequency

So, hopefully you already have a basic understanding on how energy healing works based on the 12 Universal Laws. *Everything* exists as vibration and frequency. Familiarizing yourself with the Universal Laws is a great way to start your journey to healing and wholeness.

The etheric and astral bodies

Energy healing involves working with your ethereal (etheric) and astral bodies. The etheric body is also known as the ether. It is an energetic replica or blueprint of the physical body and lies just above the physical body, a couple of inches extending outwards. It is in your etheric body where all illness and disease are said to arise. This is because it is through the ether where you are connected to your spiritual and astral bodies, and it is here, in the spiritual and subtle planes of existence, where distortion and imbalance arise. Your etheric body connects your physical body to the astral body and subsequently spiritual realm through a cord. Energy healing works primarily through the ether, your etheric body. Although subtle energy healing can be given as a "hands-on" treatment whereby the practitioner or master physically places their hands on the body, a lot of energy blockages are removed by working on the etheric plane. With regards to your astral body, the astral plane is closely linked to your subconscious and it is here where all of your thoughts, feelings, emotions, and beliefs originate and arise. The astral body can be seen as the gateway to the spiritual body, spiritual dimensions, subtle-energetic realms of being, and the etheric body closest to physical being. People who can sense things above and beyond the five physical senses, including those who are psychic and clairvoyant, are very connected to their astral body and the astral planes. Energy healing stimulates this connection and can make one more open to receiving wisdom, insight, and guidance through the astral and spiritual planes.

The best and most simple way to visually present this is through the following diagram.

Physical body: This is the very physical and tangible body you reside in. It is responsible for holding all sensory data and information and interacting with your *emotional and mental bodies*. During meditation, chi stimulates this process as does healing energy. Your physical body is essentially a transmitter and receiver of all information coming in from the mental, emotional, astral, and spiritual planes.

Etheric body: Your etheric body is located just above and beyond your physical body and creates a cord between the physical and the astral. This body can be seen as an energetic blueprint for the physical, it is a subtle replica. It transmits data and sensory info including information about your health and the vibratory state of health of each of your subtle bodies. If you are suffering with physical ailments, healing can be given to your etheric body and the effects ripple downwards (into your physical).

⇓

Astral body: This body is the plane to the subconscious and spiritual aspects and dimensions of being. Key insights into your beliefs, feelings and emotions, thoughts and deepest desires are transmitted through your astral body. It is also the plane and body where astral travel and astral projection are possible. Your astral body is a gateway to higher consciousness, spirit or the divine, and your spiritual body.

⇓

Spiritual body: This is a direct link to soul, the great spirit, the divine, higher or cosmic *(and the* consciousness, and the angelic & light realms. Everything "above and beyond" ***Spiritual*** our 3-dimensional human reality can be experienced and accessed here. It is a ***planes...)*** bridge between the human and the divine.

We can look at healing systems like *Reiki* to understand energy healing deeper. We dedicate a section to this later, but for now, Dr Mikau Usui received his healing gifts from spirit. He meditated and fasted to a point of transcendental awareness and evolved, heightened consciousness. Dr Mikau Usui spent 21 days on a mountain attempting to receive enlightenment, and his experience not only shows the power of subtle and spiritual energy but also *how* we can access it. Meditation and fasting are two powerful routes to cleansing and purification, purification of mind, body & spirit. His physical body and therefore mind were open to the subtle and energetic forces of the universe, so he became an open channel. Quite simply, his physical being was *lighter*- he was able to hold and embody more light.

This is very important when learning about the etheric and astral planes and bodies. As mind, body, emotions, and spirit are all intrinsically connected, cleansing your physical body and engaging in acts of purification also cleanses and purifies your mental body, emotional body, and spiritual body. A fast or detox can lighten you and connect you (naturally) to the more subtle expressions of being. And it is here where all psychic and spiritual phenomena and the ability to perceive subtle energy arises. It may sound like the simplest and most child-like analogy, but simply picture a feather next to a stone. Of course, the feather will rise and be lifted more easily with a mildly forceful gush of wind. Nature's breeze will allow the feather to float and even move around, whilst the stone will remain still and stuck. Natural energy can be seen as nature's breeze!

The Higher Self ('Higher Mind')

The higher self or higher mind is the *divine spark* within us. It is connected in a high energy vibrational form- or a higher vibration- connected to and in tune with the universe, God, Spirit, or Source; the source of the universe. Through our own spiritual development, we can raise our vibrations to access a higher state of consciousness, bringing us closer to Source (the divine Spirit) and dissolving resistance to the flow of the Universal Laws. The Higher Self is sometimes called the Higher Mind and is opposite to the Lower Self and Mind. The most effective way to understand the Higher Self is through the table below.

Higher Self/ Mind	Lower Self/ Mind
Enhanced cognition, original and imaginative thought, logical and intellectual thinking.	Primarily concerned with the ego aspect of the psyche- thoughts rooted in serving the "self" (emotions/ desires/ needs etc.).
Intuitive thought and advanced/evolved intuition.	Instinct and instinctual responses.

Empathy, compassion, and higher/spiritual awareness.	Lack of empathy and compassion due to focusing on the self/ego.
Connection to the divine, cosmic or god consciousness, Spirit and source energy.	"Shadow" or dark/negative aspects of self and being. *The Shadow Self.*
Transcended and evolved emotions and inner currents. Primal needs and wants replaced with higher thought forms and values.	Animalistic desires, primality and unconscious urges/physical and survival-based needs.

The Shadow Self is the part of human nature often considered as impure, dark, or undesirable. It is the things we repress, deny, or choose to prefer not to accept. Sexuality and lust usually come under the Shadow Self's domain, as do fame, power, wealth, and success (when abused and out of balance). Yet, the Shadow Self is a route to higher consciousness and the ability to *know thyself.* We are holistic, *multi-dimensional*, and primal beings, we are not just beings of light floating around on the astral or spiritual planes. We have basic needs, survival instincts, desires and a human body. We also have an ego and a psyche.

In this respect, accepting and integrating elements of your Shadow Self can lead to the things you may originally think can only be attained by suppressing the Shadow, and focusing solely on the light. Just like yin and yang, one of the fundamental Universal Laws, we are governed by both day and night, sunshine and the moon's rays, and light and dark. Something may be seen as dark due to its feminine or yin- like nature, but it doesn't mean it is 'bad.' The same is true for the ego, the ego is essential as we wouldn't get anything done without it driving our everyday human existence. It just needs to be *balanced*. Another key point regarding the Higher Self and Universal Laws is the significance of resistance. If one thinks too hard about whether this action or that is going to create abundance in our lives, we may create resistance which actually hinders the flow of abundance. It is like a universal paradox which, again, is deeply connected to the energies of yin and yang- the power of yin being a receptive and feminine quality/force which *magnetizes* things to you. There is a wise saying, "*what we resist persists*," this implies that there is an element of surrendering to the process needed in all manifesting and spiritual intentions, including healing.

Furthermore, God/the universe/Source created us with free will, so we are free to make life choices and learn valuable life lessons in each incarnation on Earth. These choices may, in reality, make it harder or easier to slip into the effortless flow of abundance, but the key is to attune to and align with the *Higher Self* as best as possible. This way, we act, think, feel, and perceive from a space of spiritual awareness, divine guidance and intuition; logic, reason, and rationality; imaginative and creative thought, empathy, compassion, and morality. Also, being in tune with our higher selves allows us to transcend and evolve past any limiting beliefs, excessive primal desires and urges, and unhealthy or afflictive emotions (which come with a disconnection from the higher mind) and further raise our vibration. Finally, when a soul self chooses a body, it makes a conscious choice to experience life on earth with specific parents, family, and other members of a soul group. An individual soul agrees to experience certain life events in order to learn and develop spiritually, thus becoming closer to God/Spirit/Source. This can only occur when we are in tune with the Higher Self and Mind.

The Higher Self and the Soul

When this vast planetary exploration began, souls coming to Earth knew they were connected to

Source. However, as lifetime after lifetime progressed, souls' vibrations lowered, and they became removed from their connection to Source. It became harder to retain and recall the connection with each re-incarnation and eventually souls forgot their connection soon after the point of incarnation. A new-born baby, for example, may sometimes appear to have a "wise" face, and look older than his or her years. This is because at the point of birth a new-born infant is closer to Source, therefore retains trace memories or echoes of a previous life. Essentially, the soul has just been existing and experiencing life on another plane, and most likely directly on or very close to the angelic, ascended masters or light deities/beings' planes. This is where the higher self is most strong- the higher self acts as a bridge to advanced and evolved portals of consciousness.

As souls experiencing life on Earth forgot their connection to Source, we felt isolated and fearful. Energy healing can restore that connection so that we can again feel supported and secure in the knowledge that we are not alone. Learning to connect with both our higher selves and shadow selves is one step towards wholeness and overcoming blocks or fears.

The Power of the Mind

A common misinterpretation of the Law of Attraction and other universal laws, including how to utilize the Higher Self and all the magic it brings, is that we can simply *think* ourselves into perfect health, abundance, or success. Thinking alone is not enough, and neither is wishing (faith/hope). We need to both set our intentions and create the space, and then surrender and be receptive. Yin and yang are both necessary- feminine energy of surrender and receptivity, magnetism and passivity and masculine energy of action. In saying this, the mind is powerful, and this shouldn't go overlooked. There are yogis, self-mastered beings, and spiritual gurus or experts who can use their minds for instant manifestation. This is due to them operating (vibrating) at a much higher frequency, through years of self-development and healing, wisdom acquisition and self-mastery. Their consciousness is advanced; therefore, manifestation occurs at a rapid rate compared to non-evolved or self-mastered humans. They are closer to Source and Spirit, and one specific gift of this is the power of healing. Healing hands and healing presence, being able to heal themselves (and others) because life force energy flows through their hands and bodies effortlessly, strongly, and powerfully.

In other words, they have done the 'inner work' and their minds are attuned to a divine and higher reality, where spiritual healing energy is strong and frequent. They're gifted with the power of thought. They're also at one with the universal energies within around. How does this relate to the mind and the higher self? *Everything* stems back to the mind and higher self; they are the source of consciousness and the root of creation. We can see the truth in this when we look at how much suffering and discord arises when we're disconnected from the higher self.

Energy Healing with the Higher Self and Shadow Self

An intrinsic part to energy healing, working with subtle energy, and getting in tune with all of your bodies; your emotions, mind, body, and spirit, is to reach a state of inner acceptance. Your shadow self is equally as important to embrace and heal as your higher self. As we explore in the next chapter, kundalini energy is the balance and harmony of all of the 7 main chakras, and the chakras need to have a free flow of energy, be unblocked and balanced and be 'healthy' for both the lower self and higher self. If there are blocks in your lower chakras there will be issues with your sexuality, creativity, and emotions. All aspects of sensuality and primality will be negatively affected. When there are blocks and problems in your higher chakras, you are less able to connect to your higher self and mind. When there is a free flow of energy through the chakra system, however, your kundalini is activated and awake, which leads to spiritual enlightenment, healing, and inner balance. One is more able to access their higher self and feel comfortable within their shadow self with an open kundalini. (More on kundalini and chakras soon!)

The shadow self is also called one's shadow personality, it is the personality traits that are seen as dark, impure, or even dirty- undesirable, and something that should be repressed. Repression and suppression of desires, emotions, feelings, and basic human needs often come under the shadow self. This usually happens when one awakens to their spiritual self, so on a path of spiritual awakening or illumination. The opposite is of course true for most of us- with all of the illusions and conditionings within society we often stay disconnected from the higher self and mind. Society and the constant distractions aim to keep us in a state of separation. We actually go into detail about the various ways to connect with your higher self and *third eye* in *'Third Eye Awakening.'* But, for now, let's look at the most significant factors keeping us separated from our higher selves and how we can overcome them.

Higher Self disconnection, and how to overcome it

1. Processed and artificial foods

Processed and artificial foods keep us stuck in a state of "heaviness," taking away from our lightness. Divine light, spiritual illumination and being able to see clearly come with embodying more light, and therefore eat less dense and heavy foods. Artificial chemicals, preservatives, additives, and sweeteners are another major contributing factor to disconnection from the higher self and mind. They prevent us from accessing our full potential and self-awareness from the effect they have on the brain, body, and emotional body. It is true that the best diet is a mainly plant-based and organic diet-wholefoods, like nuts, seeds, fruits, vegetables, beans and pulses, legumes, brown rice, and wholewheat breads and pastas. Also, lean white meats, fish, and seafood over red meat and fatty bacon.

Food choices are the number 1 thing that can connect or disconnect us from our higher selves. Diet influences everything, internally from the way we think and feel, to the way we project our inner mood and vibration externally onto others and into our relationships, career, and ability to manifest prosperity or success. The body is a holistic system and there are unfortunately so many artificial, chemical and preservative laden, and dense, fatty or sugar-ridden foods with little to no nutritional value. The higher mind needs to be an open channel. It needs to be pure and clean, clear with a healthy flow of chi (life force), and with its chakras and kundalini open or at least open to health and healing. Certain foods calcify and pollute our pineal glands, the pineal gland being a very important gland responsible for hormone regulation and the ability to connect to the third eye chakra; the seat of vision and awareness. If you want to make the necessary changes transition to a plant-based vegan or vegetarian diet. The other option is the Mediterranean diet for non-vegetarians. Follow these two options strictly and you will notice how much lighter you feel, thus enabling you to heal yourself and embody more light and spiritual awareness.

2. Calcified pineal gland

Linked to diet is the calcification of the pineal gland. The pineal gland is literally shaped as a pinecone and it's responsible for the reception and transmission of light. Without light energy, aka 'life force energy' (remember the power of Sun-gazing, reduced technological interference, and natural sunlight for sleep which leads to melatonin production) we suffer in many ways- some of it more obvious and some less seen. The below the surface, unseen elements of a calcified pineal gland can lead to depression, mood swings, irrational thinking, chaotic emotions, spiritual disconnection, insomnia, a lack of melatonin, being uninspired creatively and imaginatively, and anxiety. These of course all manifest on the surface. The best way to decalcify (purify & cleanse) your pineal gland is through the diet tips shared above, and by getting regular exercise and sunlight. Sungazing is a powerful method too while engaging in psychic and intuition development exercises strengthen your third eye chakra, which in turn heals your pineal gland.

3. Too much television and technological interference

Technological evolution is inevitable in this new age. It is man's nature to seek ways to 'better' ourselves and develop in the fields of intellect, technology, and science. Yet this simultaneously has some arguably catastrophic effects on our consciousness. Blue light is emitted from devices like smartphones, laptops and iPads. Blue light is *incredibly* harmful for our eyes and retinas. But blue light isn't all we have to be worried about, technology and Wi-Fi in general produce powerful *electromagnetic waves*. If you're familiar with kirlian photography, the double-slit experiment, Dr Emoto's water studies, and metaphysics and subtle energy in general you will know that electromagnetic interference- when exposed to it frequently and over long periods of time- causes ill-health. Disruptions, imbalances, and distortions on the mental, emotional, physical, spiritual, and astral planes are very common. And a lot of what occurs is unconscious or unseen, i.e. we don't realize it's happening!

In short, electromagnetic interference is detrimental to our health when exposed continuously. Because we're surrounded by technological and WIFI signals, phones and mobiles everywhere, iPads and laptops, computers, and now the more recent incorporation of 5G into our societies, we really need to be mindful of protecting ourselves. Blue light blocking glasses are the ideal way to protect your eyes from blue light. You should also make a conscious habit of turning off all electronic devices one hour before bed, *unless* you go to sleep listening to meditation music or binaural beat sounds (which is healing!), in which case try to put your device a couple of meters away from you. Have you heard of orgonite? Orgonite comes in necklaces and pendants and individual pieces for your room, home-office or study. Orgonite is an amazing help to combat electromagnetic interference, so it's for protective purposes. It is made up of a variety of metal shavings, quartz crystals, and other crystals and gemstones.

4. Excessive focus on materialistic desires

If you want to stay disconnected from your higher self, keep on buying excess things. Overly materialistic people tend to be disconnected from spirit, intuition, and their higher selves. This is self-explanatory; when we tell ourselves we 'need' this and that, we are closing ourselves off to other thoughts and levels of consciousness. Our mind and brain are a conduit for consciousness, consciousness is the stories we tell ourselves. Channels require energy to flow through them and we humans are channels too. What we feed ourselves in terms of mindsets, beliefs, thought patterns, and emotional responses and desires becomes our reality, but it also shapes our futures. In other words, too much focus on materialism ultimately disallows the room and space for other 'stories,' other frequencies of thought, being, and self-expression. Spirit VS material reality, Divine VS the physical world, and Subtle energy VS matter; these themes have always been a part of our human timeline providing opportunities for growth, learning and balance.

The key is to meditate and go within. Discover what you truly need and what is coming from a place of fear, anxiety, poverty consciousness (lack, always feeling like you need more), codependency, or unhappiness.

5. Disconnection from spirit, dreams, and soul

Being cut off from your dreams says a lot about one's current state of spiritual insight and enlightenment. Dreams are closely connected to the subconscious mind, this is tied into the shadow self; emotions, sexuality, primal and survival needs, karmic exchanges/interplays of energy, and past wounds and trauma. You are aware life involves light and darkness, divinity/shine and shadow. Well, dreams offer direct insight and beneficial guidance into our shadow selves and emotions. There is often a problem with the pineal gland and third eye in those of us who can't dream, or aren't interested in dreaming and learning from our subconscious minds at all. To dream is to evolve, transcend, and transform. The conscious mind and daylight is only one aspect of life and being- of our true selves. What of the subconscious mind and moonlight, nighttime? Surely this is an essential half of the whole story? True.

If you want to start connecting to your intuitive powers, spiritual gifts, and higher self you should really pay attention to your dreams. They act as a portal into higher states of consciousness and self-development. It is not just about paying attention to your dreams though, as dream recall, enhancement and development techniques should all be engaged with. For dream memory and recall, place a lapis lazuli, amethyst or clear quartz crystal under or on top of your pillow at night. Make sure it is cleansed first (water) and charged (sunlight). To access your dreams for healing, insight, and wisdom, you can meditate with a charged crystal and *program it with your intentions*. This involves placing the gemstone in your left hand with your palm flat, and then placing your right hand over the top a few inches away. Close your eyes, take a few moments to feel an energy current or pull between both palm chakras (yes, your palms have chakras too!) and project intentions of subconscious connection and healing into the crystal. Your left palm receives universal healing energy and life force whilst your right hand gives it. Thus, with an open mind and strong intention, healing energy flows through your 'giving' hand and palm chakra (right) and through/out of your 'receiving' one (left).

Shadow Self disconnection or repression, and how to overcome it

1. Past life memories

Past life memories often hold the key to many unconscious forces and influences. Time is not linear, it is multidimensional and out of body experiences, astral projection, near death experiences, and a variety of supernatural and spiritual-religious encounters provide evidence for this. People who are very in tune with their higher chakras, the third eye and crown chakras, are connected to their soul and the over-soul. There is also something known as the Akashic Records- a multidimensional 'library' existing on the etheric and higher planes (dimensions of consciousness). Past life memories and insights are available when we connect to these higher portals. Luckily, these once "out-there" concepts and beliefs have now become integrated into our material world. Past life therapy is a legitimate practice and service available in most countries, and Past life therapy practitioners have been trained through spiritual and esoteric knowledge passed down through first-hand experiences and wisdom integrated. So, you can always visit a past-life therapist for assistance.

But if you want to go on your own self-healing journey and incorporate techniques for memory access in your own self, there are ways to do so. *Fasting and detoxing* cleanses your system so you are better able to channel and embody more light. We're all channels. This opens you up to subtle energy, spiritual energy, and the ability to tune into the higher planes and dimensions. *Crystals* help to activate your consciousness and higher self and *meditation and sound therapy* enable your subconscious mind to become activated, further opening you up to a range of possibilities. You could also try herbs like Ginkgo Biloba, the oldest plant known to mankind also referred to as the 'Memory tree.' This comes in both supplement form and tincture to add to water or healthy smoothies. Overall, there are many ways to tune into the superconsciousness where glimpses into your past life self are attainable. The best way to see consciousness is by looking at an iceberg in the middle of the sea. Above the ocean where you can still see the sun and sky is your 'conscious mind.' Just where the iceberg merges with the water below is your subconscious mind,' and below this in the dark murky waters is your 'unconscious mind.' They are all connected, the iceberg itself acting as a bridge between unconsciousness down below in the darkness (where the light doesn't reach), the subconscious mind in the middle, and consciousness/the conscious light up above.

The point with this analogy is to show that there are many links available connecting you to past life memories. Consciousness is confusing yet very simple. In short, it takes a purified and cleansed channel (mind, body & spirit) to access such states of awareness and perception. Unconsciousness is where experiences relating to yourself are hidden and out of sight, yet they are equally real and true. Just because you don't see them or don't have access to them in daily life, like we do beliefs, thoughts, and emotions, doesn't mean they don't exist. The unconscious mind holds memories that lead to repression of the shadow self, collective and individual, which is accessible through the *subconscious mind*. The universe has blessed us with the ability to dream and get in touch with our psychic, clairvoyant, and extrasensory gifts, if we should so choose; the subconscious mind is the bridge between the unconscious and conscious. Therefore, we need to bring the unconscious to *conscious light* through healing, meditation and self-development, including spiritual healing, to be truly aware of shadow forces and feelings. The shadow self prefers to remain repressed, rejected and denied-until we have evolved and matured. Understanding yourself through journaling, soul-searching and introspection, therapies and spiritual awakening are sure ways to help you connect to your shadow traits, in a healthy and harmonious way.

It's important not to be overruled by your shadow. For example, out of control desires, primal urges and negative attributes such as jealousy, resentment, anger, violence, and vindictiveness. 'Shadow work integration' is accepting and having compassion for the "darker" attributes intrinsic to mankind, but integrating them with balance and self-control. It comes back to self-mastery, which is mastering your mind, emotions, spirit, and physical self, so that you can live your life in a state of health, balance, inner harmony, and wholeness.

2. Painful sexual memories and experiences

Sexual memories and experiences often come into this. Unfortunately, mainstream education doesn't teach *sensuality* in its prime and best expression. We don't learn about Shakti dance, kundalini yoga or the Goddess archetype and how to embody them in school. We aren't taught Reiki, meditation, or chakra healing; how to get in tune with our divine feminine or divine masculine, and live life with spiritual illumination and insight. An integral and massive part of being is omitted altogether. The absence of sensuality, a true embodiment of Venus energy, and also tantric practices and philosophy is very significant in our sexual encounters growing up and stepping into adulthood. I know this concept may seem quite idealistic, progressive, or bizarre, but as someone who is a part of a consciously loving, spiritual, and earth-respecting community, I see how powerful and prominent tantric ways are. Sex has become about power, lust, domination, and purely physical pleasure. Instead of making-love and exploring our sexualities in an empowering and healing way, one where we then take what we've learned from our experiences and put it into conscious and loving relationships with compassion, spiritual awareness, cooperation, and unity consciousness as our mantra- kindness and a real sense of community and oneness; we use sex as a way to receive genitalia pleasure. Quite simply, a disconnection from sensuality leads to all sorts of blocks and imbalances in sexuality.

Let's look at Venus, the planet of love, romance, beauty, sensuality, and sexuality. Many people only know Venus as the planet of 'love and sex,' but there is so much more to Venus' energy. Also, before looking at Venus let's not forget how prominent Mars has become in society. Mars is Venus' counterpart, her duality, in short. Mars represents action, willpower, force, and aggression. He symbolizes the 'lust' side of love and sex, and competition, war, violence, and aggression. But Venus is an embodiment of beauty, sensuality, romance and pleasure, pleasure in a harmonious and self-serving/loving way. Why have we taken Mars' attributes and made them so prominent in society? There's no other way to put it, but sex sells. The powers that be- governments and corporations, learned long ago that the mind and consciousness are the root of all creation, everything we see in the physical and material world is a result of our desires, thoughts, feelings, and needs. So, they sought to suppress our consciousness and true potential and control it. This isn't a conspiracy, all you have to do is look at the constant advertisements selling sex, excess things, and materialistic desires; greed, want, and need are seen as acceptable, and destroying our planet and environment (not to mention some of the horrific acts committed to animals and other humans), is more acceptable than practices such as tantra. Society is twisted, we've got our values wrong.

Back to painful past sexual memories, the only reason we have so many is due to the endless distractions and misdirection of society; a 'global economy' and consumerist society. Education isn't balanced, we aren't provided a framework for learning and growing based on Venus qualities. (Are we?) Sure, there are *some* aspects of compassion and universal love, we do have the option of Religious Education and Animal Rights, Environmentalism, and Humanitarian elements introduced into a few subjects; but, overall, we live in a very masculine and competition-based society. These are the characteristics of *Mars*, the planet of war, aggression, and lust.

Venus is feminine, nurturing, sensitive, and a lover of natural beauty and pleasure in a sensual way. Sexuality with Venus is the opposite of sexuality with Mars. Sex with Mars would involve very primal acts of passion, lust, and submission or domination. There may be actual physical violence and abuse, submitting someone against their will through physical force or emotional and mental abuse, or in less severe cases, extreme sub-dom interplays that leave one partner feeling traumatized on some level (even if they're not conscious of it in the moment). Sex with Venus, on the other hand, would include rose petals laid out on a bed, romance, sweet, and sensual caresses, and eye-gazing. Two partners and lovers come together in love, harmony, and fusion;

there is an emotional and spiritual bond, and sex is a way to achieve union and *connection*. The result of the sexual union is deep feelings of love, intimacy, warmth, and protection, as if they have found a friend and soulmate with the person they've shared sexual energy with. Hopefully you see the difference!

And this has some profound implications for the future experiences and relationships we create. We are programmed to reach adulthood with so many painful and confusing sexual experiences and emotions ingrained. It is a sad truth. It can take years to heal sexual wounds and unconscious attitudes and behaviors towards intimacy and sex, and some people never heal them. Just one small act of repression of our emotions (based on our feelings towards a sexual encounter or experience) can lead to so many problems in relationships, both romantic and platonic. And many people have much more than one. We repress, deny, and reject our feelings and thoughts, because they seem 'ugly' or 'dark,' undesirable, and impure. Yet, healing is seldom pretty, we need to embrace the darkness- our shadow self and personality- in order to heal and let go of the painful wounds and memories. It is a deep shame that tantra, tribal, and community values rooted in spirituality and conscious relationships, and more Venus-inclined approaches towards intimacy and sex aren't taught as essential to Western society, but things are looking up. The emergence of Conscious festivals and gatherings has risen, and Tantric philosophy is becoming more and more accessible. For any astrology lovers, the December 2020 Solstice saw the mark of a transition into the New Age of Aquarius. The planets are aligning in our favor! Venus and Mars have switched roles- people are recognizing the importance of community, coming together as one global family, and placing a supreme importance on caring for others, animals, and our planet. Humanitarian issues and themes are stronger than ever before and there is a significant rise in protests and peace rallies advocating human rights and social justice. The world is 'waking up!' Unity consciousness and altruism, empathy, and compassion are the main themes of this New Age, which is rooted in real planetary cycles and alignments; nothing 'woo' or make-believe. The stars are aligning.

3. Inability to express your Sensuality and a Disconnection from the Divine Feminine

The stars *are* aligning, and this brings a new set of values. Although the shadow self isn't solely feminine per se, issues with coming to terms with your shadow self stem from a disconnection from the divine feminine. The shadow self is linked to the Moon, lunar yin energy, and the subconscious, which are all feminine in nature. Continuing on from the last area of exploration (*painful sexual memories and experiences*), sensuality and sexuality are intrinsically linked. The shadow is darkness and the moon is dark in nature. It is also feminine while the Sun is 'lightness' and masculine. This means we can look to the energy of the Moon and *yin energy* for healing and wholeness. Sensual dance, Shakti dance, working with Venus' energy, and writing, drawing, journaling, and expressing yourself through art and poetry are all ideal ways to heal the divine feminine and your sensual self. This has nothing to do with being a woman, men can benefit from these activities too. In fact, a huge part in the global imbalance and suppression of both the shadow self and Venus energy and attributes is due to the imbalance in values. Men (men and women, but traditionally speaking this applies mainly to men) have chosen to connect more the competitive, action-oriented, and business-minded side of life and self. Anger and aggression have taken over and healing has gone overlooked. Spirituality is virtually non-existent on a practical and physical level, in Western society and its structures.

I intuit that if men were to become more feminine, nurturing, caring, and sensitive we would see a lot of the imbalances and injustices (to the divine feminine, women, the planet- aka 'Mother Earth') reduced, if not eradicated. It all starts with the self

41

and healing your relationship with sensuality and your own divine feminine nature is the first step to doing it. Sungazing helps to connect you to life force, willpower, and vitality- high energy levels and self-confidence and empowerment. So, *moon-gazing* connects you to subconscious wisdom, intuition, and subtle-spiritual energy within; care, empathy, nurturing, and gentleness. Poetry, music, art, and dance should be daily self-care essentials too.

Chapter 2: Core healing methods and principles

Chakras

Chakras have been covered quite a lot during our series. They are important for self-healing and achieving wholeness inside, and of course for a happy, prosperous, joyous, and abundantly blissful life! Let's cover the 7 main chakras. At the end of each there is a range of corresponding healing techniques (colors, crystals etc.) you can use to heal, unblock, and increase energy flow to the chakra. In Sanskrit, Chakra literally translates as 'energy portal,' it is the energetic replica of a physical organ or body part. Ill-health and imbalance in the chakras result in a number of possible physical ailments, and mental, emotional, and spiritual blocks.

Root Chakra

The Root chakra is also known as the Muladhara chakra. This is your center of security, roots, and physical foundations, the level of comfort and protection you feel in the world. It is representative of grounding both to your physical body and the world around. A strong and healthy root chakra means you feel protected and safe in your divine physicality, there is an absence of fear and insecurity and you generally have a strong sense of self. Sexual vitality is good and libido is healthy. A weak or imbalanced root chakra leads to the opposite. You feel disconnected from the physical and material world and there may be issues in your bodily self-image, weight, or physical health, including your mindset and emotions to your physical health. The root chakra is life force, in essence.

Colors associated are red (primary), and brown and black (secondary). Red relates to passion and the spirit of life, while being stimulating and aiding in procreative functions. Brown brings an earthy quality and element, and black is associated with the shadow self. The root chakra is symbolic of the reproductive organs and genitalia on a physical level. Each of the colors can be worked with to heal yourself. 'Muladhara chakra' in Sanskrit, the first chakra is the foundation where kundalini energy, or shakti, arises. Kundalini energy is also known as serpent power and relates to sexuality, vitality, longevity of health, and psychic abilities. physically, the root chakra is located just below the genitalia and any blockages here can lead to problems in energy flow up the spine through the other chakras.

Sacral Chakra

The sacral chakra is also known as the Swadhisthana and corresponds with your emotions, sexuality, and creativity. In many Taoist, Hindu, and tantric philosophies, the three are known to be linked. If there are issues in one the others will be affected, so the Sacral is very important. Emotional intimacy, the ability to form and maintain interpersonal relationships, and all aspects of sexuality and sensual self-expression come under this chakra. Creativity is deeply associated with sexual freedom and health as well, meaning that a weak or blocked sacral will lead to blockages in artistic and creative expression. Emotional intelligence, vulnerability, and wisdom tend to be strong in those with a healthy sacral chakra. Also, joy and the expression of pleasure and joy are strongly tied into the sacral. The ability to engage in playfulness and creativity without fear of being judged is symbolic of a strong and healthy sacral.

Orange is the color typically associated with this chakra. You can work with orange if you need to heal your emotions or relationships of any kind. Orange is warming, stimulating, soothing, and balancing- it encourages friendliness and openness to others and to yourself. Orange helps to stimulate positive physical contact, romance, platonic intimacy, sexual play, and loving energy. If you are timid, shy, or fearful or deal with frequent insecurities, orange will open pathways to self-acceptance and warmth. The sacral is further linked to the shadow self, mainly due to the shadow being emotional in nature. Issues in your shadow self or shadow aspects and traits can often be healed through deep sacral chakra healing and self-analysis. Physically, this second chakra is located around 3 inches below the navel and in the center of the belly. It is also seen to extend towards the genitalia region linking with the root chakra, believing to cover the ovaries and testicles too.

If you struggle with any of the following you might want to consider working with the sacral: addictions, codependency, sexual repressions, inauthenticity, creative blocks, jealousies, envies and resentments, fears and anxieties, wounds, traumas and feelings of guilt, shame, and victimhood.

Solar Plexus Chakra

The solar plexus is the third chakra also known as the Manipura. This energy center relates to self-empowerment, confidence, self-esteem, and willpower. It is your seat of personal confidence and authority, it's responsible for the way you project your self-image and ego into the world. The ego can be healthy too, as long as it's not out of control or destructive. Passion is the ultimate quality of the solar plexus, so a healthy solar plexus chakra creates an individual who is positively self-assured, empowered and passionate. Purpose and soul service- one's unique mission or sense of destiny- is equally linked to this chakra. People with a blocked or weak solar plexus tend to be nervous, unsure of themselves and uninspired. They lack direction and discipline and are often unmotivated to follow their passions and purpose in life- there is a sense of laziness and idleness too.

Yellow is the primary color to work with for the solar plexus. Yellow is stimulating for passion, vitality, and confidence, and self-esteem. It aids mental, psychological, and intellectual functions and is therefore perfect for all aspects of cognitive and higher thinking, inspiration, and imaginative thought. The Solar Plexus is related to the fire element, and yellow helps one to access their inner fire and spirit. Anyone suffering from envy, jealousy, resentment, or fear can work with yellow to lighten their outlook and lift them up from depression and anxiety. Also, yellow is considered a very warm and sunny color, thus is ideal to help bring a positive and optimistic outlook on life. Yellow can be quite catalytic to an underactive or overactive solar plexus chakra. A lack of personal power, courage, independence, and discipline can all be overcome with yellow. The higher vibration of this chakra is gold or golden yellow. You can work with this color to enhance wisdom and inspiration in your life. Physically the solar plexus is located in the upper part of the belly by the diaphragm. In Sanskrit, Manipura means *'dwelling place of the jewel.'*

Heart Chakra

The heart chakra is the merging point between the lower and higher chakras. It is also known as the Anahata chakra and symbolizes empathy, compassion, self-love, unconditional love, kindness, and benevolence. Generosity, sincerity, selflessness, and friendship come under this chakra's domain. All interpersonal relationships are affected by the health and vibration of the heart chakra, so romantic, platonic, business, and family partnerships and bonds will either suffer or thrive depending on the health of the heart. There is both an individual and collective aspect of the heart chakra. Self-love and the ability to find balance within codependent relationships is one important aspect; the other is how much you can experience a love and respect for nature, beauty, and the environment. Mother Earth is typically associated with this chakra. The ability to give and receive unconditional love, empathy, emotional intelligence and warmth, friendliness, and our level of self-awareness are included.

Green is the color to use and incorporate into your life and healing program. Green has a calming, balancing, soothing, and harmonizing effect. It is great for both an underactive and overactive heart chakra. Green's energy is restorative and brings peace, it can aid in tricky emotions and stimulate creativity, inspiration, and self-love and compassion. Due to green being the primary color of nature, healing yourself with green colors can open your actual heart up to new experiences and possibilities, whilst simultaneously increasing feelings of love and friendship, romance, and bliss. People with a strong heart chakra tend to be vegetarian or vegan, genuinely interested in the well-being of our environment and planet and radiate an aura of warmth and kindness. When the heart chakra is open, people project vibrations of emotional openness and (healthy) vulnerability, sympathy, understanding, tolerance, and patience; respect for all sentient beings. Pink is the secondary color of the heart chakra; pink can help with romance and loving relationships- platonic and sexual. This chakra is located in the center of the chest (not the actual heart as an organ, although they are linked energetically).

The heart is a bridge between the lower self and chakras and the higher self. We emit vibrations and interact with others through our hearts, with the heart chakra quite literally being the central point. The health state of this chakra, therefore, is very important. Signs of a weak heart include: victimhood, codependency, materialistic attitudes, selfish and narcissistic tendencies, possessiveness, obsessive compulsive disorder, spite and resentment, anger, and aggression/violence, manipulation, judgement, and a real lack of empathy, compassion, and understanding. Also, an inability to show emotions and open their heart to others.

Throat Chakra

The throat chakra is also known as the Vishuddha in ancient Sanskrit, which means *'purification.'* This chakra relates to the lament of sound, all aspects of communication, the imagination, and inspiration. Your ability to speak and communicate your truth is the throat chakra- how easily you can express your emotions, feelings, thoughts, ideas & ideologies, and beliefs too. Song, speech, written and verbal communication, musical expression, and creative and imaginative self-expression are all included in the throat's realm. People with a strong throat chakra are able to express their thoughts and internal feelings quite effortlessly. They're self-assured and confident with their speech, and usually thrive in speaking, teaching, and motivational fields. If a career were to be assigned to this chakra it would be a motivational speaker, or inspirational teacher.

There is an astral and ethereal quality to the throat chakra as well, however. The imagination is linked as is inspiration, and this includes one's capacity to connect to the angelic realm, divine assistance, and the higher chakras. This is largely because it is next to the third eye chakra (creating a natural connection). The subtle realms of spirit and intuitive abilities can be accessed with a healthy and open throat chakra.

The color to work with to heal the throat chakra is blue. Actually, all types of blue; sea and sky blues, turquoise and indigo. Blue helps to restore balance and aids in *all* aspects of communication. It eases tense or blocked energy and can loosen any stress or tension building up on an energetic and physical level. Blue is cooling, soothing, balancing, and stimulating for expression. If you struggle with thyroid problems, you should seek healing for this chakra. Blocks in inspiration and a connection to your vocation or life purpose suggest problems in the throat chakra as well, so this is something to be mindful of. A suppression of your thoughts, feelings, and emotions lead to an inability to express your truth and share your knowledge or wisdom, which in itself prevents you from stepping into full flow and alignment. For this reason, there is a sense of destiny and personal power associated with the throat. A higher vibration of the throat is higher wisdom and universal truth; therefore, indigo is a good color to work with to develop this energy. Physically, it is located at the center of the neck by the throat.

Third Eye Chakra

The third eye chakra is also called the Ajna chakra. This is your seat of vision, higher consciousness, and perception. All aspects of subtle and spiritual perception, psychic, and intuitive gifts, cognition and higher mental functioning are connected to the third eye. It is located in the center of the forehead between the brows and this shows the energetic associations. Foresight, intuition and psychic ability are the main qualities of an open and activated third eye chakra. Open-mindedness, philosophy, higher thinking and perception, imagination, and the ability to transcend duality (through observation and perception) are affected by the health of this chakra. In Sanskrit, Ajna literally means *'perceiving'* and *'command,'* it is therefore known as one's command center. We can transcend the bonds of duality and see from oneness, unity consciousness, and spiritual interconnectedness with a strong third eye. Superconsciousness is accessible.

Purple and indigo are the two colors you can use to heal this chakra. Indigo is best for wisdom and aspects relating to imagination, perception and higher cognition, while purple is an excellent color for getting in tune with your regality and inner majesty. Purple helps to open your third eye through expanding the gifts of vision, subtle and spiritual awareness and perception, and intuition. Both colors are soothing, healing, energizing, and harmonizing. Purification and spiritual clarity are the result of someone with an active and healthy third eye chakra, so imbalances manifest as the inability to see spiritually, intuitively, clearly, and calmly. Mental clarity and being able to see from the higher self arise through this chakra. Because the Sanskrit meaning of this energy center is quite literally the 'command' center, someone with a strong third eye can be described as being psychically gifted, clairvoyant, wise, intelligent, and a dreamer.

Crown Chakra

The crown chakra is called the Sahasrara and is the final of the 7 major chakras. This energy portal rests above your head, hence why it is called a 'crown.' Universal life force energy flows through the top of your head from the ether and spiritual planes, directly from the universe. Like a crown, we are channels for consciousness and divine energy- we're conduits. Divine, universal, cosmic, and spiritual consciousness are the crown chakra. Physically, it relates to the pituitary gland and also the pineal gland and hypothalamus. The crown is therefore closely associated with the endocrine and nervous system, but it is also connected to kundalini energy; the free flow of awakened spiritual and psychic energy which is a result of a balanced and harmonious chakra system. Kundalini moves from root to crown and vice versa. Thus, people with a strong crown chakra tend to be balanced, loving, healthy, and spiritually perceptive individuals. This chakra ultimately connects one to the spiritual world where subtle vibrations and dimensions of being are accessible. It can protect us against psychic attack and negative energy and open us to the beauty and transcendental awareness of the spiritual and energetic universe.

Gold, white, and clear light are the colors to work with here. Violet can also be used to soothe the nervous system and any mental disorders, headaches, tensions, or migraines that may arise from a blocked or imbalanced crown chakra. Pure light flows through the crown with the first three colors. Self-realization, enlightenment, the recognition of other planes and dimensions, compassion, universal love and compassion, unconditional love, and a connection with the divine... all possible! Color healing leads to a sense of home and belonging too due to the crown's link with the kundalini. Grounding and spiritual illumination are both equally available. Spirit is grounded into the human body through kundalini energy and an open crown. Universal symbols and associations of the crown chakra include Christ and Christ consciousness, Buddha and enlightenment, Krishna consciousness, the diamond, angelics and ascended masters, and spiritual guides. White, gold and clear light color frequencies help to raise one's vibration to match the potential of the crown. Finally, there is a sense of limitless, sacredness, and benevolence; faith, hope, and divine union and presence.

Knowing your chakras is one of the most effective ways to heal yourself. In addition to the 7 main chakras, you also have your palm chakras and feet chakras, and the thymus chakra and soul star chakra. It is through your palm chakras, located in your hands, where healing and life force energy flows; and through your feet and sole chakras where life force energy grounds you, connecting you to the earth and ground. The thymus is believed to be the 8th chakra located in-between the heart and throat chakras, and the soul star chakra is just above the crown. This is a connection or 'bridge' to the oversoul, akashic records, and highest planes of consciousness.

Kundalini activation

When your chakras are in a state of health and harmony, open and activated free from blocks and imbalances, your kundalini energy is awakened. Kundalini is the life force 'serpent' energy which flows from Root to Crown. It symbolizes psychic, spiritual, sexual, and creative energy. It is known as a serpent-like energy because it moves in the shape of a snake up and down the spine, like a spiral (imagine the spiral shape snakes make when they move). Kundalini can be activated through yoga, tantra, dance, healthy food, spiritual healing, meditation, and a variety of self-development exercises. It is important when embarking on a self-healing journey to be aware of kundalini and the effect it has on your life. Kundalini is responsible for longevity, holistic well-being, and your ability to manifest and attract. Working with your chakras is a sure way to activate kundalini, as chakra healing opens your 7 main chakras for life force to flow.

The main pathways to kundalini activation

1. Herbs and good diet choices

Eating foods and herbs high in life force are one of the best ways to awaken and activate your kundalini.

Superfoods like macca, cacao, spirulina, wheatgrass, chlorella, baobab and ginseng can be taken in supplement form or added into smoothies (in powder form) and are high in vibration. Fruits, vegetables, nuts & seeds, beans, pulses, legumes, and wholewheat or brown alternatives (rice, pasta, bread, oats) are also ideal choices. It is true that we are what we eat, so eating foods high in vibrational life force help to raise our own inner vibrations; we can embody more light and therefore a higher frequency with superfoods, herbs and a plant-based diet. Life force is stimulated through nutritious, organic, wholefood and less dense/heavy foods.

2. Kundalini yoga

Kundalini yoga is an original form of yoga expanding from the traditional hatha yoga you may already be aware of. Kundalini yoga helps to raise kundalini energy, activate and unblock your chakras, connect you to your inner spirit, and heal the mind, body, & soul. It works on an emotional, psychological, physical, and spiritual level and regular kundalini yoga practice increases chi levels within. Chi is of course life force energy- healing energy. Kundalini yoga is great to use alongside diet and meditation, spiritual healing, and connecting to Source. If just the idea of kundalini yoga resonates with you, you may want to research some poses and techniques online!

3. Tai Chi, Qi Gong and Martial Arts

Martial arts that take a more spiritual and yin approach assist in kundalini activation. Actually, all martial arts help, but spiritual and 'yin' ones such as tai chi, qi gong and aikido are perfect for getting in tune with your whole self. Other ones tend to be more combative. Aikido, for example, translates as "the way of the harmonious spirit" while tai chi's name means wholeness and completion. Qi gong is focused on 'qi,' vital life force…. Spiritual and gentler forms of martial arts are suited to everyone regardless of physical size, sex, or strength. They also allow for inner healing through focusing on emotional and spiritual health as well as physical vitality. The beauty with martial arts is that they are both an Art and a Healing modality, they provide a framework for spiritual growth and healing on the physical, mental, and psychological planes.

4. Meditation and Sound therapy

Meditation and sound therapy should be added to your self-healing list. Both assist in raising kundalini energy, activating memories on a cellular and spiritual level, releasing past wounds, pains and blocks, and opening channels to healing and higher consciousness. A lot of the imbalances and blocks we experience are psychological, emotional, and mental- and of course spiritual- which means we don't see them. It is these apparently 'invisible' blocks and energetic distortions that lead to so many of the problems we see. Meditation and sound therapy help one to go within, expand self-awareness, and reconnect to one's intuition, heart and higher mind in order for internal issues and everything behind the scenes to be overcome.

5. Dance and sexual healing

Dance, body movement and self-expression, and sensual and sexual healing are important too. Any way to allow your body to move and express itself is ideal, and freedom of expression is incredibly beneficial for the healing process. Kundalini is like a serpent, snake-like and subtle with the ability to flow, shift, adapt, and respond. You respond to physical sensations and external stimuli on a daily basis, all the time and consciously and unconsciously. Moving your body to move your emotions, thoughts, inner impressions, and beliefs is a powerful method of removing (releasing) stagnation in these areas. In other words, *movement is medicine*. Sensual play and sexual healing can be used to release past wounds and attune with self-alignment. Dance can stimulate your sense while activating life force. You can use visualization to assist in any movement medicine and sensuality you should choose to engage in.

Crystals

Crystals are also known as gemstones or rare gems and have been around for thousands of years. Ancient cultures and civilizations knew about them and their power, such as ancient Egyptians, and modern-day scientists and researchers have discovered their power too. We use quartz crystals to power watches, for example, due to the unique gravitational pull and connection they have with the earth's energy field. Crystals have metaphysical, healing, and spiritual properties. Regardless of whether you choose to see from a more 'left brain' and scientific perspective or a viewpoint more holistic and spiritual (the 'right brain'), we can learn a lot from crystals. Other books on the topic may refer to gemstones as the Crystal Kingdom, but we prefer to call it the Crystal King & Queendom. Like the Sun and Moon, light and darkness, and day and night, there is more than one significant force influencing us and our lives here on earth. Crystals embody both masculine and feminine energy. We can therefore learn about the healing properties and powers of individual gemstones so that we can choose the correct ones in our healing journeys and meditations. Also, you should know that crystals are *conscious*- on a level. They have been formed through planetary influences, astral energy (of the Moon, Sun and other planets and celestial objects) and the earth's core energy.

To cut a very long topic short, these are the key things you need to know about crystals for self-development.

1. They have a unique electromagnetic energy field which interacts with our own. When we hold, tune in to, or meditate with a crystal we *merge*. A crystals' aura or electromagnetic energy field interacts with ours and creates a specific vibration (frequency) around it.

2. Crystals are programmed with a specific and unique blueprint of information, which is also known as their healing properties, based on the individual planetary influences during the creation process. The *color* of the crystal will also affect the type of healing energy the gemstone is instilled with.

3. Crystals need to be cleansed, charged and programmed before use. This is important! To cleanse a crystal, allow it to be washed in cold running water for up to 15 minutes.

Sometimes a few minutes with your intention is all it needs. It then needs to be charged in sunlight, and potentially moonlight too. Sunlight is the main one (anywhere up to 12 hours). Finally, you can program a crystal or gemstone by placing it in your left palm with your right hand over the time, a few inches away. The right hand is your giving hand and the left your receiving one, so vital life force energy flows through your right hand and into the crystal and your left palm. You should program your crystal with any intention you feel is right: intuition, healing, guidance, wisdom, protection, letting go of the past, releasing emotional pain, etc.

The concept of *frequency and vibration* applies to the crystal queen and kingdoms. Refamiliarize yourself with the universal laws if you are unsure. 'As above so below.'

Let's break this section down into something easy to understand and implement.

Grounding (Earth energy)

- *Root*: Garnet... Garnet helps to connect you to your body through increasing passion, sensuality, confidence and positive energy. It is a stimulating and grounding stone and inspires devotion and love, balances libido, and strengthens survival instinct and courage. It can enhance inner strength and physical strength and vitality simultaneously.

- *Sacral*: Carnelian... Carnelian aids in emotional warmth, inner harmony and happiness, self-esteem and emotional negativity. This is a very warming stone that can alleviate the pain of past relationships, while connecting you to a desire to be sociable and seek harmonious connections, friendships, and intimate bonds. It sharpens perception and self-trust, alleviates envy, anger and resentment, and promotes courage and creativity.

- *Solar-plexus*: Chrysoprase... Chrysoprase can help to ground you and connect you to your body by its healing properties. It promotes hope, inspires truth, heals codependency issues, stimulates creativity and draws out your talents. It is a very detoxifying, activating and energizing gemstone and encourages independence and commitment to your goals and dreams.

- *Heart*: Jade... Jade promotes peace, harmony and wisdom. It has the qualities of balance, serenity, tranquility and purity- it is a deeply protective crystal that can enhance love and nurturance. Jade attracts good luck and friendship whilst promoting self-sufficiency and self-autonomy. It is therefore highly effective for bringing stability and positive feelings into your relationships and physical environments.

- *Throat*: Blue Lace Agate... This crystal is perfect for positive thinking, connecting you to joy, and bringing peace and tranquility. It helps to soothe the mind and emotions, and is ultimately a stone of calmness, hope and protection. Purification and cleansing come with blue lace agate which leads to the ability to speak your truth and express yourself.

- *Third Eye*: Sodalite... Sodalite enhances and amplifies intuition, perception, logic and intelligence. It allows you to see the world clearly and with rational thought, objectivity and truth, so that you can make important choices in your life. It is grounding through its ability to connect you to wisdom, calmness of mind, and self-trust. Emotional balance is increased and the self-trust that comes with wisdom and intuition enhancement opens new doors to opportunities.

- *Crown*: Kyanite... Kyanite connects you to your body and the source of inspiration and the divine. It is wonderful for meditation and higher self attunement, aligning you with altered states of consciousness and inner serenity. Kyanite aligns all of the chakras and subtle bodies, balances yin and yang within, dispels negativity, and removes energy blocks. It brings tranquility and enhances consciousness- it also promotes vivid dreams.

New Beginnings (Earth energy)

- *Root*: Bloodstone... Bloodstone helps to promote new beginnings on a physical level through alignment, abundance, and purification. It cleanses, re-aligns, balances, and protects you from harmful intentions and negative energy. Bloodstone leads to idealism, generosity, good fortune, and heightened intuition, therefore allows you to move to new chapters with ease and strength. It's a powerful vitalizer and can also enhance creativity, dreams, and selflessness.

- *Sacral*: Rhodonite... Rhodonite is a stone of compassion, inner balance, and harmony. It promotes emotional balance, calmness, nurturance, and love while clearing emotional wounds, trauma, and past pain. It is grounding while connecting you to your heart and highest potential. Self-love, forgiveness, and healthy codependence/independence are amplified. Elegance, grace, and alignment with your path and purpose are strengthened.

- *Solar-plexus*: Green Tourmaline... Green tourmaline increases tolerance, understanding, happiness, healing, strength, serenity, and compassion. It aids in confidence and self-esteem and allows you to understand others better. This is a very balancing and holistic stone and can therefore be used to spark energy in your solar plexus so energy can flow more freely into your heart and higher chakras.

- *Heart*: Rhodochrosite... This gemstone enhances friendships, harmony, healing, comfort and self-love and compassion. It is warming and stimulating, energizing, and cleansing. It stimulates love and passion whilst enhancing your connection to spirit and your soul. Depression can be overcome, and optimism, positivity and creativity are amplified.

- *Throat*: Celestite... Celestite is powerful for promoting new beginnings and fresh starts. It enhances self-awareness, intuition and subtle-spiritual perception. It helps to transition into peaceful states of awareness and inner calm, its spiritually enhancing.

- *Third Eye*: Sapphire (Blue, Indigo and White) … Sapphire brings wisdom, enhanced intuition, psychic gifts and abilities, and personal power. It is a stone of meditation, luck and creative expression. Spiritual confusion and stress can be overcome, and mental clarity and serenity are enhanced. It is also known as a crystal of prosperity, so opens pathways to healing, independence, abundance, and dream fulfillment. Aspirations can be realized, and love, loyalty, and generosity embodied.
- *Crown*: Clear quartz… Clear quartz inspires new beginnings, clarity, psychic abilities, harmony, and positivity. It is known as a 'master healer' crystal, meaning it can be used on any of the chakras and for kundalini awakening/activation. It dispels and draws out negative energy and cleanses, purifies and aligns. It's for the soul and spirit but can also stimulate the immune system and self-healing mechanisms- it can be programmed with multiple intentions and qualities.

Emotional healing and balance (Water energy)

- *Root*: Smoky quartz... Smoky quartz is powerful at cutting through tricky and chaotic emotions. It promotes inner peace and contentment, serenity, positive thoughts, and emotions, intuition and healing. It is cleansing and purifying and helps to ground you while protecting you from negative, harmful vibrations, and stress and anxiety. It aids in a practical approach to life whilst soothing emotions simultaneously.

- *Sacral*: Aventurine (Yellow)... This gemstone heals indecisiveness, issues in self-control, and oversensitivity. Hypersensitivity can be alleviated and soothed with yellow aventurine. It increases manifestation too as it helps one to focus intentions, leading to enhanced abundance, prosperity and creativity. *Green Aventurine* can also be used for the heart chakra for emotional healing. This one promotes feelings of well-being, love, warmth, and friendship. It dissolves negative emotions and protects you from electromagnetic harm and interference.

- *Solar-plexus*: Citrine... Citrine allows you to experience sensations of warmth, happiness, prosperity, pleasure, truth, and self-alignment. It is an excellent stone for connecting you to your true path and purpose, aiding in self-confidence, strength, and self-empowerment. Your chances for connection, creativity, and success are increased- citrine can lead to inner strength and self-esteem that allows you to heal yourself. It's energizing, charging, emotionally balancing, and stimulating (joy, wonder, enthusiasm, zest for life…).

- *Heart*: Rose quartz… Rose quartz is quite literally a gemstone for the heart. It brings the vibrations of unconditional love, self-love, universal-love, healing and compassion. It is warming, stimulating, balancing and integrating at the same time, it helps to amplify harmony in relationships and trust, caring, and kindness. Rose quartz purifies, calms, harmonizes and dispels negativity and bad emotions; anger, resentment, envy, hate, judgement, intolerance, and clingy-possessive tendencies.

- *Throat*: Aquamarine… Aquamarine is a soothing, graceful and cleansing crystal which enhances peace, prophecy, tranquility and inspiration. It is excellent for enhancing intuition and psychic gifts that can lead to deep insight and understanding. Inner power and strength are amplified, and courage, perception, tolerance and intellect &

intuition are enhanced. It promotes self-expression and can be used for meditation, clairvoyance, aura and chakra healing, and mindful empathic communication.

- *Third Eye:* Moonstone… Although primarily for the Sacral, moonstone can be used for the third eye too. Moonstone promotes new beginnings through healing past wounds, pain and trauma. It provides calmness, clarity, emotional warmth and balance, nurturance, good fortune, and spiritual insight. It is very psychic-ally and spiritually stimulating, sparking profound intuitive insights and self-realization. Love, hope, abundance, and selflessness can all be achieved with the unique vibration of ancient wisdom.

- *Crown*: Calcite… Calcite is wonderful for enhancing memory, wisdom, intuition, psychic protection, aura strengthening, astral connection and encounters, and channeling higher wisdom and consciousness. It is cleansing, purifying and amplifying- it clears your chakras all the while protecting you from negativity and harmful intentions. It helps to strengthen boundaries and boosts intellect, spirituality and a connection to soul. Healing is offered through the deep spiritual insight and wisdom sparked.

Releasing the Past (Water energy)

- *Root*: Obsidian… Obsidian is powerful at helping you overcome blockages, negative energy, trauma, and hard emotions. It is great for healing, transformation, purification (of mind, body, emotions & spirit), and increasing self-compassion and inner strength. Practical affairs can be dealt with smoothly and it both blocks you from psychic attack and increases manifestation abilities.

- *Sacral*: Moonstone and Pearl… Moonstone and Pearl are both ideal to use for releasing the past and healing emotional wounds. Pearl enhances purity, innocence, honesty, and integrity- it amplifies meditation, tranquility, and wisdom. It connects you to ancient wisdom and the subconscious realms, the subconscious being where insights into emotions and the shadow self are strong. The same is true for Moonstone. Pearl is called 'the stone of sincerity' and Moonstone is 'the stone of new beginnings.'

- *Solar-plexus*: Topaz… Topaz can be blue or yellow. Topaz in general helps with communication, luck, good health, and fortune. Attraction, love, prosperity, and abundance can be increased with Topaz. It is healing, soothing, and stimulating; it leads to an increase in openness and honesty in relationships- and to yourself, self-realization and relaxation, the reduction of stress, and anxiety. Yellow topaz is particularly effective for the solar plexus while blue topaz can be used for the throat chakra.

- *Heart*: Emerald... Emerald amplifies the qualities of love, romance, inner harmony, joy, clairvoyance and intuition, serenity, truth, and intelligence. It is a beautiful crystal for all aspects of love, friendship and platonic love, romantic love, self-love, and family bonds. It dispels negativity while connecting you to your heart space, your source of power and unconditional love. Forgiveness, healing, compassion and faith are all amplified with Emerald. Further, it helps to increase self-awareness, perception and intellect- mental clarity and wisdom combined with a higher truth and intuitive sight.

- *Throat*: Turquoise... Turquoise promotes positive thinking, harmonious and balanced emotions, inner serenity and peace, wisdom and sensitivity. Romantic love and friendship can both be enhanced with this gemstone. It is a stone of purification and self-realization;

it sparks recognition of greater truths and brings clarity into your life. It also protects you from negative energy, mood swings, and anxiety.

- *Third Eye*: Lapis Lazuli... This one was revered by ancient Egyptians for being a gemstone of truth, higher wisdom, and psychic and intuitive gifts and abilities. Spiritual insight comes about with Lapis lazuli and dreams are enhanced; dream recall, memory, and the experience of having vivid dreams, and receiving insight and guidance from your dreams. It enhances inner truth and clarity of perception, ancient wisdom, universal awareness, purification, manifestation, and personal power. It further shields you from psychic attack making it excellent for dealing with emotional trauma and abuse. You can express your feelings and emotions more freely with lapis lazuli too.

- *Crown*: Selenite... Purification, serenity, peace of mind, emotional harmony, and self-alignment all come with Selenite. This crystal increases and amplifies universal love, higher/universal consciousness, spirituality and connection to spirit, integrity, psychic development, and positive mindset. It helps to expand your awareness with a focus on spiritual and subtle realms and energy, and memories of your past lives. It can lead to a release of judgement while allowing you to see the bigger picture. It is therefore excellent for releasing the past and gaining clarity on your emotions and internal currents.

Manifesting Wisdom (Air energy)

- *Root*: Tiger's eye... Tiger's Eye can actually be used for the first three chakras, the Root, Sacral and Solar Plexus. It is powerful for grounding, wisdom, integrity, willpower, personal courage and strength, and self-confidence. It has a protecting, shielding and cleansing effect. For the root chakra, Tiger's Eye helps to connect you to your source of wisdom and ability to think and perceive clearly and rationally. It aids in logic, self-expression, and self-autonomy while amplifying self-empowerment.
- *Sacral*: Amber... Amber and Yellow Jasper can be used for the Sacral and Solar plexus, they're interchangeable. Amber has a unique energy as it is technically a fossilized tree resin, but is also used in crystal healing. Amber sparks romantic love, inspiration, purification, and cleansing, energy and

vitality, joy, and balance. It is popular among intellectuals, teachers, and students due to its effect on the mind. It promotes peace and clarity of perception, concentration, and focus, whilst simultaneously increasing a genuine desire to learn and gain new knowledge. It enhances passion! Spontaneity, zest and good luck and success can be developed with Amber.

- *Solar-plexus*: Yellow Jasper... Yellow Jasper calms and soothes emotions and mental patterns while protecting you from electromagnetic pollution. It has a neutralizing effect. It also aids in relaxation, mental clarity, tranquility, healing and inner contentment. Wisdom is enhanced through these qualities.

- *Heart*: Peridot... Peridot is a very soothing and healing gemstone which allows for creative inspiration and self-expression. It brings a feeling of renewal and purification, rebirth and personal growth- intellect and wisdom enhancement can both be developed. Peridot sparks internal change and transformation so that we can see things in a new light, with clearer eyes, foresight and greater wisdom. This gemstone amplifies self-responsibility and vitality in order to take control of your life.

- *Throat*: Angelite... Also, *Aquamarine, Sodalite, Lapis Lazuli, Turquoise, Blue Lace Agate* and *(Blue) Kyanite* are perfect to use here as well. Angelite has a unique energy that helps with astral travel and projection, channeling (divine wisdom, inspiration), and hope, faith, and unconditional love. It is an excellent gemstone for artists, poets, musicians, and philosophers, creative people of all kinds who also like to think and be intellectual. Spiritual insight and connection can be developed, and telepathy, psychic ability and evolved empathy are achievable- all aspects of advanced communication. Creativity and inspiration are the main benefits of working with Angelite, but tranquility of mind, logic and intellect can all be enhanced too. (You can also use it for your Third Eye Chakra.)

- *Third Eye*: Azurite... And *Amethyst, Fluorite* and *Sodalite*- these are ideal choices too. Spiritual wisdom, communication, clairvoyance and psychic abilities, and deeper clarity and perception come with healing with Azurite. It can be used for both the third eye and throat chakras and works well for inspirational pursuits due to it aiding in the increase of self-awareness, intuition, and wisdom. It is great for philosophical, intellectual, artistic and cognitive/problem-solving pursuits.

- *Crown*: Diamond... Diamond is a symbol of purity. It clears the mind, chakras and subtle energy bodies so that you can think and see clearly, and with vision, clear sight, and developed intuition. It is considered a precious gemstone and is obviously revered for its connection to love, romance, friendship, and marriage. On a metaphysical level this is all true, but it also enhances loyalty, devotion, prosperity, abundance, manifestation, and soul. It's effective for manifestation and luck attraction. Diamond also helps to connect us to the higher self- the higher mind- for soul alignment, greater awareness, and new levels of insight and observation.

Making Shifts and Changes, Transformation (Fire energy)

- *Root*: Onyx... Onyx enhances strength, stamina, self-control and self-confidence. It is truly a stone for the root chakra, relating to all aspects of grounding, physical strength and personal power. It can amplify wisdom for decision-making and making the right choices in life. There's an aspect of self-alignment and prosperity enhancement. Also, *Garnet, Red Jasper, Obsidian, Black Tourmaline* and *Bloodstone* can be used for the Root chakra for important shifts and changes.

- *Sacral*: Sunstone… Sunstone is wonderful for enhancing personal freedom, originality, sensuality and good luck and fortune. It aids independence and luck and energizes all of the chakras. It can help you shine through enhancing intuition and personal authority, and alleviating stress and anxiety. Sunstone is great for increasing vitality, confidence and self-esteem- it connects you to your happy place with an emphasis on optimism and positive emotions. *Carnelian, (Orange) Calcite* and *Moonstone* are ideal choices as well.

- *Solar-plexus*: Pyrite helps with all aspects of logic, reason, intellect, creativity, and memory. It is great for focus and concentration and can therefore increase personal confidence associated with learning, aligning with your life purpose, and/or psychic and spiritual development. Practicality, intuition and self-responsibility are enhanced while channeling abilities increase. Pyrite allows you to connect to your source of inspiration, creative self-expression, and intuitive & logical insight. In addition, *Citrine, Tiger's Eye, Yellow Jasper, Topaz* and *Amber* work perfectly.

- *Heart*: Malachite and Amazonite.... Malachite is a stone of protection. It protects you from psychic attack, negative energies and electromagnetic harm. It is powerfully transformational and can spark wisdom, peace, understanding, spiritual insight and alignment, and healing. It promotes loyalty and positive thinking and emotions in relationships and enhances comfort and your connection to others and the natural world. Amazonite is another beautiful gemstone which amplifies the following qualities: sincerely, honesty, peace, mindful communication, self-love, integrity, eloquence and grace, trust, clairvoyance/psychic gifts, perception, and honor/morals & ethics. It inspires truth and is generally considered perfect for all matters of the heart. You can also use *Rose Quartz, Rhodochrosite, Rhodonite, Emerald, Green Aventurine,* and *(Green) Jade*.

- *Throat*: Any of the throat chakra stones already mentioned; Aquamarine, Angelite, Lapis Lazuli, Turquoise... (Please read descriptions.)

- *Third Eye*: Tanzanite… Tanzanite helps us to slow down and get in touch with our truth and internal compass. Intuition, universal truth and wisdom, deep insights and spiritual integrity are all available with Tanzanite. It amplifies our vibrations and connects us to higher dimensions, spirit and the divine. Divine inspiration and spiritual guidance can come about, thus making it an ideal choice for powerful change. Karmic and toxic love patterns are effective for being worked through with Tanzanite's assistance. Psychic abilities increase, and we can move forward with our lives with a sense of inspiration, optimism and purpose. *Lapis Lazuli, Amethyst* and *Sodalite* are great for personal transformation too!
- *Crown*: Phenacite… This is a very powerful and rare crystal many people aren't aware of. Phenacite enhances shifts in consciousness and meditation, promotes lucid dreaming and astral projection, calms the mind, heightens the senses, sparks advanced intuition and psychic gifts, aligns you with your true path, power and destiny, and clears negative or harmful energy from your aura and energy field. This unique crystal cuts through cords of attachment and toxic patterns very effectively. It aids in compassion, self and

universal love, and community ties and bonds- soulmate love and kindred spirits can be developed and enhanced with Phenacite. It also helps with forgiveness and releasing the past to make space for a new, brighter future. Other crystals to use for the Crown include *Selenite, Sugilite, Clear & Spirit Quartz,* and *Howlite.* Sugilite brings the vibration of connecting to the higher, spiritual and angelic realms, and the ability to channel divine and ancient wisdom. It promotes self-awareness, meditation and spirituality, so any aspect of tension, discomfort or disharmony can be overcome. Howlite is an amazing gemstone for artistic and imaginative inspiration, abilities and channeling. It amplifies creativity, intuition and the imagination while bringing feelings of inspiration and purpose. New opportunities and connections can be formed with Howlite's assistance.

Reiki healing

There are many forms of energy healing we could have chosen to include here. But from my experience, reiki healing offers the most encompassing wisdom and perspective. Reiki literally means *universal life force*- life force energy, and in any form of energy healing a practitioner works with chi, source energy, subtle life force, or spirit. They are all one and the same. So, Reiki as a natural healing system seems to be a great foundation for you to understand how energy healing truly works. Do please note however, learning the wisdom and esoteric knowledge doesn't make you qualified to teach Reiki, or to call yourself a practitioner. Due to the important concept and practice of "lineage" in Reiki one needs to receive Reiki attunements from an experienced Reiki Master Teacher in order to be classed as an (official) practitioner or therapist. But Reiki energy is the energy used in all forms of energy healing, so you can use the techniques and knowledge shared in Reiki for self-healing. Life force flows through every living thing; some people call it prana or chi, others call it reiki, or spirit or source. Spirit doesn't judge!

Reiki History

To understand the power of healing energy you should be familiar with the history of this beautiful system. Reiki was introduced by Mikau Usui, a Buddhist monk who was studying in a temple in Japan. Mikau Usui went on an intensive fast and meditative journey, fasting for 21 days on a mountain near the monastery. His intention was to achieve a state of transcendental awareness and spiritual enlightenment. This happened on Mount Kurama, a cave known at that time for its spiritual significance- many monks would use that cave for meditation and deep contemplation. For 21 days in 1922, Mikau Usui fasted, prayed and meditated; it is believed that he used stones to count how many days he spent in the cave, and this is highly significant as you will see later regarding Reiki's link and connection to the elements of nature and natural cycles.

On the morning of the 21st day M. Usui received a flash of light and insight, directly from the universe. Ultimately, enlightenment. Not only did he see and experience this light frequency, but he also began to see ancient Sanskrit symbols through the ether, through the subtle planes of existence. He had access to higher dimensions of consciousness and was 'astrally activated,' his light body (energy body) was vibrating high enough to both receive the light projection and see sacred symbols.

In addition to these two magical experiences, on his way down from the mountain-top cave Mikau Usui tripped and hurt his big toe. Upon reaching out to soothe himself, he felt a *rush of energy* flow through his hands, and then he experienced an extraordinary sensation that instantly made his large toe feel better. Thus, he was blessed with the gift of healing. Dr Mikau later went on to call this 'Reiki' and developed an entire system around it. The energy itself, once again, is also referred to as source energy, spirit or life force by many.

What are the key points we can take away from this? Well, many people who embark on a path of healing and spirituality have similar experiences to Mikau Usui. They all feel the need to fast and detox their system- mind, body & spirit; and they all receive flashes of insight, light and divine inspirations. Seeing symbols and visions through the ethereal and astral planes are also common. And this is why we've chosen Reiki as an energy healing essential; it is the perfect foundation in which to familiarize yourself with the process of subtle healing energy.

The Reiki Principles- what can we learn from this Japanese healing art?

Reiki also has a number of principles or precepts, aspects, and elements. If you're interested, the original lineage is Mikau Usui, Chjiro Hayashi, Hawayo Takata, and Phyllis Furumoto. These are the *original masters* of Reiki, meaning that everyone and anyone ever attuned to the healing system would have been taught and trained by one of these people. Let's explore the significance of this. The four Aspects of Reiki are 'healing practice,' 'personal development,' 'spiritual discipline,' and 'mystic order.' This basically sums up the purpose of energy healing! Reiki is primarily a healing practice with the offering of treatments aka reiki sessions. These treatments or sessions are given by a Reiki practitioner or Master and include a series of specific hand-movements and positions. Treatments can include directly healing the physical body or working above on the aura, or etheric body. There is said to be an "energetic blueprint" of our physical bodies, where all illness and disease is birthed, just above and beyond the physical body. Reiki healing can take place on the subtle and astral planes or directly on the physical body, therefore. Whether the channeler (practitioner or master) provides hands-on healing or etheric/astral healing all depends on the desired effect and intention.

The first Aspect shows us what we ourselves can do with life force energy. When we begin to work with subtle energy more, healing ourselves on all levels and releasing blockages and imbalances, we start to become a channel for healing energy. This happens completely *naturally and organically* (just like Mikau Usui's experience!). We may not even be conscious of it at first. But, over time- and often quite quickly too, our palm chakras start to open. Many people think there are only 7 or 8 chakras, yet we also have palm chakras. Universal life force healing energy flows through our palm chakras. You may have heard of the term *healing hands* or *healing presence*; these arise with spiritual growth and healing. The second aspect links to this, personal development. Reiki leads to self-development, personal transformation and self-discovery. Self-evolution is an integral aspect of Reiki, Reiki energy stimulates the body's self-healing mechanisms and activates consciousness on unseen levels; both the subconscious mind and Higher Self can be sparked through the life force energy of Reiki. In turn blocks and imbalances are released and removed on the mental, emotional, physical and spiritual planes. Personal development and self-healing are initiated through connecting us to our cores, to our true nature, inner spirit and soul selves.

Spiritual discipline is next, and this is something that can help you on your path. Reiki as a healing system has an intrinsic connection to spirit, thus it is a spiritual path and discipline. Linked to the second aspect is that Reiki initiates an increase in spiritual gifts, such as intuition and intuitive sight, psychic ability and awareness, and connecting to your soul and evolved expressions of self. These "self-evolved" expressions may be the ability to communicate telepathically, perceive subtle energy, access dream states, or channel healing energy oneself, more powerfully if already a practitioner or simply by being naturally attuned and awakened if receiving a treatment. You don't have to receive a Reiki attunement to channel healing energy. Many receivers of reiki who have never been attuned to the system report feeling unique sensations in their palm chakras and in the Third Eye chakra- the energy portal and center associated with spiritual and psychic gifts, and vision & sight. Finally, Reiki is a deeply mystical experience and order in itself. Once attuned, you become part of a unique system working towards a common practice, common goals, and shared intentions. This is the intention and why Dr Mikau Usui chose to pass his gifts on. What this means for us, non-Reiki practitioners, is that we can recognize the divine and mystical aspect of reiki energy (life force, healing energy, subtle energy) for health and well-being.

Remember the diagram shared earlier about the different bodies and planes of existence.... A lot of illness and disease begins on a subtle level, from some sort of spiritual disconnection or separation from the soul- from the core of your being. Ultimately, healing energy can be given to everything and Reiki teaches that we can channel the subtle life force energy for mental, emotional, physical and spiritual health. We can also "energize" (send healing and health to) fruits, water, animals and trees, food, animals, and nature. Energy healing involves the experience of recognizing that we are a part of something 'higher,' something above and beyond the individual "I" or "me" reality. Reiki teaches the exact same thing, it is actually known as a *Healing Art*, or a *Mystic Art*. We can learn a lot from it; union of self, union with others, union with the planet or universe as wholes, and union with spirit can be achieved and experienced. Through the mystical essence of the system, a sense of interconnectedness is felt and observed just like the wisdom and teachings of the Universal Laws. Furthermore, an awakening to one's inner spirit always occurs through being attuned to Reiki energy, or by simply receiving it for the higher chakras. Chakra and kundalini awakening are connected to receiving Reiki energy healing.

Then we have the 9 elements. It is interesting that there are nine elements as 9 is symbolic of completion. The 9 elements in Reiki are:

1. Oral tradition: It is passed on directly from Master to student through Attunements. *What does this mean for us?* ~It shows how we are channels for the divine, healing energy, and spirit. Spirit flows through us and the more we work on ourselves, clear and unblock our chakras, and work with crystals, special gemstones, meditation, and other significant tools and techniques, the more we can access this beautiful energy.

2. Lineage: The original masters are included in every Reiki lineage, from 1925 to 2020. It doesn't matter which year you receive Reiki; you will always be connected to the original channel/receiver (Mikau Usui) of Source's gift. *What does this mean for us?* ~The factor of 21 days is significant here. The 21-day meditation and fast is what led to enlightenment and being able to channel healing energy. There is an ancient, timeless, and transcendent wisdom we can learn here.

3. History: The history of Reiki is ultimately about the energy itself- Reiki, source, spirit, life force…. How it was gifted to a man with pure intentions from God or the Universe.

What does this mean for us? ~This element of Reiki shows us our true potential and power. Infinite possibilities are available when we make the right decisions in harmony with our ultimate health and highest vibration. Detoxing from everything that doesn't serve a higher purpose, committing to a spiritual practice, and purifying our physical systems, which of course means purifying our mental, spiritual and emotional systems simultaneously.

4. Initiation: 'Sacred ritual' and 'rites of passage,' one can't be attuned to Reiki without them. *What does this mean for us?* ~It signifies that frequency and vibration are at large and strong! The universe finds multiple ways to show us the power and importance of vibration and frequency, operating at our best, and connecting to our souls. Self-mastery is key with energy healing.

5. Symbols: Reiki as a system taught to others to access their true potential involves symbols. Symbols come through in the form of powerful imagery, visions, or visuals. Many of them are Sanskrit in origin but some are more generally from the collective consciousness- universal archetypes and visual projections of consciousness. *What*

does this mean for us? ~They teach the significance of the subtler realms, dimensions and planes of consciousness. They show the power of thought, frequency and intention, symbols are used to amplify, energize and expand healing energy. They're also energetic keys or portals and doorways into higher states of consciousness.

6. <u>Treatment</u>: Specific hand positions are used to heal self and others. *What does this mean for us?* ~We can heal others through self-healing. We must first raise our vibrations so that we can stay attuned to a compassionate, empathic, wise, and strong and centered version of ourselves.

7. <u>A form of teaching</u>: There are different levels to Reiki, generally understood as level 1, 2 and 3 with level 3 being the Master Teacher level. *What does this mean for us?* ~The teaching element helps us to come to terms with the presence of a spiritual and metaphysically accepting community. Esoteric fields of thought and things that were once considered "woo" are becoming more and more well-known and sought after. Ancient wisdom can be shared in a grounded way.

8. <u>Monetary exchange</u>: Honor is an essential teaching in Reiki. This natural healing

system supports the value of commitment, respect, and valuing Reiki energy and the Masters in the lineage, which, of course, means respecting and honoring Spirit (also God, the Universe, whichever higher power you believe in and know to be true). *What does this mean for us?* ~We can learn the concept of energy exchange; everything involves a natural flow of giving and receiving energy. Subtle energy and universal life force are a gift and blessing. We humans should honor and cherish this gift!

9. <u>Principles/precepts</u>: Principles to live by… there are some minor variations, but these are generally considered: 1. I will not worry. 2. I will not anger. 3. I will be grateful and count my blessings. 4. I will do my work honestly. 5. I will honor my elders and teachers. 6. I will be kind to every living thing. The principles are actually written and spoken as mantras, beginning with "*Just for today, I…*" So, 'Just for today, I will not worry. Just for today, I will not anger.' etc. What does this mean for us? ~This one's self-explanatory. Compassion, empathy, respect, truth, honesty, kindness, and a range of positive emotions and feelings, the principles are channels for self-discovery and awakening,

personal transformation and growth. They are healing in themselves and are presented as mantras so that we can use them as a sort of *self-affirmation*, affirming to the universe (and ourselves) what kind of vibration we wish to embody, create, and project. 'Just for today' represents the cyclic nature of life, signifying that each day is a new cycle and a new chance for wholeness (healing).

"How can I use Reiki for myself and potentially others?"

If the Reiki topic has fascinated you, I would honestly recommend finding a practitioner or experienced Master and receiving a Reiki attunement and course. A traditional course includes all of the wisdom, techniques, and knowledge necessary to start channeling healing energy for self and others. It really is a beautiful and authentic system and I've never met anyone who passes on Reiki attunements and teachings who isn't committed to a spiritual practice. There is a sense of purpose and soul alignment in Reiki healing.

For now, you can start to practice 'self-healing techniques' at home. One may call these *vibration raising techniques*, *channeling*, or *connecting to your source of personal power.* Energy healing is the goal and intention. Before we go into these, there are some other therapies you might want to research.

Other forms of healing you can participate in or seek include:

- Psychoanalysis and Cognitive Behavioral therapy (CBT)
- Herbalism/herbs for holistic well-being
- Acupuncture and Acupressure
- Reflexology
- Aromatherapy
- Shiatsu
- Holistic Massage
- Trigger Point therapy
- Meridian Psychotherapy
- Hypnosis/hypnotherapy
- Indian Head and Face Massage
- Hot Stone therapy and Hopi Ear Candling
- Dream therapy
- Yoga and tantric yoga
- Kinesiology
- Neurolinguistic Programing (NLP)
- Tai Chi
- Past Life therapy
- Cranial-Sacral Massage

This list is not exclusive, the point to bring into awareness is that western medicine and healthcare is not the only way to achieve health. There are many systems and modalities that work with subtle energy. Therapies such as the ones named above actually provide a more *holistic* approach to treatment and in many can heal the root cause, as opposed to just the symptoms. The root cause in emotional problems lie in a disconnection from your body, sensuality and senses, and sexuality- and/or past sexual memories and experiences. The root cause of psychological blocks and fears, illusions and insecurities stem from issues on the mental planes. The root cause of manifestation problems lies in your levels of thinking and perceiving the world around... Holistic-healing modalities have an encompassing approach to achieving *wholeness* as they consider the human being as a complete and complex individual. In this respect, they are specifically effective for regaining your personal power; they benefit the mind, the emotions, the body, and the spirit.

If you feel inclined to learn and train in any of the above, either for self or to evolve the wisdom, teachings and practical applications into a service to help others, the *School of Natural Health Sciences*[1] is an established, professional and friendly online

---

[1] https://naturalhealthcourses.com/

college with a range of holistic therapies. It is highly recommended!

Self-Healing Techniques

There are a range of self-healing techniques available on the internet. Here we go into some of the *most effective* which are suitable for beginners and those more experienced alike.

Chi ball

Creating a chi ball is one of the fastest ways to heal yourself. It can be done anywhere, at home, on a work break, or when going about your day-to-day activities for a reboot. You can also use it alongside any other vibration raising, healing and psychic and spiritual development exercises. Chi, as you're aware, is universal life force energy- it flows through living things from the food you eat, to the environment around, plants & flowers, animals and cells inside your body. A chi ball is a 'ball of chi,' created through your intention and your palm chakras. The 7-chakra system is the most spoken about reference to chakras, but the palms have chakras too. Universal life force energy flows through your body like a circuit; your left hand is known as the receiving hand and your right hand is the giving one. *Left is receiving, right is giving.* Together they make a circuit for healing energy to flow more strongly. This piece of knowledge is something to bear in mind for later.

For making a chi ball, the idea is to focus the energy into an "invisible" and energetic ball of life force. Both hands must come together in a cupping motion. This can be performed anywhere as mentioned, to recharge your energy levels when out and about. For example, if you are feeling stressed or anxious you can make a chi ball and place it over your *heart chakra* to calm your emotions, or over your *third eye chakra* to instill feelings of deep peace and clarity. If you've just suffered an argument or heated discussion and are feeling angry, triggered and worked up you can create a chi ball and place it over your *crown chakra* for spiritual awareness and inner contentment (or over your third eye and heart chakras for the reasons shared above). There are a number of ways chi balls can benefit you in daily life.

Assuming you are wanting some techniques for a well-thought-out self-healing program at home, the following should be done.

1. Find a quiet spot where you won't be disturbed. You may want to put on some healing and vibration raising music, such as binaural beats or nature sounds with Tibetan chimes and singing bowls. 432 Hz and 528

Hz are perfect binaural beat frequencies to play.

2. Get in a meditative space and take some deep and conscious breaths. Find silence and peace within, and make sure your breathing is steady and your mind calm.

3. Bring your hands up to the level of your heart chakra. Make a cupping motion as described previously. Your palms should be facing each other an inch or two away. If you're already an experienced energy healer or Reiki practitioner, you may find your hands naturally begin a few inches away. This is because of the purpose of the chi ball- chi grows and expands within your hands.

4. Start to breathe and project your intention into the ball of growing energy in between your hands and palm chakras. Stillness of mind and inner calmness helps this, so allow the universe's natural light and energy to do its thing. Keep your intention set and visualize a ball of beautiful light growing within your hands.

5. The color of light should be pure white or golden. (You can use different colors which we explain later.)

6. With each inhale, picture the beautiful healing light and energy growing and expanding within your hands. With each

exhale see this coming out of your palms and 'energizing' the energy inside your hands. A cyclic motion and visual should be formed.

7. This exercise can be performed for as little as 5 minutes and up to one hour, however long feels comfortable and right for you. The average amount of time I would suggest energizing your chi ball is 10- 15 minutes.

8. Once your hands have started to feel a sufficient gravitational pull, i.e. they have moved further apart due to the built up ball of energy growing inside (you will actually be able to feel your chi ball circulating around!) slowly bring the ball up to either your heart chakra or your crown, just over the top of your head. These are the two main energy centers that benefit from a chi ball.

9. Finally, once you feel ready, 'pour' the energy into or onto your chosen chakra. Watch it spill and flow into your heart or crown. The beautiful healing light energy is filling your vessel, radiating it's love and light into your being. Visualize it and feel it happening at the same time…

To conclude, gently rest the palms of your hand over the chakra with your left palm flat on your head or heart, and your right hand over the top. Keep your hands there for a few moments while feeling the warmth of healing light flowing through you. At this stage you can say thank you- the act of gratitude amplifies the experience more. Thank the healing energy and light and allow yourself to feel the bliss of the chi, the universal vital life force and healing light, flowing through you. To finish, rub your hands together a few times as if you are sparking them against one another, and then bring your hands down onto your knees in a meditative position.

This is the basis of a chi ball! You can get creative with your chi balls too. You can make one for each of your chakras and set an intention for each. Or, if you have a specific ailment, block or issue you can work on two interlinking chakras. For example, your sacral and throat for emotional healing and being able to speak your truth, express your feelings and emotions, and communicate your inner thoughts. Or your third eye and solar plexus for increasing self-confidence and being able to see intuitively with spiritual sight.

Generally speaking, there are specific combination for chakra healing: -

- Root and Heart
- Sacral and Throat
- Solar Plexus and Third Eye
- Heart and Crown

Chi Balls for the Chakras

Root Chakra

To create a chi ball for your Root chakra, visualize the color *red* and set the following intentions. Security, stability, and feeling safe and connected to your body. A chi ball for the root chakra will enhance the qualities of grounding and being connected to the physical world and realm. This is particularly effective for anxiety, fear or feelings of discomfort and disconnection, any sense of feeling unsafe and insecure in your surrounding and physical environments. Root chakra healing with a chi ball allows energy to expand and release blockages from irrational fears and worries; you can become more at ease within your reality and self. Making a chi ball for your root chakra is effective for increasing passion, vitality and life force too.

Sacral Chakra

To create a chi ball for your Sacral chakra, visualize the color *orange* and set the following intentions. Emotional healing, overcoming sexual blocks and past painful memories, and enhancing creativity. Emotions, sexuality and creativity can be healed and energized through creating a chi ball for the sacral chakra. Issues in relationships and connection can be worked through with gentleness and kindness (self-compassion), and the self-awareness that comes with activating this energy center. The sacral relates to the water element and emotions, and although the color associated is blue, orange is the color to work with and visualize for your chi ball. Create a sacral chakra chi ball if you are dealing with emotional chaos and deep sexual or intimacy issues.

Solar Plexus Chakra

To create a chi ball for your Solar Plexus chakra, visualize the color *yellow* and set the following intentions. Self-empowerment, confidence, self-esteem and purpose. A chi ball for this chakra is a great way to increase self-esteem, personal power and authority, and willpower. Energy and intentions projected into your solar plexus allow for a better alignment with your purpose or destiny, service and life path. Create a solar plexus chi ball if you're feeling disempowered, low or uninspired; equally lacking in direction and focus. Issues in self-worth and the ability to walk in your truth can be overcome as well as the confidence to go after goals, dreams and aspirations.

Heart Chakra

To create a chi ball for your Heart chakra, visualize the color *green* and set the following intentions. Empathy, kindness, beauty, compassion and love. Self-love, unconditional and universal love, and all forms of love- romantic, platonic, sexual and family bonds & friendships can be activated and amplified. Heart chakra chi balls are perfect for giving you a 'boost,' connecting you to your higher self and heart. This is because the heart, love as a frequency, is the source of creation *and* a direct link to the higher chakras. A chi ball here will open your heart and break through patterns of distortion and destruction (regarding feelings, emotions and relationships). Romance, beauty and a love and respect for nature and the planet as a whole increase with chi ball chakra healing. You can overcome blocks and past wounds to help with intimate bonds and your connection with Mother Earth.

Throat Chakra

To create a chi ball for your Throat chakra, visualize the color *blue* and set the following intentions. Communication, self-expression, purpose and inspiration. Chi ball healing for your throat amplifies all aspects of communication and self-expression. It is great for opening communication channels leading to inspiration, imagination, intuition, the exchange of ideas and intellect, and the ability to express your emotions and feelings. A chi ball here is perfect if you're seeking inspiration and currently feeling unmotivated or lacking in self-alignment. Although primarily associated with communication, the throat chakra relates to the higher mind and imagination and the ethereal and astral realms; subtle energy and the realm of spirit. Energizing this chakra with a chi ball will open portals to higher consciousness and activate your third eye, or at least initiate the process.

Third Eye Chakra

To create a chi ball for your Third Eye chakra, visualize the color *purple* and set the following intentions. Wisdom, insight, intuition, perception, purity and spirit. A Third Eye chi ball can be a powerful catalyst for psychic and spiritual development. It helps to open up portals to the subconscious, enhance subtle and spiritual perception, and spark intuitive wisdom, insight and guidance. Cognitive abilities and imaginative thinking can be enhanced too. You can also create a chi ball here for stress, anxiety or fear and irrational thinking. Chi balls will help to break down illusions and align you with clear sight and clear thinking. A meditative mindset will be achieved. It can therefore also help with depression and mood or temperament disorders.

Crown Chakra

To create a chi ball for your Crown chakra, visualize the colors *violet* or *white* and set the following intentions. Spiritual illumination, cosmic consciousness, divine connection, self-realization, and transformation. A chi ball for your crown will simultaneously activate your Soul Star chakra, the chakra believed by some to exist just above the crown. This connects you to your superconsciousness, the angelic, ascended master, and light being realms where the most advanced spiritual gifts and levels of awareness are available. If you're feeling spiritually disconnected in any way or like you need a reminder of the beauty and transcendental bliss of the universe, create a chi ball for your crown chakra. It can spark memories and activate kundalini energy so that healing energy will naturally start to flow through all of your other chakras. Stress, tension and anxiety can further be overcome and healed.

Visualization meditation (light)

Visualization can be used to heal from a number of blockages and internal issues. The key thing to be aware of is the power of light. There are so many words and phrases when learning about energy healing and spirituality, the Healing Arts. Chi, source, spirit, subtle energy, life force, healing energy, divine energy, divine light… one of the main ways to access these is through visualization light. This is because everything exists as a light frequency, whether it be a specific color or pure light as it is. Recognition of everything being light (divine light, healing light) automatically connects you to the light within and around. Visualizing light creates shifts and change and transformation, it is one of the fastest ways to connect to Source energy and Spirit. Lots of mental, emotional, psychological and physical ailments and issues begin on a soul level; an astral, ethereal, spiritual or soul level- something 'unseen' and 'invisible' (but very real!). Enlightenment is seeing the light and not only seeing it, but feeling, sensing and experiencing it. And potentially hearing it! Light is the source of all creation, just as OM is the sound of all creation.

This signifies that any visualization you incorporate into your self-healing practices will have profound effects. On a subatomic and subtle level, the healing process begins straight away. It must be stressed that nothing connects you faster to health and wholeness that light, as light is the root of everything. If we slow time down and see life and the universe as a holographic visual, an interconnected multidimensional web, and an infinite reality where the time and space complex is always 'now' and timeless; we see the truth in this. Everything comes back to the one original light, the Source. Thus, we create worries, imbalances, blockages, problems, stresses, distortions and illusions from our minds- from the thoughts and projections we give things. Visualization instantly initiates healing. And this means that we can start to break down our illusions, fears and anxieties through the powerful light frequencies radiating into our cells and very being (the *core* of our being). Whatever we've accumulated, be it mistruths, false beliefs or mindsets, negative thinking patterns, worries and confusions, it will come up for healing and self-evaluation. It would be wise to remember the well-known phrase 'knowledge is power' here. Self-awareness arises through visualizing light frequencies. The mind, body and spirit are designed to work in harmony, and this means visualization meditation brings hidden things from the depths to the surface.

Imagine a flashlight shining into the darkness. All that was previously in the dark will be visible and surrounded by light with a flashlight. This torch is symbolic of our conscious mind, and the effect of going within (meditation) and envisioning Source, divine or spiritual energy (light/visualization) onto and into a specific area. Again, this area may be a chakra, a plane or body (mental plane/body, emotional plane/body, etc.) a body part and organ or system (nervous, immune, circulatory system…) or a life theme and cycle. There are so many dimensions and elements to being human. We're spiritual beings having a physical human experience. Familiarizing yourself with the colors of the *Chakras* is the first key step to utilizing the power of Visualization. Once you know which energy portal relates to what color(s), you can start to heal yourself on the most intimate and holistic of levels. Without a holistic approach and understanding some aspect of yourself will suffer, which means you won't be able to attain complete healing, health and inner wholeness. Kundalini is, of course, pure light; source energy and divine white light.

Sound Therapy

You may not think it, but *silence* is a form of sound. Do you remember the Universal Laws? Yin and yang, passive and active, feminine and masculine….

Well, what about silence and sound?! Sound therapy involves a range of techniques and pathways to healing yourself and feeling more content each day. Meditation and mindfulness are the main routes associated with silence. Quantum physicists have found that within every atom is virtually 99.9% space, which means everything in the universe is essentially empty space. Physical reality, therefore, becomes defined by the thoughts, feelings, and emotions we give them. Meditation can be used to change the 'story' and the realities created in your life. You become the observer allowing yourself to detach from chaotic emotions and thoughts, unhelpful conditioned beliefs and responses, and all other conflicting internal energies. Meditation has so many health benefits. There are also masses of studies that have been conducted to show the power and validity of both meditation and mindfulness. In fact, when researching established universities, scientists and peer-reviewed, or recognized, experiments done there were so many I decided to take a more minimalist approach. It also led me to conclude the following…

The key with healing is to actually experience, to *feel* and to go within. Sometimes, too much focus on the "proof," "evidence" or overly analytical and "left-brain" need for hard stats can take from the experience. This subsequently leads to important lessons and real change being achieved. Feel and experience, don't over-rationalize or reason real sensations and emotions out of existence. What does this mean? Connecting to your source of personal power and feeling the energy flow through your veins requires some spiritual perception. This is a realization that physicality is essentially formless, empty space, and- ultimately- an illusion. 'Reality' is subjective, so it's not just physical matter and we aren't just flesh and bones. We are spirit. We're also divine with subtle energy available to us in each moment. This is the key when it comes to relying too much on scientific proof or evidence; it takes away from real and first-hand experience. To put it another way, if you're always thinking how can you expect to feel? We are *human beings*, not human doings.

So, being, feeling and going within to directly experience is important. There is a lot of research, however, for those more 'left-brain' and in need of scientific support.

Here are some forms of meditation you can work on incorporating in daily life:

- *Transcendental meditation:* This is transcending the state of one's mind into a blissful, almost eutrophic and heavenly way of perceiving and experiencing the world. Senses become heightened, self-awareness increases, and there is an overall feeling of being connected to one's purpose and something greater than them. This meditation is usually experienced through a combination of *fasting*, *detoxing*, *visualization, deep pranayama breaths*, and *sound healing* like *binaural beats or Tibetan singing bowls and chimes*.

- *Mindful meditation:* (as explored in the next point).

- *Silent meditation*: Silent meditation is mindfulness; it's being silent and present within oneself to explore and understand thoughts and feelings and belief patterns. This is effective for making sense of any situation or experience presented in life. It is a chance to slow down and get in touch with your inner being, free from the chaos of the mind and self-judgement. Silent meditation helps in observing your inner sensations and feelings so you can master your breath, so that you can further move onto more advanced healing techniques.

- *Focused meditation*: This is contemplating on any chosen topic or intention. *Focused intention* is the key here. If you have a recurring issue, are currently struggling with a tricky life situation, or need to free yourself from fear, trauma or anxiety, focused meditation helps to get to the root cause of the issue. Picture, visualize and release/let go are the key steps with this meditation, as are self-compassion and patience, non-judgement and forgiveness.

Mindfulness is linked to meditation too and many would argue they are interchangeable. Mindfulness is exactly as the name implies, it is becoming mindful, conscious and aware of internal and external sensations. It's about the empty space and the thoughts and impressions inside. By practicing mindfulness, *being mindful*, conscious and developing awareness, our thoughts become clearer and an inner peace and sense of bliss results. Our manifestation powers also increase tenfold. When we are mindful, we are paying attention to our thoughts- instead of being the boat, aimlessly drifting around the sea, we become the engine, the compass, and the captain. We can steer our lives in the right direction and take charge of our lives and self.

Mindfulness can be as simple as contemplation, meditation or (healthy) introspection. Being conscious of our thoughts and impressions allows us to break down any negative and detrimental thought patterns and conditioning, into a way of perceiving which is in harmony with ourselves, others and the natural world. People in tune with their inner source and power, henceforth, no longer feel separate or receive pain from those distractions and sensitivities, and instead experience life with an inner calm and understanding.

Mindful meditation on healing & health: On the topic of healing, mindful meditation on healing is meditating with the intention of releasing blocks and pains that may be preventing you from achieving wholeness and recovery. You can look inside yourself, through intuitive wisdom (that arises through space and silence), patience and compassion. All meditation and healing exercises can be used to develop mindfulness with increased and integrated health as a goal, such as nature sounds, sound therapy, Reiki, mantras, and transcendental meditation. Mindfulness is the foundation. Just as our thoughts affect, create and shape space, setting your intention to exist in a state of perfect health 'sets the stage' for future steps and endeavours to come. Mindful meditation for healing and health can be seen as switching the light switch on. You may still have to do a lot more to get that light, like check the wiring and electrics, change the bulb from time to time, and balance light with darkness, but you clicking the switch is an important part of making sure your 'light' stays on.

Empathic mindfulness: Empathic mindfulness is really good to practice and include in a self-healing routine or regime. This is going about your daily life with the *specific intention and focused awareness of being empathic*. Embodying an empath nature will come naturally once you have begun including meditation as a daily practice. Why an empathic nature? Because, empathy and compassion are some of the greatest roots of health and raising your vibration. We can only vibrate at our best and highest when we are in a state of flow and harmonious energy, when we have self-love, love, self-compassion, and compassion. Empathy is a powerful force. Empathic mindfulness will help you remember (re-member, i.e. to re-group! ~think of a community...) that you are a creator of your world, and no one can inflict harm unless you allow them to. No-one can dull your sparkle, put out your light, or diminish your gifts and talents. Empathic mindfulness can be done as simply as walking through nature, reflecting or contemplating life on a park bench, or sitting outside in the fresh air and sunshine whilst listening to birds chirping.

Mantras

Mantras are words or phrases repeated for effect, such as '*I am in a state of perfect health, I am in a state of perfect health, I am in a state of perfect health.*' They're a form of self-affirmation, you affirm a truth or desire to the universe. Mantras can be spoken, sung, hummed or thought. They can be used with meditation, as a 'mindfulness mantra' or simply when walking about in day-to-day life. Mantras increase manifestation and your connection to the Universal Laws. They enhance your spirit and speak a story to your cells. They're ultimately a type of *self-talk*, you're telling your body and your inner being what you want to be or achieve; how you wish to vibrate.

Sing, hum or speak them wherever you go or take the time to create a sacred space and align with a mantra practice. You can get creative with your mantras! Always remember the power of your intention and mind to shape physical matter, sensitivity to subtle energy is a gift and transforming it into a higher awareness through mantras is a very effective way to develop and strengthen your true nature.

Here are some examples of mantras for health and healing you may wish to incorporate into a self-care practice.

1. 'I am healthy, happy and content. Spirit flows through me effortlessly.'
2. 'All that exists is now, and in this present moment I am safe and protected.'

3. 'Life is magical when I open to the source of creation.'

4. 'Divinity flows through my cells and being, I am full of life force!'

5. 'My body is a sacred vessel.'

6. 'Mind, body, emotions and spirit work harmoniously for me now. Bliss enters my life.'

7. 'I take control of my health and recognize the power of my mind.'

Sound therapy

Sounds can be used to change neurological activity and structures in the brain. Neuro Linguistic programming, binaural beats, positive self-talk, mantras and affirmations, musical instruments, singing; these are just a small scope into the ways we can utilize sound waves for healing. We use sound every day, even when we don't consciously realize it. Neurons create interlinking pathways so that the body can send signals to the brain and mind, and vice versa. Scientists have achieved an amazing feat by making physical objects levitate. They call it *acoustic levitation* and it works through high speed acoustic vibrations (sound waves and particles) being directed at an object in an enclosed space. But it's not only sound waves that can alter physical matter, of course- our minds and emotions are powerful too. Focusing on sound therapy, when our brain's neurotransmitters pick up on certain sounds and frequencies our consciousness is affected. Extending beyond the mental plane and mind, thoughts and impressions in the immediate now, the effect sound has on consciousness also relates to our beliefs and subconscious programming. In essence, sound therapy can change the structure of neurons to re*shape* and re*create* our core level programming, cellular health, and the vibratory frequencies of our various systems. (Immune system, circulatory system etc.) Remember that everything exists as vibrations and frequencies.

The various forms of sound therapy to incorporate into your life, for great results, are:

- **Nature Sounds** including bird song, rainwater, forest sounds, whale and dolphin songs and waves crashing against the shore. All of these have a calming influence and can be used for study, meditation, contemplative activities and connecting to the natural world to enhance health and speed up the healing process. Holistic health is getting in touch with your mind, body, emotions and spirit; your soul too! Sounds of the natural world are one of the fastest ways to bring you back into a state of inner peace and serenity.

- *Shamanic drumming and/or tribal drumming*. Drumming acts as a 'universal heartbeat,' a natural rhythm that automatically evokes feelings and sensations of unconditional love and compassion. Tribal drumming is healing, energizing, empowering and centering, the "heartbeat" effect helps to align you with the core of your being whilst reminding you of an ancient and primordial power. Ancient wisdom and deep flashes of insight often arises through drumming. It can also be used to synchronize your breathing, journey inside oneself, and to enter a trance state for healing, insight and subconscious encounters.

- *Shamanic journeying* takes you on an inner journey inside yourself, psyche and heart space. Because shamanism is rooted in our connection to Mother earth, the universe and our physical bodies, the heart chakra and higher self are associated with shamanic journeying. This Sound therapy involves a range of musical instruments, voice, sometimes plant medicine, and visualization techniques. Techniques to connect to spirit guides, ancestors and spirit animals are often used in synergy with shamanic journeying. This is a great avenue to try if you're looking for a deeper connection to spiritual realms and your subconscious mind, need to heal your shadow self, sensuality, or sexuality, and are working through any difficult past pains, wounds or trauma. Special insights, intuitive guidance and wisdom shine through and the aim is to connect you with the highest possible vibrational aspect of yourself, without repressing or neglecting your primal, animalistic and shadow tendencies (personality/self).

- *Tibetan singing bowls, bells, and chimes* are used by monks and by many in the spiritual community to reach wholeness and healing, and access transcendental inner states. They can be used directly in meditation and also combined to OM chanting, other forms of sound, and mantras or self-affirmations. These are effective at removing blocked energy from your chakras and connecting you to your heart space (the heart chakra) and third eye.

- *OM chanting*. Speaking, singing, humming, or thinking 'Om,' Om being the universal sound of creation, can bring great healing on many levels. It can connect you to your heart, higher self, and inner power through intentions also aiding in self-alignment, practicing healthy boundaries, and allowing you to overcome limiting beliefs and mindsets. Because Om is known as the sound of the creation- it's the initial and original sound in which all other sounds and frequencies expand from, regular Om chanting opens portals into the self and higher dimensions. But it also has a grounding effect and can help with releasing painful or chaotic emotions, getting to the root of physical ailments or situations in your current life cycle, and bringing clarity and wisdom to life's events.

- *Gongs and musical instruments* are wonderful for *sound journeys* where one explores many aspects of their own mind, psyche, subconscious and self. Sound journeying once again has a holistic effect, whereby the sound journeyer accesses multiple layers of themselves; the emotional body, physical body and sensations, spiritual body and soul essence. Mental and astral planes can be connected with too. People usually report a feeling of multi-dimensionality, especially those who are already on a spiritual path or committed to healing, or a meditation practice. Heightened sensitivity and intuition occurs while simultaneously grounding one within.

- **Silence** is, in itself, a form of sound therapy which has already been covered. It is also known as contemplative or silent meditation.

Elemental Healing (Working with the Elements & Nature therapy)

This book wouldn't be complete without looking at the positive effects and healing benefits of nature, also *elemental healing*. The elements of nature exist in our planet and within our bodies. We are all made up of fire, earth, air and water- the elements flow through us and influence our health, well-being, and longevity. Western science and medicine doesn't teach this, but this doesn't take away from its truth. You may be doing everything 'right' in your eye, eating all the right foods, exercising, meditating every day and being disciplined. Yet you could still suffer from imbalances and self-sabotaging behaviors you're completely unconscious of, with no clue as to why there are still health issues and problems in your relationships. This is the beauty of being aware of universal energy and the elements. First, however, let's explore nature healing.

Nature therapy

Nature is healing, cleansing, restoring and rejuvenating. It recharges emotions, replenishes energy and heals on all levels. It can bring feelings of love, warmth, and protection, and generally wraps one in a massive ethereal hug. Nature is one of the simplest yet complex ways to heal yourself. Self-alignment, increasing boundaries, dealing with emotional and psychological issues, and spiritual growth can all come about through spending time in nature. You can achieve this by taking walks in nature, such as a local outdoor space, forest or nature reserve. Sitting on a bench and listening to running water of a stream, birds chirping, or the rustling of leaves and trees are quick-fixes and being exposed to these frequently and over long periods of time help to build up your inner strength and self-healing mechanisms.

Some of the main benefits of nature include:

- Increased energy levels, vitality, holistic well-being, and zest for life.
- Emotional 'reboot' and cleansing, balancing and harmonizing of emotional issues.
- Centering and alignment increase in boundaries and self-protection.

- Mental clarity and clearing of old 'stories,' shifts in mindset and self-talk, and improvement of communication.
- Improved physical health and vitality.
- Normalizing circadian rhythms.
- Improving hormone-related symptoms, pineal gland and thyroid functioning, etc.
- Protection and shielding from electromagnetic interference and technology.
- Protecting and cleansing the aura (the invisible energy field around you).
- Increased self-healing mechanisms and improved immune system.
- Sleep enhancement, overcoming insomnia, and improved dreaming.
- Reduction of stress, anxiety and nervous tension.
- Reduction of headaches, neurological disorders, irrational thinking and fears, and recurring emotional and psychological issues.
- Increased cognitive functioning, original thinking, intellect and problem solving.
- Creative genius and imagination enhancement.
- Increased spatial awareness, self-awareness, intuition and instincts.
- Increase in life force and vital energy.

- The ability to perceive subtle energy, connect to dream states and the subconscious, and see life from a spiritually aware and connected viewpoint.

Each point has its own story so there is a lot that could be said here. You may want to choose a few that you feel you need help on and contemplate the qualities in nature. Mindfulness, mindful meditation, and 'soul-searching' (introspection, conscious self-reflection and contemplation) are effective routes to personal transformation and healing. Choose some of the points and meditate on the qualities. This is one of the most effective ways to connect to the power of nature therapy, as nature's energies are restorative and healing on their own; you only need your intention and an open and still mind to succeed.

Now let's look at the elements.

Elemental healing

Discovering potential imbalances and internal blocks through understanding the elements is a very profound method for healing and self-analysis. We can look to *Astrology* and our *Natal (Birth) charts* to get a clearer picture of unseen forces affecting us, but we can also look to foods we eat, the amount of exercise we engage in, libido (or lack of it) and so many other aspects and themes present within life.

For example, if you have a lot of water in your Birth chart you will be emotional, sensitive and adaptable. If you have a lot of fire you will be passionate, self-expressive and courageous. Someone with much earth energy will be grounded, security and order loving, and responsible, and a person with lots of air energy will be defined as being imaginative, intelligent and perceptive. These are the general traits, but the point with sharing this is how each of the elements has *unique qualities & characteristics* that help to make and shape a person. Knowing the wisdom of the elements enables self-evaluation and self-discovery on a whole new level.

Fire Energy

Star Signs: Aries, Leo and Sagittarius

Main qualities: Boldness, courage, zest, life force, passion, creativity, artistic talents, fun-loving, spirited, friendly, outgoing and playfulness.

Being a fire sign or having a lot of fire in your natal/birth chart tells you a lot about your personality and the challenges and successes you will face in life. Fire is bold, inspiring, courageous and highly passionate. It relates to the qualities of pragmatism, inspiration, devotion and life force, zest and excitement for life. People with lots of fire energy are charming, charismatic, outgoing and social; enthusiastic and optimistic too. They prefer to be as positive as possible and like to keep things upbeat and light. There is a bounce in one's step, a vitality and unique energy to wake up each morning. Passionate, self-expressive and generally intuitive, fiery people are able to express their ideas and wisdom effortlessly. They're also wonderfully creative with immense creative spirit and artistic vision.

What does this mean for healing and achieving wholeness? ~

Too much fire can lead to a lack of water. One can't communicate or connect with depth and the emotional intelligence and vulnerability of water. They (people with too much fire/excessive fire energy) lack gentleness, grace and tact. There is also a disconnection from the subtle and spiritual realms, and one's true feelings and emotions. Inner currents like soft energy, moods, feelings, emotions and ethereal energy are replaced with constant chatter, external talk, or a largely extroverted nature. There is an ability to be introspective, 'go within,' and connect with the inner worlds of self and being. Physically too much fire can lead to high metabolism and burn-out if not careful.

Too much fire can lead to a lack of air. There is an inability to speak one's truth effectively, with transparent and calm communication. Too many

126

ideas and a tendency to be on the move or in constant motion can result in not focusing their ideas and intellect into a dedicated path. There may be a disconnection from one's true path and purpose with a lack of air energy. One's destiny or legacy may suffer- so much fire and excitement can have the opposite effect, paradoxically manifesting as being stuck in the 'inspiration & idea/concept' stage. There is a vision, but self-talk and outward communication is jeopardized by lack of communicative gifts.

Too much fire can lead to lack of earth. Visionary qualities are emphasized to the point of 'having too many eggs in too many baskets.' There is no direction, focus or *grounding*. Projects and passion pursuits are scattered and not grounded into a secure and stable foundation; physical structures are neglected and sacrificed. Motivations and intentions often lack the applied action needed for success on the earth plane- projects are started and not finished, significant bonds and relationships are cut short, and there is a general frivolity and flightiness with regard to people, projects and places. Commitment and responsibility fall short.

Positively, when in balance and attuned to the fire qualities and strengths... One can inspire others and motivate them to new heights! High energy levels allow for significant advancements in creative and artistic projects. Imagination, intellect and intuition soar and there is a sense of fearlessness that allows one to take on any challenge in life. Original thinking and problem-solving make a fiery person full of passion and excitement, optimistic thinking and positive energy. Fire promotes action and a success mindset while adding vision to the grounded qualities of earth, inspiration and an optimistic outlook to the logical qualities of air, and self-empowerment to the sensitive qualities of water.

Crystals to enhance and integrate fire include: Ruby, Obsidian, Opal, Peridot, Rutilated quartz, Sapphire, Tiger's eye, Pyrite, Sunstone, and Fire agate.

Earth Energy

Star Signs: **Taurus, Virgo and Capricorn**

Main qualities: **Practicality, responsibility, down-to-earth, order, structure, organization, duty, wisdom, grounding, honesty, patience and security.**

Earth energy is grounding, stabilizing, security loving, and practical. Duty, responsibility and a love of structure and organization define a person with a lot of earth energy. They are connected to ancient wisdom and primordial earthy power. They're also sensual and instinctual with a fierce sense of protection, motherly or fatherly love and nurturance.

These people tend to be caring, sensitive, sincere and artistic in a grounded and down-to-earth way. Earth energy is modest and generally humble, mainly wise and perceptive with unique skills in observation. Success, achievement and accomplishment rooted in reality- in the physical world- come with balanced or strong earth energy. They can be both kind, generous and selfless and ambitious, practical and security/structure focused simultaneously; honesty, patience and resourcefulness define them.

What does this mean for healing and achieving wholeness? ~

Too much earth can lead to a lack of fire. Inspiration, vision and passion are often sacrificed with excessive earth energy. There is a large emphasis on security and creating physical structures and foundations, and this takes away from spontaneity and 'big vision' thinking to integrate new ideas or original concepts. There is a slight lack of imagination with excessive earth. One can become uninspired, unmotivated and lacking in original and artistic thinking, or simply shy away from excitement and creative self-expression. On a physical level, a lack of fire can result in lethargy, idleness, and laziness, and weight gain and stagnation.

Too much earth can lead to a lack of water.
Emotions suffer and vulnerability is compromised in
the name of physical strength. One becomes
detached from their inner moods and currents.
Personal, intimate, romantic, and platonic
relationships may be sacrificed in the name of duty
or physical responsibility. There's too much
emphasis on achievement and seeing physical
results, 'living in the now' and being present with the
joys and pleasures of life are diminished. One also
becomes distanced from their own emotional
intelligence and sensitivity with a lack of water
energy. Intuitive and imaginative qualities suffer
dramatically too.

Too much earth can lead to a lack of air.
Inspiration and original ideas are decreased. There's
an inability to see and think clearly, rationally, or
intelligently. Communication breaks down and one
becomes stuck in their ways, there's a disconnection
from the mind and self. Physically, one may gain
weight or suffer with heaviness and bloating. Ideas,
emotions, feelings and impressions aren't free to
flow, and repressions can result. Wisdom isn't
allowed to shine, and self-expression suffers. One
also becomes limited in perception with a lack of air
in relation to too much earth. Overall, "lightness" of
self and spirit is replaced with being solely
connected to the physical body and world.

Positively, when in balance and attuned to the earth qualities and strengths... One can show others what it means to be a truly grounded and responsible adult. A sense of duty, service and helpfulness towards others and communities take precedence, and personal victories on a personal and/or professional level manifest as a result. Balanced and integrated earth allows for the inspiring and visionary qualities of fire to be grounded, the emotional vulnerability and intelligence of water to be nurtured and nourished, and the intellectually gifted mental qualities of air to be held in physical foundations. Support, nurturance, security and stability are provided to the strengths of all the other elements with earth energy.

Crystals to enhance and integrate earth include: Cornelian, Chrysoprase, Jade, Smoky Quartz, Bloodstone, Garnet, Red Jasper, Hematite, Moss agate and Onyx.

Air Energy

Star Signs: **Gemini, Libra and Aquarius**

Main qualities: **Intelligence, cerebral gifts, intuition, imagination, perception, observation, communication, language, mental agility, wit and sociability.**

Air energy is purifying and uplifting. It relates to all aspects of communication, intellect, mental and psychological gifts (and health) and perception. Intuitive, imaginative, subtle and logical perception come under the air element. Logic, reason & rationality are the main qualities of strong air energy. People with a lot of air tend to have a keen eye for detail and perception and advanced observational skills. They're witty, clever, inquisitive and open-minded. Sociable and friendly, they have an introverted and introspective side too. Self-expression, speech, poetry, writing, publishing, public or motivational speaking, and teaching are all associated with air energy. Cerebral gifts too, deep and philosophical thinking combined with the capacity for original thinking. There is a scholarly energy with air.

What does this mean for healing and achieving wholeness? ~

Too much air can lead to a lack of earth. Focusing too much on the mind and intellect often leads to an absence of grounding, focusing less on security, stability and physical foundations to secure one's ideas and knowledge into. Physical vitality and nourishment may suffer as a result. There may be too much emphasis on the exchange of ideas and communication with a neglect of the body, health and movement or exercise. Diet choices may be poor when there is a lack of earth energy. Also, there is a chance of being flighty and a scatter-brain or being prone to gossip and mindless chatter.

Too much air can lead to a lack of fire. Being stuck in the 'idea' stage without the inspiration, passion or zest to back it up. Having fire inside- a direct result of the airy inspiration and imagination- but not being able to implement it due to misdirection or a lack of optimism. People with too much air and not enough fire give into negative thinking, pessimism, and illogical or irrational thinking. Intuition can suffer as a result. There is the aspect of having amazing ideas and a firm understanding of topics or concepts, but not being able to communicate them properly. The same goes for feelings and emotions.

Too much air can lead to a lack of water. A lack of emotion, depth and sincerity arises with diminished water. Air signs and energy tends to be superficial; the 'shadow' aspect of air is false communication, manipulation and deception- intentionally distorting the truth. Water energy is sensitive, empathic and compassionate; transparency and living with heart and soul (therefore genuinity) is strong and developed. A lack of water can lead to the inability to communicate with grace and authenticity. Dishonesty may arise and emotional depth and openness are sacrificed. Further, too much air implies an overemphasis on thought, reason, intellect, and rationality & logic. Intuition, 'free flow' of ideas and information/wisdom and evolved creative genius (and imagination) lack.

Positively, when in balance and attuned to the air qualities and strengths... Air is inspirational in a wise and purifying way. It is able to communicate with ease and share wisdom, knowledge and ideas to empower and uplift, and connect people within a community. Airy people tend to be very friendly and sociable. Air adds an extra dimension of wisdom and original thinking to the creative visions of fire, rationality and reason to the adaptability and transcendental feel of water, and imagination and open-mindedness to the structured and organized qualities of earth. Balanced air energy can enhance all of the other elements by providing wit, quick-thinking, the ability to rationalize and conceptualize, and being more open to the exchange of an eclectic range of topics and interests.

Crystals to enhance and integrate air include: Amber, Amazonite, Citrine, Topaz, Emerald, Diamond, Malachite, Fluorite, Lapis Lazuli and Amethyst.

Water Energy

Star Signs: Cancer, Scorpio and Pisces

Main qualities: Sensitivity, compassion, empathy, intuition, psychic gifts, spiritual awareness, gentleness, devotion, imagination, creativity and artistic abilities.

Someone strong in water energy is intuitive, emotional, sensitive and artistically gifted. They're both imaginative and intuitive, creatively gifted and compassionate, and intelligent and wise. Water is emotional and serves as a direct connection to the subconscious realm and subtle energy. Water can navigate life's currents with ease and grace, attuning to an emotional frequency. Emotional wisdom, intelligence and vulnerability are strong in people with a lot of water. There's also a psychic and clairvoyant element to water energy- it is able to pierce through life's illusions and get to the root of truth. Universal truths, a connection to the divine, transcendental union, and advanced empathy and intuition are associated with this element. Universal archetypes and ideas, and insights into the meaning of life, the universe and human nature; are strong. Visionary qualities combined with a sense of unconditional love and universal compassion are evolved.

What does this mean for healing and achieving wholeness? ~

Too much water can lead to a lack of air. Too much water and not enough air means there is a disconnection from logic, thinking, rationality, reason and scientific thought. One tends to feel and experience reality through emotions- emotional intelligence is strong but communication may suffer. Reality becomes primarily about the feelings, instinctual responses and overall 'vibe' one senses and feels, and other aspects of making sense of relationships and situations are sacrificed. People with a lack of air energy can become overwhelmed by intense emotions and internal currents if they can't express their truth or emotions.

Too much water can lead to a lack of earth. There's an inability to ground one's wisdom, passion, imagination and creativity into physical material structures. One may be stuck in the dreaming or philosophical stage, or be focused so much on visionary, spiritual and psychic qualities and gifts that they don't apply themselves in life. Too much water at the expense of earth energy means dreams and goals can never be fully realized. Success, financial abundance and prosperity, personal achievements and accomplishments may be sacrificed, and talent can go to waste. Also, there may be a disconnection from the world and one's body. Bloating and weight gain can result without sufficient physical exercise.

Too much water can lead to a lack of fire. Water is sensitive, emotional and intuitive- it can lack the passion and inspiration of fire. Not enough fire manifests as wandering through life with a dreamy aura, being "away with the fairies" or simply looking as if one is going to float away. Passion and sincere positivity for life and projects may not be expressed, so others may think one dull, bored or passionless. Internal feelings, thoughts, and moods can't be shown or projected externally in a way others respond to; a disconnection from spirit and life force can take over. A lack of fire ultimately makes one over or hyper-sensitive and potentially irrational in interpersonal relationships.

Positively, when in balance and attuned to the water qualities and strengths... Our bodies and the planet are made up of over 72% water. Water is cleansing, purifying, spiritually illuminating, and enlivening, it energizes and soothes simultaneously. This is why watery people are often psychic and have heightened and evolved senses and intuition. Water people inspire others through their love, compassion and empathy. They're sensitive to the needs of others and make excellent caregivers, nurturers, healers, psychics, dreamers, empaths, poets, philosophers, musicians and artists. Water provides depth and sensitivity to the bold qualities of fire, emotional intelligence and wisdom to the intellect (and wit) of air, and soulful bonding and spiritual perception to the modest, practical and grounded aspects of earth. All in all, water channeled positively allows the higher self to be connected through the emotional body and instincts.

Crystals to enhance and integrate water include: Opal, Coral, Moonstone, Pearl, Sugilite, Aquamarine, Rhodochrosite, Lapis Lazuli, Amethyst, Jade, and Fluorite.

Intuition and Psychic Development

We've already looked at the higher self... Intuition and psychic development are intrinsic to healing with subtle, ethereal and spiritual energy. When life force flows through you your chakras are unblocked and energized, which in turn stimulates your higher chakras- your third eye where intuitive and psychic energy is strong. If you aren't already familiar with the '4 clairs' it may be useful to quickly run through these. Everyone's heard of clairvoyance, but are you aware of the others?

Clairvoyance

Clairvoyance is 'clear seeing.' It is the gift of sight beyond the physical sense. Clairvoyance is essentially an open and active third eye, subtle and spiritual perception with an ability to see beyond illusions. One can get to the root and truths of matters with clairvoyance. 'The veil of illusion' is broken down and there is a clear light guiding you. Precognitive powers are incorporated, you may be able to see upcoming events or sense them profoundly or know when something good or bad is about to happen, or when someone new is about to enter your life. A clear example of clairvoyance is having a thought that you know and feel within is real (even if your rational logical mind can't explain it) and then it happening, such as someone coming into your awareness then seconds to moments later that person walking into the room, calling you, sending you a text message, or you hearing a significant story about them.

You may literally "see" it with your physical eyes, yet the sensation arises below the surface, with your third eye. The ability to see auras and swirls of energy is connected here. Psychic and spiritual vision is switched on in people with clairvoyant abilities, so it is pretty hard to fib or lie to them. These people are more often than not committed to a higher truth and reality- their higher self is strong and in control. Deception and manipulation can be sensed a mile off and imaginative and artistic visions come to them frequently. In dreams, one may have precognitive dreams while being aware of imagery and symbolism that relates to waking life.

Clairsentience

Clairsentience is 'clear feeling.' This gift is associated with empathy, the ability to feel what it's like to be in another's shoes. This is a form of reading people and seeing inside their mind, soul and core self- one can feel emotions, thoughts and subtle energy through clairsentience. Advanced forms of empathy are telepathy and psychic ability, in essence; the capacity for knowing exactly what it's like to be someone else, through your ability to feel on a deep level. Another person's health or ill-health can be felt, and all aspects of mind, emotion, physicality and spirit can be experienced too. Clairsentience doesn't just apply to feeling other people's inner being, it is also the ability to *merge* with them on all levels, taking on and making sense of a particular physical ailment or internal imbalance, or any hidden aspect of someone else's life. So, if someone has an upset stomach, they would be able to feel it. If someone is suffering from a foot injury a clairsentient person would 'just know' (through instinctive feeling).

Empathy comes in many forms. Clairsentience involves receiving information and knowledge from people, places and objects. One can touch an object and pick up on its story, and this applies to its history, significant people or figures who are connected to the object, and various 'behind the scenes' forces that have shaped the energetic memory of the object. Referring to places, one may walk through a sacred or religious site and feel its history and background. You can *relive the memory* through evolved clairsentience. Experiencing goosebumps, Deja Vu, or unexplainable sensations are common. Simultaneously the same applies to negative experiences, like walking into a room and feeling strongly how there is tension or that something is wrong.

Claircognizance

Claircognizance is 'clear knowing.' It links to the other two as to see and feel you must 'know.' It's important to know that the four clairs interlink, they are all similar in meaning and essence. You may get a sudden insight, an absolute conviction that I *just know*, without any physical or logical reason. You may have certainty about events that occurred in the past, or may occur in the future, and you are able to recognize when someone or something is dangerous. People lying, telling the truth, or even distorting the truth ever so slightly can all be sensed. Creative and imaginative ideas are rich and frequent with Claircognizance and inspiration flows freely. There is a lot of cerebral, intuitive and cognitive activity! Sacred geometry and quantum mechanics are two topic areas associated with this Clair, as knowing is being self-aware and intelligent; but with a deep awareness of the universe. Flashes of insight, problem-solving, being able to figure out tricky puzzles and brain-games, and seeing beyond the veil of illusion are developed in Claircognizant people.

Psychic downloads are common too. During conversation, you may interrupt others through knowing the "perfect time" to share an insight or piece of information. You're attuned to a universal clock and are deeply intuitive. You possess personal power and presence, your mind is attuned to a higher frequency and your knowing might sometimes be mistaken for arrogance, ignorance or hearsay from people who don't see (possess clear & psychic sight). The hunches you experience are largely true and so on point that your wisdom is in line with some divine power and higher knowing. Finally, you have the extraordinary gift of absorbing information from books, writing, meditation, and documentaries or podcasts, in a way most humans don't possess. There's an aspect of 'cosmic downloads' linked to Claircognizance and the other three Clairs.

Clairaudience

This is the gift of 'clear hearing.' You can hear sounds coming from alternative frequencies and dimensions. You hear tones and frequencies above and beyond the normal scope of sound waves. This includes being woken up by angelic voices or people with a strong benevolent energy calling your name. The space in between waking life and dream world is thin, there is an overlap- this is known as the astral realm. People with Clairaudience receive guidance or simply messages of presence and love through people they know (a mother, grandmother; someone with unconditional love in their hearts) through the ether. It's not only during sleep where the veil is thin that this occurs. It can also occur in waking life, one may hear a loved one call out to them seeking their help or attention; it is common for spiritually awakened people with their psychic powers activated to hear their lover, close friends or family speak to them telepathically. Telepathic communication is developed with clairaudience.

One also receives messages through sound, speech and internal noise. These are sounds that you know aren't coming from the physical space around you, but from another dimension. Your consciousness is heightened and activated so time and space doesn't exist, or in other words isn't linear. Time is multidimensional. Space is multidimensional, timeless, and infinite. There is an invisible cord that connects us all and people close to our souls often communicate in the subtle realms. We're connected through thoughts, feelings, emotions and the power of our hearts and spirits, therefore a loved one may project an intention or thought, and we hear it. The other main aspect of Clairaudience is hearing ringing or chimes and bells- again, as if they're coming from far away (another plane of consciousness/dimension). People often report the feeling of Archangel Michael and angels, light beings and spiritual entities existing on different planes. Music playing is a common occurrence as well. Intuitive messages come to you through means that can't be explained logically or rationally, and telepathy is evolved to new levels. Additionally, one can communicate with plants and animals, hearing what they say through the energy and vibrations they emit (thoughts, feelings, subtle energy, etc.).

It's useful to be aware of the four Clairs as they can lead to great healing and personal growth. You can use this knowledge as a healing exercise by journaling and writing down your thoughts, feelings and memories. Often, a lot of what we experience is *unconscious*, i.e. supernatural or extraordinary things happen that we can't explain, or don't yet have the wisdom to understand. But we know it to be true intuitively, for example having precognitive dreams or knowing when someone close to you is about to call or enter the room. The examples shared above with Clairvoyance, Clairsentience, Claircognizance and Clairaudience are advanced occurrences, yet one thousands to millions of people experience on a regular basis. Life really is magical and multidimensional.

So, journaling and expressing yourself through self-reflection, introspection, and wound, trauma and childhood healing (looking to your past, both positive and negative memories) aids in connecting to this psychic and intuitive part of yourself. This then opens new neural pathways for further healing and self-discovery. Life is cyclic, everything is interconnected. A memory can trigger a powerful process of self-healing and awakening which further aligns you, or reconnects you, with core aspects of yourself you've forgotten. Working with Amethyst is an effective way to connect to your psychic and spiritual gifts. This is the color of the third eye (chakra healing is also advised, specifically for the Third Eye!), and Amethyst is perfect for intuition, clear-thinking, subtle perception, and spiritual insights. It is known as a crystal for poets, artists, psychics, seers, shamans, philosophers and both teachers and students. This crystal opens portals to the higher mind and self whilst connecting you to universal truths and wisdom.

Chapter 3: Overcoming blocks, releasing past pain, and healing from trauma

Energy healing involves overcoming blocks, releasing pain, and healing from trauma, as the chapter title suggests. Blocks are imbalances in the energy bodies. Distortions and energetic blocks can manifest on any of the 'bodies,' the mental, emotional, physical and spiritual planes. A lot of what we experience internally shows externally, and sometimes it's unconscious and other times conscious to us. Emotional blocks and distortions, for example, can lead to mental stress and psychological anxiety, or physical aches and pains through a buildup of tension. On a spiritual and holistic level, holding onto emotional pain also leads to imbalances in key areas of life, from finances to career, relationships and love. Trauma is even worse as unresolved trauma can lead to more severe and long-term issues, ultimately affecting all areas of life. A core wound in sexuality, as another example, will lead to unconsciously projecting your fears and insecurities onto others, sometimes the people who are already evolved and operating at their best. They could be a true soulmate or kindred spirit, only have our best interest at heart, and vibrate on a frequency of love and purity, or kindness and sincerity; yet through our unhealed wounds we project negatively onto them and cause further disconnection. This is why it's so important to heal ourselves and be conscious of the mind, body and spirit.

In this chapter we will explore some of the main challenges presented to us on the human journey.

Presence is key

One of the most common blocks to healing and wholeness thousands to millions of people experience on a daily basis is not living in the now, being present. Staying stuck in the past, or thinking too far into the future, will only lead to an inability to be present with our feelings, emotions and needs. When our needs aren't met, we unconsciously project onto others, being too "future focused" can take you out of the present moment and away from mindfulness, and this is the root of most breakdowns in relationships and communication which is essential for harmony and loving unity. Learning to become present in each moment with your partner and others allows you to become present with yourself, with your thoughts, feelings, emotions and inner truth. We can't be authentic or real in relationships unless we are first honest and real with ourselves. So, mindfulness and presence are the key. A prime example is how we sometimes treat our partners when unevolved and less mature. You may be completely "loved up," relaxing with your sweetheart after having just eaten a lovely dinner, in a romantic and cozy space; but then something in the mind kicks in that prevents you from enjoying this warm and affectionate space, further taking your attention into the future. It may not sound like a big deal or problem initially, but, in reality, this action allows in a lot of room for confusion and illusion. Fears, anxieties and disillusionment takes hold, and the beautiful and warm authentic connection you could have experienced is replaced with unconscious wounds and trauma projections.

Illusions arise when we are not being present with ourselves or our partner. When we mentally project into the future a number of things happen. Firstly, we become disconnected from our body and our physical surroundings. Our intuition and wisdom *knows*, it is perceptive, sensual and intuitive- we can sense our partner and lover's intentions, which, unless dealing with a true narcissist or toxic character, are in harmony with the loving and genuine feelings you desire. Thinking too far into the future and coming out of presence disconnects you from your body and divine intuition and power, and it is from this space where illusions and distortions in mind and emotion originate. Secondly, the energetic space surrounding us also known as the *aura* starts to allow negative thoughts and energy in. The aura is known to science as the electromagnetic energy field, and it is an energetic "bubble," if you will, responsible for all thoughts, feelings, emotions, beliefs and subtle impressions. It is in this energetic bubble where illusions and faulty perceptions otherwise known as distortions enter, i.e. when we lose contact and touch with the self. Mindfulness and being present in the moment prevent this from happening, but when it does happen, we open ourselves to subconscious and unconscious influences. And the realm of the subconscious and the unconscious, is where "shadow elements" can come through.

The subconscious is closely linked to the shadow self, the parts of self that are dark, seen as ugly and often repressed or denied. The unconscious or unconsciousness is also where repressed and hidden or rejected aspects are stored and although we are not conscious of them, they still influence all aspects of waking life. So, when you come out of presence and living in the moment with your partner, all of the various "things" behind the surface come through in full force! Unseen and past traumas and wounds still floating around in unconsciousness, or your subconscious mind, make their way into the forefront of your conscious mind so that they affect your thoughts and emotions in the present. The *mistake* lies in confusing these ethereal and astral influences for truth or reality; they are not reality; they are merely mental projections and emotional distortions. You need to be aware that reality and human emotion is a complex and confusing thing. The "darker undertones" may not be reflective of what is actually happening in the present, or with the exchange of energy and connection you share with your friend, lover, partner or acquaintance. We are all plagued by our fears, childhood wounds and insecurities, and potential illusions and distortions, therefore opening yourself to all of these various "potentials" is, again, a mistake. The *block* lies in your inability to live in the present moment and have focused attention on your relationships.

Past wounds, childhood traumas, shadow influences, unconscious currents… *thinking too far into the future* allows these in. Fortunately, there are many steps to recovery and ways to heal from this block, and this is a very significant block to realize. Developing presence can be achieved through meditation and mindfulness and all of the various healing tools in this book. The first step is being aware of the illusory nature of 'reality.' Through meditation and self-healing, you can cultivate greater awareness, empathy, self- compassion, intuition and spiritual or psychic insight and awareness, further filling yourself with chi, the universal life force energy responsible for health, vitality and longevity.

Codependence VS Soul-dependence

There is a massive difference between being harmoniously codependent and having an unhealthy codependent mindset. Codependency is something that is generally viewed as negative and harmful to the self. It is self and counterproductive, implying you rely too much on a bond and connection with someone which takes away from your sense of independence. Self-autonomy, self-sovereignty, and self-esteem are often sacrificed with unhealthy codependency. In Western society, there is a lot of emphasis on 'things,' need, wealth and greed. We buy too much and desire too much materialistically, and this makes us seek comfort in people and places too. Having a healthy codependent mindset- or strong soul-dependence (soul-independence), however, implies a sense of mindfulness and being in control. You actively and consciously choose to engage in codependence; therefore, the positive associations of cooperation, compromise and consideration are present. Being conscious is the key here. When you possess a harmonious codependent mindset you have made the conscious choice to engage in codependency and develop a bond with *focused intention*; you aren't ruled by unconscious forces and, generally speaking, you possess positive emotions and thoughts. This intention includes making the decision to share love, affection, living space, resources, money, and emotional and material bonds. One of the greatest mistakes and blocks to holistic health and longevity lies in the lack of such choices, and of course being too codependent.

Spiritually, we can call this "being stuck in your root chakra." The root chakra is an essential aspect of self. It relates to survival, security, sexual reproduction and feeling grounded in the world and in your body. But codependency with all of its unconscious pulls and negative consequences (arguments, excessive needs and greed, projecting onto others, etc.) relies too much on a 'root chakra reality.' Where's the heart chakra (unconditional love, empathy, self-love), third eye and higher self (connection to spirit, divine reality, psychic gifts and intuition), or crown chakra (spiritual illumination, transcending the go, overcoming excess materialistic desires)? An overactive root chakra makes one too grounded and peace and joy come from the ability to feel secure in the world. But this is a twisted truth, as is one truly happy or at peace? Always desiring more 'things,' feeling like you never have enough, seeking to control people and relationships, and the hundreds of other examples we could share... this isn't happiness. This is being stuck in a state of need and lack.

Soul-dependence is a good word to adopt and incorporate into your vocabulary. It's also something to meditate on and seek to cultivate (increase). Being soulfully independent signifies relating to others in a balanced and harmonious way, steering away from negative/unhealthy tendencies and behaviors such as possessiveness, jealousy, insecurities and excessive clinginess, mothering or smothering. You also see yourself in a healthy and whole way, a way in which you are balanced and whole within which further reflects into your connections. Being soulfully independent within a healthy codependent mindset means that you naturally steer clear of the negative codependent behaviors. Thus, recognizing codependent behaviors can help you overcome previous mistakes and attract the love, abundance, health and opportunities you want. You may want to get deep with your understanding of codependency.

Codependency can be defined as the following: -

1. *Becoming a martyr*: Martyrdom is sacrificing your needs for others- to an excessive extent. You may fall into pleasing and appeasing or being too selfless,

losing yourself (your "self") in the process. Sacrifice and extreme appeasement can include sacrificing your mental, emotional, physical or spiritual health, or losing sight of your morals, values and own empathy in the pursuit of making a toxic relationship last.

2. *Equating love with lust*: Equating or confusing love with lust is another common sign of codependency. You may become wrapped up in this idealized or fantasized vision of love, that you make yourself prone to illusion and the reality of your partner's intentions, motivations and actions. Lust can also apply to yourself and how you present yourself within a relationship.

3. *Taking on your partner's addictions*: Possibly one of the most obvious effects of being unhealthily codependent; taking on your partner's addictions is a sure step to rejecting true and lasting love out of your life. You may think that sacrificing your health or sanity is helping your man, but, in reality, it is doing the complete opposite!

4. *Alternating between polarities*: A case of extremes... duality is inherent within all of life, alternating between polarities in terms of codependency can relate to being overly practical and responsible in one instance, and then lacking all responsibility in another. You may have chaotic emotions and a frantic mindset, further jumping from completely different personalities in moment to

moment, or day to day. This is due to your desire to adapt, merge and fit into what you believe your partner wants. Yet, a lot of this stems from insecurity and "precognitive thinking"- the people in your circle or a partner may be a lot more stable and emotionally and practically secure than you are assuming.

5. *Ignoring problems*: Repressing real issues in your relationships leads to many problems and eventually the breakdown of a significant bond. Romance, intimacy and sexual desire are built on the foundations of trust and honesty, and these can't be achieved without open and transparent communication. In the short term, ignoring problems results in the breakdown of communication and tension building up in your relationship. Long term, you can develop minor, severe or extreme forms of depression, anxiety, trauma and/or repression- repressions which build up into core wounds that require deep healing and therapy to recover from.

6. *Excessive comparison and self- criticism*: Comparing yourself to others doesn't do anything for your self- esteem, nor will it help well-being or positive feelings of love and affection to grow. Comparison is the seed of jealousy, envy and resentment, and these can lead to toxic displays in your own behavior and speech. Unhealthy comparison and self-criticism imply that the attention is always on someone else, so less energy

and focus can be given to yourself and your own issues or real-life "flaws." If you want to be whole, healed and balanced focus on yourself. You are unique and beautiful.

7. *Low self- esteem and self- worth*: Low self-esteem, self-worth and confidence are major detrimental effects of codependency. Having a healthy codependent mindset will help you to develop the self-esteem and self-empowerment necessary for a thriving and authentic relationship.

8. *Lack of self-love and self-care*: Self-love and self-care are integral to the success and longevity of health and partnerships, but being overly codependent diminishes opportunity for these.

9. *Reactive, not responsive*: Learning to *respond* and *not react* is one of the keys to health and healing. When you respond, you acknowledge, rationalize, empathize and recognize. When you react, you respond in a certain type of way, a way that is most often not in harmony with your best self. Reaction can involve harsh words, unnecessary judgment and a sense of chaos and mental or emotional distortion; you don't see and speak with harmony, cooperation and just compromise in mind. Responding is a bit more *mindful* and involves greater levels of awareness, compassion and empathy.

10. *Sexual issues*: Issues in one's sexuality usually signify fears and blockages in intimacy and opening up on a deep level. Sexual problems can include

being terrified of intimacy, allowing past wounds and pain from sexual relationships to affect your current self, and either taking on an extreme dominating or submissive role in the bedroom. Your tendency to self-sacrifice and appease or please can spill out into the bedroom, so working on this tendency if you possess it can help to develop a healthy codependent mindset as opposed to being codependent.

11. *Depression*: Depressive tendencies may develop through codependency. Relying on one person for all of your needs means that you become naturally down and sad inside, and this is because true happiness comes from yourself. Codependency misaligns you with your true self further placing sole emphasis on external situations, environments and people.

12. *Suppression of dreams and aspirations*: Finally, your dreams and aspirations may become suppressed and take a back seat. Codependency creates a disconnection between your soul, spirit, life path or purpose, and goals, dreams and aspirations, and your desires and passions. Desire shifts towards your relationship, partner or materialism to the point where nothing else seems to matter.

Toxic love patterns and Karmic bonds

If you are familiar with the New Age, spirituality or holistic and alternative health scene you will most likely have heard of toxic love and toxic relationships. Toxicity is something which is deeply associated with unhealthy romantic and sexual bonds, and a reality that affects a lot of people, specifically younger people or those less spiritually evolved. Toxic love is the opposite of soulmate love, a soulmate bond and connection. It is also known as karmic love as karma implies an exchange of energy whereby learning and growth is inherent. This is a fundamental part of toxic (and soulmate) love- both partners use each other as a mirror to learn, heal, grow and evolve. Great transformation comes through toxic love, but first the subjects involved must transcend old cycles and ways of being and transform through the test and challenges presented. This includes many things including the ability to apologize, losing the need to be right, learning to compromise, accepting change and growth, developing empathy and understanding, displaying compassion within a romantic relationship, and many others. Of course, any one of these things leads to major blocks, imbalances and issues in health and well-being. Toxic or karmic love can be seen as the opposite to soulmate love for a number of reasons. Understanding the aspects of a soulmate love and bond can contribute to the healing process, enabling you to see where you might be going wrong and what you need to change to be the best version of yourself.

A soulmate love and bond

Soulmates are a reflection of us. They are here to teach us about core aspects of ourselves, and this the key difference between a soul bond and a toxic love bond. Soulmates can be seen as *mirrors*, reflections of our innermost self. A soulmate bond shows itself so we can learn, evolve and heal, transcend lower vibrational ways of being, behavior and thought. In terms of everyday practical implications, this means that you experience depth, intimacy and emotional openness and authenticity in a soulmate (non-toxic) bond. Empathy is strong and you navigate your relationship with self-awareness. Soulmate bonds come into our lives for deep healing and releasing. We may still be holding onto emotional blocks, issues and trauma that a soulmate can help us to release. Alternatively, you may have outdated, limiting or self-destructive beliefs and mindsets preventing your evolution and self, or spiritual, development. A soulmate connection helps to transcend this, showing you the "unseen" and invisible parts of self. We also have deep friendships with our soulmate, in addition to a romantic connection. Non-toxic relationships, i.e. soulmate bonds, are characterized by friendship, mutual respect, and recognition of one another- you recognize their strengths, talents, energy and beautiful qualities and don't seek to take these in a way common in toxic relationships. If you weren't romantically or sexually involved, you would be wonderful friends and experience platonic intimacy! This is the key and the foundation to true love blossoming. And it's a well-known fact that love and intimacy lead to the production of feel-good hormones. Hugging and physical contact produces oxytocin, dopamine and serotonin, neurotransmitters essential for well-being and positivity.

You may also share a spiritual or even psychic connection with your partner in soulmate love. Many soulmates are literally connected through the thing that defines them… soul. We all have access to spirit and the divine and we all have a spiritual body. You could very well experience telepathic connection in the form of telepathy (telepathic communication) or simply share a spiritual-psychic link and bond. You may know when the other is about to call or enter the room, without physical warning, and further sense things above and beyond the "norm." Your awareness of one another's presence is deeply heightened and sharing thoughts, speech and

161

emotions are not uncommon. There is also most likely an element of reading one another's minds too, literally possessing a clairvoyant gift to tune into your partner's energy field and aura. What does this mean for health? It signifies we can open our kundalini and heal our chakras, the energy portals responsible for health and longevity. It is in the aura, the electromagnetic energy field surrounding us, that thoughts, emotions, beliefs, subtle impressions, mental projections and one's state of vibratory health (your personal vibration or frequency) can be seen, experienced and sensed. Soulmates often have an invisible and profound bond with one another on the subtle planes of being.

Seeking to strengthen and develop these core and essential aspects of a *soulmate bond* will help you to overcome any toxic love patterns, and finally attract the health and love you desire. Let's now look at the elements of karmic or toxic relationships.

Toxic love patterns

Below are some key examples of a toxic love relationship or connection: -

- Clinginess, possessiveness and jealousy. These 3 are sure signs that there is toxic energy in your relationship. Brief and passing moments of any or all of these are OK, and perfectly normal, but displaying them as frequent patterns of behavior and thought are not. This is when and where it becomes toxic causing severe disruptions in your relationship. The same applies for all of the following...

- Needing to be right!
- The inability to say sorry or admit mistakes.
- Being an energy vampire, i.e. sucking the life force out of your partner and draining them of their love, affection, sincerity, resources, happiness, confidence, money etc.
- Falling into any of the codependency traps and mistakes outlined in the Codependency section.
- Spitefulness, deception, manipulations, mind games, vindictiveness, and narcissistic tendencies.
- Selfishness and a lack of sincerity, emotional depth, and authenticity. Not being transparent or real- lacking "vibes," heart, soul and depth.
- Repetitive problems and issues recurring in the relationship, without the willingness to work through them.
- Communication breakdowns, specifically with the absence of mindfulness and conscious action and speech.

It's easy to assume that 'energy healing' only involves practical and physical steps towards healing and recovery. Yet, a lot of what influences us (positively or negatively) occurs in real time, within our relationships, attitudes, thoughts, emotional patterns, and inside feelings, moods and impressions. Attitudes towards money, love, relationships and career all come under energy healing, so getting to the root of blocks and mistakes is highly important. *Knowledge is power.*

Illusion: Beyond the 3-dimensional reality

Illusion is the basis of the three-dimensional realm and world we find ourselves living in. The truth is, we are all interconnected, one and connected on a subtle plane and dimension of being. Your thoughts, feelings, beliefs and emotions influence and affect those you love, those around you and the world as a whole. The collective consciousness- the global energy field- and the thoughts, feelings, emotions and impressions of others affect and influence you directly too. Thus, we are not separate or disconnected from one another and it is the belief or mental distortion that creates most to all of the illusions we see today. Disconnection and a faulty belief that we are separate forms the basis of all of the blocks you see in your health and lifestyle patterns. To live in illusion is to live in a state of separation, and this could literally be manifesting as physical separation on so many levels. Subliminal messages from society, foods and substances aimed to suppress our consciousness and destroy our pineal glands, and the 'consumerist sell society' tactics mentioned in earlier books. Also, not taking a holistic approach to health and just focusing on muscle mass, cardiovascular health, and physical systems. In the East, for example, meditation and mindfulness are considered *essential* to health-they're not just an option. People who live by a plant-based wholefoods diet would tell you that they don't need meat to survive and thrive because of it. They live off beans, pulses, fruits, nuts, seeds, vegetables and herbs, sun-gaze (potentially) and get their energy straight from nature, which in turn provides for their longevity and health, energy and vitality. There is a glow in the eyes with the appearance of light shining in these types of people.

The point is, illusion and confusion is everywhere. That's why meditation, sound and nature therapy, energy healing and working with spirit and subtle energy are so important. And just look at relationships without spiritual perspective or two beings committed to self-mastery. It is often the case that the women and girls (no sexism intended, but we do live in a patriarchal society) play-out some pretty strong illusions within romantic bonds. *"He is a man, surely he should be the one protecting me?" "Men should be the bread-winners, of course he should pay."* These are common! Also, there is a real problem in our society with men showing emotion and empathy. Women want their lovers to be softer, emotionally open, and compassionate; yet when it comes to real opportunities and situations for growth and self-evolution, unconscious blocks prevent this from happening. Girls/women wish to receive emotional love and support from their man but aren't as equally selfless in giving it. Your partner may shower you with love, affection and support when you need it, yet, when he truly needs it you shrug off his true feelings as if they mean nothing. Unfortunately, many women nowadays do this, specifically and especially when younger and in toxic or karmic relationships. The exchange of energy is not fair nor just- the woman seems to think it is OK to "demand" all of the love and attention she desires, but not give it in return when the guy truly needs it. This is disillusionment and what creates so much hidden trauma, wounds and resentments that are taken into adulthood.

Illusion 1: men don't need the same affection and care that women desire, they should be strong, 'manly,' and masculine. If they aren't, they're weak or are "acting like a girl."

Illusion 2: when a man is being truly vulnerable and in tune with his femininity (which is what has been requested of him), his girlfriend or partner pushes his feelings aside and gets irritated for not being more 'manly!'

He can't win.

This is just one example and there are a lot things we could say about women, how they're seen as the cleaners and home-bodies, nurturers and family support system (emotionally, domestically); and that if they choose a career or business path they're 'too masculine,' etc. Now if we look at health, being overweight, fat or obese is a legitimate health issue. There are constant advertisements, campaigns and products telling us how important health is, and doctors have some pretty clear advice about weight and well-being. YET, someone who is coming from a place of love, kindness, compassion and spiritual awareness could say something- solely from a pure and self-empowered (and gentle, genuine and caring) space, and society jumps down their throats! "You can't say that, you're judgmental." "You're fat shaming." "Shame on you! Leave her alone, she looks beautiful." This is disillusionment at its finest. Being obese to the point of frequent and perpetual health issues is *not* in alignment with Creator's vision for humanity. The universe is benevolent, loving, compassionate and truly has our best interest at heart. Spirit is loving and caring too, we are given so many opportunities for healing and self-alignment in this life. So, why is it okay for corporations and generic ads to scream in our faces how things should be, but a spiritual and sincere person says the same thing with care and they're abused and insulted? Targeted and projected on?

The witch trials were real. Spiritual people have been persecuted throughout our history too. Hopefully you understand how much illusions can influence us on the earth plane. It may be useful for you to sit down in meditation and contemplate some of your own potential illusions and beliefs, to see what is really 'truth' and connected to a higher perspective; one in harmony with the divine, soul and your higher self, and what is distortion.

Finally, something specifically which contributes to the "illusions block" is the effect movies, magazines, television and mass media has on us. The *subconscious mind* picks up on subtle cues, messages and signals being projected through these platforms, the projections of us not being good enough, needing to look a certain way, and wear certain items of clothing to be "sexy" or attractive.

168

Our *conscious minds* pick up on the more obvious and direct cues & commands literally (actually!) telling us how we need to act, look and behave. Yet a lot of these signals are not rooted in natural beauty and essence. It should be established by now that natural beauty *shines* and is one of the most powerful forms of power, beauty and magnetism we females can exhibit. A lot of these superficial looks and images presented to us are formed from the idea and notion that we need to sacrifice certain elements of our core and true selves, simply to fit into a society created "mold" of what we should look like to please men. But men aren't robotic, emotionless, unintuitive or disconnected creatures wandering aimlessly around with their penises where their third eye should be... many men are empathic, spiritually aware, conscious-minded and soulful, or at the very least with "vibes" and an appreciation for natural beauty within. Thus, illusion starts when we take everything the media says as literal, or the only option and route to sex appeal and being beautiful. *Beauty is in the eye of the beholder...*

Self-worth, self-esteem and positive reflection

A lack of self-worth is one of the main blocks you may be unconsciously facing that inevitably contributes to the rejection of perfect health out of your life. With self-worth comes self-empowerment, self-confidence, self-esteem and self-sovereignty- all of the 'selves!' The ability to step into your own power and light and shine occurs when we take care of our health. When we make good choices, we feel good about ourselves which instantly makes us want to treat the people in our lives better and heal. Vice versa, the cycle spirals round so there really isn't an end or start; feeling good about ourselves makes us want to take care of our health. This is why it's often easiest to stay disciplined and committed to a health practice when you're already in flow and feeling positive. Energy healing works the same way. Even small changes start a cycle of self-empowerment and personal transformation, one minor improvement in emotional well-being will inspire you to make changes to your mind or body. One profound realization into a past issue or block motivates you to heal other parts of your life. *Interconnectedness*, remember?

Kindness, compassion, selflessness, generosity, humility; these are just a few of the essential qualities that come with a healthy and strong sense of self-worth and self-esteem. The *Law of Attraction*, as established in chapter 1, works on the power of positive thinking, belief, faith and knowledge of the power of your mind, thoughts and mental projections to affect and shape reality. If all successful people truly believed they didn't deserve financial prosperity, success, fortune, fame, abundance, or love, do you really think they would be successful at all?! The answer is they wouldn't- they would have a *block* against success and prosperity, and the exact same laws of quantum physics apply to healing, wholeness and self-mastery. If you want to truly begin your path with energy healing be mindful of how you feel about yourself- work on cultivating self-esteem and self-worth. Also, transform projection into *positive reflection*. Projection is the act of projecting negative or undesirable qualities in self or another, while positive reflection is reflecting beauty and positivity, the things and characteristics you wish to increase (or see embodied in others). *Positive mirroring* is something you can work on. Approving negative projections means that you aren't conscious or aware of the projections you yourself are creating, or if you are conscious of them you don't wish to heal or change! Self- acceptance and recognition of your own shadow personality traits, and then further making the decision to transcend past them, can help with this. 'Shadow work integration,' in short. It also allows you to stop projecting those "flaws" into your partner and family. Just as our planet goes through cycles of light and dark, day and night, and receives energy from the sun and moon, your shadow self is your inner darkness. Projection is birthed from this self-denial or lack of awareness and acceptance, a rejection and dismissal of the shadow aspects of self. But the purpose of life, evolution and self-development is to balance, integrate and make whole- to *unify* the varying aspects of ourselves. If we can't embrace certain aspects of ourselves, how can we expect to see or accept them in others? Further, how can we have compassion for others when we don't treat ourselves with the same level of self-love and compassion...? The answer is we can't.

If the opposite of healing is to unconsciously project those unhealed and unwhole parts of our true nature and personality into others, then energy healing means healing our whole self -the shadow self included. Journal, write, express yourself musically and poetically, practice self-care and self-love, take regular controlled fasts and detoxes, and treat yourself with the same love and care you would want to treat others. Moon-gaze as well, the Moon is *feminine* in nature and connected to the subconscious and the realm of emotions.

Know your strengths, and your yin or yang!

Being born man or woman has some implications on the type of energy you embody. Men are more masculine and yang in nature whilst women are more feminine and yin. This is just the way things go, but this doesn't mean you can't seek to bring more unity and harmony to these polarities. Energy healing is deeply associated with healing yin and yang, your inner energies. The Moon is feminine and yin in nature with a link to the subconscious, intuition, astral forces, and dreams. It also corresponds with emotions. The Sun is masculine and yang with a connection to the conscious mind, willpower, vitality and self-confidence. The Moon can be seen as one's "inner" moods, emotions and currents and the Sun as the "outer" self, the ego and conscious mind. If you aren't already familiar with yin and yang you should really wise up on these qualities, they influence you every day!

Women, for example, have periods and men don't. Men on the other hand have taken on a governing and leading role in society, seen by patriarchy over matriarchy, men succeeding in business and government, and men being the providers and protectors while women are the nurturers and family-keepers. Feminine energy is empathic, caring, sensitive and intuitive, so it's no wonder that women have been given the role (traditionally) as homebodies and the support system and primary care-providers for children. As masculine energy is assertive, forceful, dominating and active in nature, it's also no surprise that men adopt business mindsets and have had more of an active role in society until recent years.

This is where things get interesting... the evolution of our consciousness can be seen to be reflected on an individual and collective level. The more we wake up to our true selves, in harmony with soul and spiritual illumination (a unified and loving global reality) the more we see powerful changes within society and nations. Patriarchy and matriarchy are being balanced just as the roles of women and men are fusing. We explore this concept more in depth in 'Third Eye Awakening,' but this is something you may want to keep in mind for self-healing.

For now, consider meditating on these qualities. *Ask yourself*: -

1. 'Where am I currently vibrating now?'
2. 'Where am I stronger or weaker?'
3. 'What could I work on increasing and integrating more?'

Feminine energy (Yin)	Masculine energy (Yang)
An affinity with the Moon and nighttime	An affinity with the Sun and daylight
The subconscious mind	The conscious mind
Empathy, compassion	Self-assertion, forcefulness
Magnetism, receptivity & passivity	Dominance, forcefulness & action
Caring, selflessness & nurturance	Success & achievement, competition
Instincts and emotions	Thoughts and intellect
Intuitive wisdom and inner feelings	Rationality and logic

Love or lust?! (Tantric perspective on sex & intimacy)

Sexual healing is integral to healing oneself. This is quite a broad topic and one we go into in '*Kundalini & Sexual Awakening.*' Overcoming blocks, releasing pain, and healing from trauma can all be achieved through healing your sexuality. Sexuality is the primal force of the universe and creation; we are born from sex; birthed into this physical existence through the act of 'love-making.' Is it making love or primal desire? Sexual intimacy, foreplay, sexual union, kinkiness and an exploration of your sexuality and sensuality are core aspects of most people's life lessons and experience. Even if you don't have a particularly active sex life, you will still experience desires and fantasies through porn and masturbation. In fact, a desire for sexual intimacy and union is one of the most primordial and powerful pulls in this universe, at least for us humans. The root chakra is symbolic of our reproductive organs, physically. It relates to sex, lust, security and survival and it is from this first and 'root' chakra, located at the base of the spine, where life force energy flows to stimulate kundalini. Kundalini energy is of course necessary for our spiritual awakening, longevity and vitality.

Primal instincts are a major driving force. Sexuality and sensuality allow us to grow and evolve as spiritual animals, enabling us to connect to both our wild and primal, animalistic selves and our divine and spiritual ones. Without sexual and sensual self-exploration, we would be "closed" off emotionally, mentally, spiritually and physically. Healing your sexuality and sensuality are extremely significant to living an abundant and successful life. If you know anything about kundalini you will know that creativity, sexuality and emotions are linked. They are the 3 points in a triangle with the triangle being the shape of the third eye chakra. Blocks in any one of these leads to blocks and imbalances in the others. If you feel disconnected and uninspired creatively, you will have a tricky time expressing your emotions and feelings. You'll also be closed off to romance and intimacy. If you suffer with sexual wounds and painful memories or repressions, you will close yourself off to connections built from emotional vulnerability and openness, also creating a discord with your creativity. Feeling separated from your emotions and ability to express yourself will equally lead to an inability to engage in creative and artistic self-expression and be empowered sexually. They're all entwined.

Tantric approach suggests that the mind, body and spirit are interconnected and when someone has achieved a state of spiritual illumination, balance and harmony within; they can meet another on their wavelength. Sex becomes an act of love and unification, unifying the two soul's as one.

Here are some main ways to heal your sexuality. We won't go into the detail of each as we cover these in other books (or throughout this one) but be aware of how significant each is in aiding self-healing.

1. **Kundalini yoga**
2. **Tantric breathing**
3. **Tantric sexuality philosophy**
4. **Holistic movement**, like **tai chi**, **qi gong** and **dance**
5. **Shamanic healing** and **shamanic journeying**
6. **Sound therapy**
7. **Spirit animal connection**
8. **Chakra healing**, particularly working on your **Sacral**
9. **Self-therapy**, **counselling** and **meditation**
10. **Art therapy**, **music therapy**, **nature therapy** and **creative/artistic expression**

For meditation and self-therapy of any kind, you may want to explore how your perception may be clouded, based on past wounds and pain. One negative experience can affect us in so many ways and lead to a future self whereby fears and insecurities around intimacy and sexual union are strong. Examples include...

1. Feeling like you have to dress a certain way to appear sexy to your partner. You can't possibly be desirable in your natural form, or with your natural curves, flaws and imperfections. You have to continuously cover up, put on concealers or certain items of clothes or accessories to 'mask' your naked form. Quite simply, natural beauty is replaced with a superficial type of "beauty."

2. You become overly submissive in the bedroom, losing touch and tune with your sexual power. Sensuality may be lost altogether and the types of scenes you see in porn or in overly sexualized commercials or ad campaigns becomes your sole version of intimacy and connection.

3. You forget that you are also worthy and deserving of real pleasure and sexual intimacy, and you sacrifice your own needs for your partner's (or multiple partners). It becomes all about how you can pleasure and turn the other person on, and in the process, you start to become more needy,

codependent and weaker in your convictions. Self-empowerment suffers, as does your self-esteem and confidence. In short, you give away your power and diminish your intuitive and instinctual self.

4. Your perception of love becomes similar to that of the movies, television or media. The classic "fairytale" fantasy love takes over in your mind's eye and the consequences are that real issues and problems in your relationship are overlooked or repressed and pushed below the surface. Intimacy suffers and so does your sexual life, as your mindset is taken over by an unrealistic and limiting belief of love.

Chapter 4: Mysticism and Spirituality

Defining Mystic healing

There is a reason why mysticism is considered a taboo subject in wester society. Generally, it's considered "woo," crazy-talk or something spiritual and ungrounded- something rooted in a disconnection from reality. Yet, this couldn't be further from the truth. Mysticism is a deep and ancient philosophy, awareness and practice *rooted* in our connection to the real world; to spirit and the divine. Life is sacred, divine and transcendent, there is a subtle and spiritual energy that connects all of us here on earth, and the stars and planets in the greater universe. There is nothing make-believe about very real energy currents! Shamans and tribal cultures have been aware of this spiritual and timeless energy for some time. It is infinite, limitless and expansive. It exists within ourselves and our planet yet beyond us simultaneously. Mystical energy is a benevolent force of the Universe, of Spirit, Source, God and Creation; it is real and currently being felt and connected to by millions.

Mystic healing has many other names. Shamanic energy healing, spiritual healing, healing with chi-vital life force, universal energy and subtle energy. It is known as the divine, cosmic consciousness, universal consciousness, and God or the universe-whichever higher power you believe in. Spirit is timeless and universal while being available to everyone. It's also infinite, expansive and non-physical but still flows through us on a very physical and down-to-earth level. There is a magic associated with mystic healing and connecting to our spiritual selves. And this is why it's necessary to realize our cosmic nature and connect to natural energy in this lifetime. There is more to life than the physical realm just as there is more to life than the five physical senses... Again, life is multidimensional, which means there is a world of opportunity and possibility awaiting us. Healing ourselves through accessing this mystical and spiritual energy allows us to connect to our true power and potential, transcend outdated beliefs and patterns of conditioning, thinking and behavior, and rise to new heights. Healing occurs on multiple planes of existence, the mental, emotional, physical, spiritual and astral/energetic planes and dimensions; there's so much more that occurs behind the scene on the "invisible" planes of consciousness.

Supernatural gifts and awareness, psychic phenomena, channeling, extraordinary levels of creativity and imagination, a connection to the divine, telepathic communication... Healing ourselves with subtle energy creates new neurological pathways and energy channels within. We can further look to both ancient and tribal cultures, like Shamanism and ancient beliefs in healing, and modern day practices and scientific findings. *Mystic healing* doesn't mean closing ourselves off to science, technology or the modern age- it is a unification of old and new, ancient and modern, and spirit and science. A holistic and unified approach is what is needed to achieve true health, harmony, happiness and success on the earth plane.

What's the point?

So, why explore the various methods and routes towards healing with subtle and spiritual energy? If you've read the first book in this series you will already know the answer to this. Life is multidimensional and we are made of mind, body & spirit. Actually, we're more complex than this, as we also have emotions, internal feelings, a subconscious mind, a soul and a body- and with each comes a huge array of sensations and experiences. This is the point of energy healing techniques, they help to connect us to our true selves and to our whole selves. Mind, body & spirit, lower self and higher self, shadow personality and higher mind, heaven and earth… life involves duality, polar opposites. The ultimate goal is to find unity and harmony within and around.

Reminding ourselves of the basics of Energy Healing

Let's quickly recap everything we've learned.

1. The Universal Laws

The 12 Universal Laws act as a guide for how we're supposed to live our lives. They provide wisdom, insight and guidance into our own human nature and the nature of the universe. The Universal Laws of: Divine Oneness, Vibration, Correspondence, Attraction, Inspired Action, Perpetual Transmutation Energy, Cause and Effect, Compensation, Relativity, Polarity, Rhythm and Gender, aim to assist us in realizing our full potential. They serve as a general guideline, instilling information into 'secrets' of the universe.

2. The Higher Self & Mind

The higher self is our higher mind, the part of self that relates to intuition, psychic and spiritual gifts, clairvoyance, cognition, problem solving and original thinking, and advanced and developed forms of mental expression. Imagination, intellect, wisdom, perception and the ability to receive insight and knowledge from our dreams all come under the higher self's domain. Without a connection to our higher self, we would be mainly primal, lustful, and animalistic versions of ourselves- operating on a bsis survival and instinctual level. There is nothing wrong with this, but we do need balance and a strong connection with the higher mind in order to function properly. We also need the higher mind and self to form deep and meaningful connections, connect to our true path and purpose, and live life with compassion, understanding, self-awareness, empathy and wisdom. The higher self is a direct link or bridge into divine and spiritual consciousness, and beautiful qualities such as generosity, selflessness, purity and grace.

3. The Shadow Self & Personality

The Shadow self is equally important. This is the 'lower' aspects of self and mind- primality, animal urges and desires, instincts and everything related to survival, security and sexuality; basic human impulses, needs and drives. At a higher vibration the shadow self is our inner need for connection and emotional bonding. Emotions and our ability to form deep and meaningful connections come under the shadow self, as does sexuality & sensuality. The way we're able to express our sexuality and sensuality is determined by the state of health of the shadow self; for example, how well have we been able to integrate it's lessons and teachings… In addition, the shadow self is connected to our dreams, the subconscious mind, and our primality in a positive way. It can inspire us to reach new levels of creativity, intuition and imagination through the wisdom and awareness it brings.

4. The Chakras

The Chakras are the energy portals that link to our physical body and some of our physical organs. The term 'Chakra' is ancient Sankskrit in origin, literally meaning "energy wheel." There are believed to be 7 main chakras which run through the body, starting at the pelvic region and ending at the top of the head. There are also other chakras which aren't generally taught but can still be felt and experienced through energy healing and a sufficient spiritual self-development practice. These are the feet chakras (connecting to the earth), palm chakras (where chi and healing/universal life force energy flows through), thymus chakra (located between the heart and throat), and soul star chakra (the chakra linking us to superconsciousness and the highest possible realms/dimensions known to mankind; which is located just above the crown chakra). Blockages or imbalances and distortions in the chakras lead to a variety of ailments and ill-health. Problems can arise on the mental, emotional, physical and spiritual planes, and general/holistic health and well-being will suffer if left undealt with.

When healed, opened, and balanced a healthy chakra system manifests as spiritual connection, evolved creativity and artistic/imaginative ability, vitality and longevity, and a strong life force. All aspects of life and it's themes are improved with a free flow of energy through the chakras.

5. Kundalini energy

Kundalini is the serpent-like energy that flows through the seven main chakras. It begins at the *Root* chakra, which is located by the pelvis region, and ends at the *Crown* chakra just at the top of the head. Kundalini leads to spiritual awakening and illumination, divine self-realization, creativity and artistic abilities, strong and well-developed life force, sexual vitality and libido, and psychic abilities. Someone with an active and awakened kundalini is known to be deeply intuitive, wise, insightful, healthy and spiritually open. They also have passion and zest for life, and will be confident and self-empowered as to their life purpose and path. The best way to remember kundalini meaning is to consider this trio: *Sexuality*, *Spirituality* and *Creativity*.

6. The Main Pathways to Healing & Wholeness

There are some energy healing 'fundamentals' you can remember and seek to embody and integrate. These include Crystals, Reiki (working with subtle and spiritual energy), Sound therapy/healing, Nature therapy, Elemental healing (working with the elements), and of course Chakra and Kundalini healing. Any type of boundary and aura strengthening, psychic development and protection, and karmic healing technique and path to health works wonders too!

Chapter 5: Spirit Animals and Significant Archetypes

Spirit Animals

Spirit animals are an intrinsic part of spiritual enlightenment and the journey one takes to get there. There is a whole world of opportunity and insight awaiting through spirit animal connection, and there are many unsen guides and helpers happily waiting to offer their assistance!

Spirit animals are the animals that show themselves when we are vibrating high enough to connect with them. They often appear when our third eye is open, and when our heart and higher self is operating at a high enough frequency to tune in and receive the wisdom they wish to share. Spirit animals are spiritual guides, in essence. They exist on the subtler planes of existence and are here to show us the beauty and infinite potential of the energetic world. They can instill us with wisdom, inspiration, guidance and direction- beauty, peace, happiness and a sense of self-sovereignty and personal empowerment. Great healing comes about when we connect to our spirit animal guides.

So, how does it work? How are we able to tune in to an apparently 'invisible' force? The key is to know that they are not invisible, they are simply existing on a subtle plane and dimension. In fact they are always around us, they're always available if we should so choose.

The purpose of Spirit Animal connection

- They offer unique insight, wisdom and guidance into our live path, purpose, strengths and talents.
- They help us to overcome past repetitive cycles and negative/destructive cycles.
- They can help us get to the truth of shadow personality traits, outgrown life cycles, and limiting thinking.
- They aid in personal growth and transformation, and our self-alignment.
- Power, integrity, self-autonomy, confidence and self-empowerment can all increase with the help and assistance of spirit animals.
- They also show us the unlimited potential and possibilities available through the reality of multidimensionality, subtle planes of being, and divine spiritual connection.

Animals often visit us through the astral realms when we are in tune with our soul self, connected to our spirit body. Through astral projection we can project our consciousness onto that of one of our animal helpers or guides. When we astral project and consciously open ourselves up to the astral worlds we need to make sure the entity, being or animal we are connecting to is actually in alignment with our best interest. One wouldn't connect with a crocodile for example, which embodies the energy of the root chakra, something more primal and instinctual, when wanting to connect to the higher self for vision or higher guidance.

The beauty with the animal realm is that the human journey can be found and represented in the entire animal queen and kingdom species. Of course, *every* animal has an astral body. Some animals relate to the higher self, such as the Eagle or the Hawk, and others to the lower chakras and more primal aspects of being. We can journey through the chakras- the energy portals that construct our own physical and energetic body- and find an animal we hold a strong resonance with to call upon for guidance and healing whenever we may need it. Just because an animal may provide 'medicine' and be available to connect with during astral projection, this does not mean that you will feel to tune in to its energy. A prime example is the Tiger- a beautiful, powerful and fierce spirit animal to have. I know many who have a strong connection with the majestic tiger and work with her on a daily basis. Yet, others don't; they may ask to connect astrally to the tiger only when they need to develop the qualities of strength, passion and courage. This is because the tiger spirit animal links to survival and can therefore be seen as very primal, often resonant with people who have strong passions and a sense of healthy fierceness!

Another example is the Swan. This spirit animal represents grace, gentleness, and purity- there are many who consider the Swan a close spirit animal and guide But some others will only request to tune into the Swan's energy when they need to increase the qualities they lack. Hopefully you understand the concept of Spirit Animal assistance through these two examples... we're all different and unique. What applies to one may not necessarily resonate to another. Some people are more connected to their primal instincts and emotions or physical body than their higher self, subconscious mind and self, and inner spirit. And vice versa. Some people are more masculine in energy and nature while others are more feminine. Each animal species provides a certain healing energy, a medicine, that will appeal to us in different doses. The term *working closely* with your spirit animal is for when you have already discovered which animal's medicine and energy resonates with you, and is close to your heart and soul. Simultaneously other animals are here for you to draw on for strength in times of need, for example when you may have become out of balance with yourself- or are lacking in a certain quality.

We can connect to the energy of animals we have little to no affinity with when we need to develop certain qualities. These can be "one off" or rare astral connections, however the ones we have a real deep soul resonance with we can remain connected to on a daily basis and in our dream, multi-dimensional, healing and astral work. The key to connecting astrally to your animals is to know who you are and what holds true for you. We all have our own specific frequency and blueprint and our animal guides are always available to make themselves present in times of need. You may even find yourself becoming one during your astral projection exercise! Oh yes, many of us have such a soulful bond and deep, timeless connection that we start to awaken to memories and realizations when connecting with spirit animals. You may have been a specific animal in a past life and thus the cord has maintained. When open to the realms of spirit and soul, anything is possible. You might also start to see how your 'core frequency,' the unive vibration and soulprint you've entered this life with is intrinsically connected to an animal. You share a *soul resonance* through the energetic meaning and healing powers of the animal.

Before going into some of the most well-known spirit animals who often visit people on a spiritual and healing path, here is a simple but very powerful exercise of connection to your spirit animals and helpers.

An exercise to connect to your Spirit Animal

You will need:-

★ Drumming- a 'heartbeat.' Tribal or shamanic drumming creates the vibration of a universal heartbeat.

★ A Sacred, quiet space- somewhere you won't be disturbed and can really go within to connect to source.

★ Intention and a sense of knowing, the knowledge and awareness of the spiritual subtle realms.

Close your eyes, merge your heartbeat with the drumming, the heartbeat, and focus your intention on speaking with your spirit animal. This all takes place on the astral planes, the ether and spiritual realms. Set your intention of connecting with your spirit animal. You may want to take a few moments to think about the qualities of the animal, or meditate on a picture of the animal. Having a picture or drawing in front of you helps, although this isn't a necessity.

Now tune into the frequency of the animal's medicine. Visualize its natural habitat. Visualize being submerged in a natural place such as a cave, waterfall, ocean, mountain or a forest. You will know which one is correct based on your intuitive feeling. Start to take some deep breaths and still your mind...

Feel your awareness merging with nothingness, with the silence and space of spirit and the empty universe. It's in silence and emptiness where sound and space arise.

Once you are in a space of surrender, trust and pure openness, allow your animal guide to bring you the insight, direction, or simply just connection you need. Make your intentions known- actively ask for help. Project feelings of love and harmony. Be vulnerable while remaining strong in your light and truth simultaneously.

It really is that simple. Meditation, self-healing, psychic and intuitive development, and getting in touch with your true self and core nature will all help amplify this experience. You may want to consider engaging in a conscious fast or detox, which lightens your physical and spiritual body. Spending more time in nature and getting to know your own inner nature- such as through astrology and numerology, your life path, will aid greatly. Anything that connects you closer to your soul, truth and personal power will increase your chances of not only connecting to astral animals, and communicating with them, but also the vividness and quality of the experience. Think in terms of *connection*, how would you make sure you connect with others on the best possible level? Well, you would make sure you were in an open, transparent, modest and present space.

To make this topic easy to learn and the wisdom easier to integrate, the Spirit Animals have been shared in categories. These are:-

- Primal & Instinctual
- Serene and Emotionally Balanced
- Down-to-Earth and Grounding
- Wise and Insightful
- Higher Self Connected
- Spiritually Evolved
- Creatively Gifted and Inspirational

Hopefully this will make this topic easily accessible!

I've chosen to include 44 Spirit animals, with 44 being a significant angel number. There, in fact, 100s of important spirit animals you can look to and call upon for your healing journey. Every animal has a symbolic meaning and energetic significance, these are the ones I felt most necessary to share for their powerful medicine (wisdom, energy and insight).

Primal and Instinctual Spirit Animals

Crocodile

The crocodile, or the alligator too, is a symbol of primal power and strength. This animal is very much linked to your emotions, instincts and inner feelings, the realm of emotions and physical senses relating to intimate relationships. If this is your spirit animal, so if you resonate with the crocodile, you have heightened senses and psychic abilities. The crocodile relates to psychic powers which arise from primal instincts and the ability to be in tune with one's surroundings. Water links here, and water is connected to feelings, emotions and feminine energy- nurturance, magnetism and sensitivity. This animal isn't just passion, courage and physical strength; the croc is also instinctive in a nurturing and protective way. Self-discovery can occur with the crocodile's assistance. Getting in touch with your feelings and instincts are very important, essential for your well-being and for relationships to thrive.

Psychic abilities and spiritual awareness stems from the water element as well. You must have courage and fearlessness in revealing your feelings, expressing your emotions and truth to others. This is the message of the crocodile/alligator. Issues in sexuality, painful memories, past wounds and trauma, and ancestral, family and karmic wounds often link to the crocodile. Dealing with your past and tricky emotions you've left unhealed and unresolved is the key to successful relationships. It's time to look to your primal and ancestral self.

The overall message of the Crocodile: Speak your emotions clearly, get in tune with your gut feelings and instincts, and heal the past.

Horse

The horse represents freedom and change, movement and travel. You're gifted with opportunity and a chance for movement and travel right now. Take a risk, have courage and venture forward- be open to adventure. Journeying can be emotional, spiritual, psychological or physical. You may be going on an actual journey, or planning one, or making significant change in your life right now. Free will is yours. Opportunities come with surrender and openness to change, don't become stagnant or fearful of the future. Personal power and authority is another key message of the horse spirit animal. It's time to broaden your horizons! Sexual empowerment and sensual expression may be in store, or you could be developing the self-confidence to step full into your power- which often links with sexuality and liberation. There is a unique sense of nobleness and majesty in the way horses run too. They're free and physically strong, live in the great outdoors, and love nature. This all reflects your own nature. Physical vitality, movement and exercise are called for in addition to self-development in the self-esteem and self-worth areas. Your confidence comes from self-empowerment, so embrace your divine and strong-willed nature. Don't give in to people-pleasing or appeasing others either, restrictions and limitations aren't beneficial to you.

The overall message of the Horse: Freedom is yours, embrace change and take back your personal power.

Lion

The lion symbolizes courage and devotion. This animal is majestic, regal, confident and self-expressive. You will often find lions lazing around in the Sun- they love their rest and sleep! But, they're also incredibly strong and courageous, bold and determined. They're fiercely protective with a deep love of family, community and brotherhood. These are the qualities the lion animal can teach and inspire. Also, a healthy sense of self-worth, self-esteem and personal authority; self-autonomy and sovereignty can be developed with the lion's assistance. You are divine, a majestic, sensual and intuitive creature with powerful instincts! Like a King and Queen you have a crown, an energetic and ethereal crown (chakra) sitting upon your head. Be proud of your gifts and talents. There is a difference between being egotistical or arrogant and possessing pride, pride can be healthy and useful to your path. Humility, modesty, pride and integrity are called for with the lion too. Honor and cherish family members, friends and elders; community values and bonds are very important in your life. Respect yourself with regards to your talents and gifts as well, because sometimes people will want to try and take your crown, or undermine your worth and divinity. Inner strength is developed from self-realization and self-love. Finally, generosity and benevolence are associated with the lion.

The overall message of the Lion: Live courageously, shine bright, and step into your regal power.

Panther

The panther has many different healing energies and messages. Firstly, this animal is a symbol of power and self-sovereignty. The panther is majestic, sensual and powerful with penetrating emotions. There is a depth of spirit and soul connected to this

201

beautiful creature, the panther is insightful and instinctive. Secondly, she is linked to the astral realm. Dreams, healing and the subconscious represent the panther's medicine and energy. This animal brings a unique wisdom with much insight. The panther's in tune with the universe, with feminine energy, emotions, feelings and unseen realms. There's comfort in the darkness, and this is where deep intuitive insight and wisdom arise. Subtle perception is available when you feel comfortable in the dark. Darkness is, of course, symbolic with the subconscious realms and the shadow self. This also calls for fearlessness. Courage and inner strength should be developed so that you can access the unseen and invisible, astral and spiritual realms, for self-discovery. Intuition and instinct are then birthed from this palace of self-sovereignty. Feminie energy is further amplified, including the qualities of fierce protectiveness, nurturance, empathy, generosity and receptivity. Be open to the astral energies of the universe and natural world at this time, as they can offer much inspiration and knowledge into your calling or destiny.

The overall message of the Panther: Reclaim your power, love fearlessly, and step into your soul's service with courage and boldness.

Wasp

The wasp is an interesting spirit animal and one not many may initially associate with energy healing. The wasp brings the energy of struggle and setbacks. Sometimes life can sting, and that's just how it goes! Life involves duality, there is light and darkness within everything. PAin and suffering have a purpose, struggle and temporary "stings" lead to our growth and self-development. Not everything nature creates is easy to love, but we are part of nature just like the wasp. Yes, wasps can sting- some people are even allergic and suffer minor to severe physical reactions, but they also contribute to the ecosystem. Wasps keep insect population down and thus help plant life, they lead to the earth's sustainability and survival. Just like our own hardships in life, not everything will be joyous or pleasant. But they will teach us the lessons we need to grow. The wasp spirit animal can help you to appreciate the beauty of nature in both its shine and its shadow.

The overall message of the Wasp: Life sometimes stings, but the pain and struggles help you grow.

Wolf

The wolf is a deeply instinctive and intuitive creature representing primal instincts, family and the balance between independence and codependence. This animal portrays your own 'inner animal,' your primality and basic instincts. You should trust in your higher self and the guidance orsingith your intuition wishes to birth. The wolf is connected to shamans and subtle-spiritual energy. They have a psychic sixth sense, they can even communicate telepathically. Wolves, therefore, teach you the power of the human mind and spirit. Telepathy, psychic ability, and an advanced and evolved intuition verging on clairvoyance are main themes of the wolf. Listen to your inner voice, trust in your instincts; this is the key message. Loyalty and a fierce protectiveness over loved ones are also key messages of this spirit animal. You may be highly independent but you are still part of a community & family. The wolf inspires family and positive karma bonds while keeping a strong independence. Also, pay attention to your dreams because the wolf provides hidden gems of wisdom and insight into your deepest yearnings. All matters of emotions, feelings, desires and internal motivations are secondary associations. Be open to new knowledge, learning from mentors or elders, and stepping into a role of self-leadership and skillful mastery. Mystic energy is strong and spiritual illumination is available, in addition to evolution of your emotions and physical being- emotional intelligence, empathy, physical stamina and vitality.

The overall message of the Wolf: Empower yourself, transform knowledge into wisdom, and fine-tune your emotional and psychic sensitivities.

Serene and Emotionally Balanced Spirit Animals

Deer

The deer represents gentleness, grace and spiritual harmony. This animal can help show you the true meaning of peace and feeling content within your surroundings. Deers are beautiful animals to watch... They are one with nature and the wilderness, with an aura and demeanor of harmony and contentment. They are respected and revered by many, spiritual people recognize deers as divine and sacred animals. Yet they're hunted for their flesh by others. In this sense, the deer can be seen to be a symbol of the human nature. We are both primal animals with a "root" (chakra, essence) focused on survival and spiritual creatures. The deer represents one's capacity to remain calm and grounded. Senses can be heightened and fine-tuned, and inner peace should be developed now. This is the deer's message! Grounding, perception, purity of spirit and emotional harmony are the main themes. The deer is also a message of hope with a warning against violence, be it violent communication or physical or emotional violence. Regardless of what other people may be attempting to throw your way you should remain peaceful and non-combative. Stay true to your heart and higher self, as the soul speaks. Fertility and rewards for inner strength and perseverance will come to you when you stay true to yourself. Self-alignment, gentleness and sensitivity are essential qualities to possess.

The overall message of the Deer: Be gentle in spirit, action and mind… blessings come to those with a pure heart

Dolphin

The dolphin symbolizes playfulness, community and harmony. This animal fits into the *Serene and Emotionally Balanced* category because the dolphin is also a symbol of telepathy, emotional intelligence. The dolphin's telepathic abilities are so advanced that they can communicate with other dolphins through a supersonic radar. They're also known to be amazingly sensitive and empathic, compassionate and able to show real and sincere emotions. The dolphin is deeply intelligent. This animal is intuitive and gifted in the realms of subtle and telepathic communication. It also has a serene and calming presence and aura. Dolphins love to play. Because of the link to the water element, this spirit animal suggests you are comfortable with your feelings and emotions, your inner world. If you're looking to this animal for healing and self-development then you need to make peace with your emotions, feelings and inner currents. Subconscious forces influence our lives, it's inescapable; thus, being in denial or repression isn't healthy, nor does it add to your unique destiny in any way. Relationships, talents and communication can all be developed with honesty and emotional vulnerability. Duality is another lesson learned through the dolphin. You can see beyond the veil of illusion and observe how multiple truths can exist simultaneously, finding unity within duality, for your own wisdom and personal gain. The dolphin spirit animal can help you to master your communication, speak your truth, and get in tune with your feelings.

The overall message of the Dolphin: See the many possible truths in a situation, embrace your inner world (emotions & feelings), and embody serenity and mental clarity.

Dove

The dove is a symbol of purity. Spiritually luminous, the dove reminds us just how important peace is in our daily lives. Peace is the source of inspiration, personal power, insight and wisdom. It births transformation, abundance, the development of soul gifts and talents, and positive manifestation. Peace creates and helps to transcend chaos and destruction. The dove is peace and purity personified. Calmness breeds more calmness, and with serenity comes clarity of mind and purity of spirit and emotions. The dove can help with detoxing and cleansing too, purification of any kind. Embody tranquility and aim for purification. Cleanse your life, of toxins, chemical, bad or destructive food and lifestyle choices, negative mindsets and chaotic emotions. Seek purity, inner harmony and balance in everything you do. Meditation and rest will help you in multiple areas of life. The dove inspires introspection and contemplation- spiritual retreat, meditation and self-alignment through soul-searching or healing. There is beauty and harmony all around you if you have eyes to see! Compassion is a powerful force that comes with peace and quiet contemplation. The dove also teaches the significance of spirit.

The overall message of the Dove: Be present, connect with your spirit, and strive towards peace.

Hummingbird

The hummingbird represents presence. Being in the 'here and now' is what this animal teaches. The hummingbird symbolizes spirit and a deep connection to the emotional and spiritual planes. There is beauty and sweetness all around you, time is essentially timeless, infinite and eternal. You are an eternal being. Divinity can be seen in nature around you; the flower, ant, tree's roots or sun. There's a divine simplicity in the natural world which serves as a reflection to your soul. It's important that you direct your energy to things that serve your highest self, anything that aids in your soul nourishment and divine connection with Source. The dragonfly also reminds you that there is inspiration all around and unlimited potential. Silence and stillness are other key meanings. It's important that you develop silence within so that you can connect to your source of self-awareness, intuition, and higher mind. Spirit flows through everything and the hummingbird will remind you of this truth.

The overall message of the Hummingbird: Be here now, immerse yourself in divine "I Am" presence.

Swan

The swan represents grace, purity and true love. This is an extremely peace and serenity bringing animal with qualities that enhance and uplift the spirit. Swas are graceful and poised. Depth of intimacy is associated with the swan, so if this is your spirit animal (or if you feel drawn to calling on the energies of the swan) you are emotionally balanced and intelligent. Humility, integrity and dignity define the swan… Self-awareness arises with getting in touch with your emotions and feelings, inner currents are highlighted. It's time to take the plunge into the depths of emotion and awareness of your deepest desires. Soulful longings are often hidden behind unconscious fears, or illusions and false motives or manipulations of others. There is an "unseen" and "invisible" reality and world. And this is where your true self and soul shines. The swan spirit animal aks for intimacy and complete honesty; vulnerability, openness and authenticity in mind, thought, speech, emotions and actions is what is desired. Intimate relationships will thrive when you are completely honest with yourself and others. Remember to live gracefully and modestly, with integrity and a commitment to personal truth. You are the creator of your own destiny. Additionally the swan also represents soulmate and true love-romantic and love bonds. When a swan mates they mate for life.

The overall message of the Swan: Dive deep into the realm of emotions, inner feelings and currents; live with grace and integrity.

Turtle

The turtle is a symbol for our need to slow down and be patient with ourselves and with life. Patience is a virtue, slow and steady wins the race! Small steps are sometimes necessary to realize the big picture, or your full potential. This is the message of the turtle. Don't rush anything. Projects, a new relationship, a talent or skill you're working on mastering, health and virtually every aspect and theme of life- be patient. Take your time and trust in the divine power. If your intentions and motivations are aligned to a higher truth, to your best reality, and your higher self they will occur in perfect timing. Self-alignment is birthed from trusting in the universe and a higher purpose. Inspiration is associated with this animal, as is purpose and power; taking shortcuts isn't an option. Achieving your goals and dreams, seeing your aspirations through to completion, and attaining success comes with hard work and virtues. Shortcuts or 'cutting corners' will only lead to diminished integrity, and a polluted social status or public image. You want to be your best, so keep a steady pace and commit to integrity and self-empowerment. Your higher self will love you for it in the end!

The overall message of the Turtle: Patience is a virtue, trust in the process and stay aligned to your path.

Down-to-Earth and Grounding Spirit Animals

Bat

The bat represents rebirth and transition. There is a sense of new beginnings, which is grounding and connecting to both the body and the earth. The bat will help you to understand grief and get in tune with past lives, or past versions of yourself. There is an aspect of initiation, of awakening to your true self and path! New ideas and intelligence come through the bat's wisdom, and this spirit animal is particularly helpful for assisting you with releasing the past to make space for the new to emerge. The bat is a symbol of rebirth, fresh perspectives, and new energy. Transformation of ego is another meaning of the bat's symbolism. You can let go of parts of you that are no longer needed and no longer serve your best interest; old chapters must close for new ones to benign, in other words. Because the bat can see in the dark, increased vision and sight is available through the bat too. Vision and sight can be physical which help in the material world, but they are also referring to the third eye and intuitive, psychic sight. You have an opportunity to connect to subtle levels of perception, see through illusions, and use your 'extra'-sensory abilities to connect to the voice of reason and truth. There is an earthy wisdom with the bat that is also connected to your higher self and clairvoyance.

The overall message of the Bat: Rebirth is assured, new beginnings are on their way; release the past and old chapters.

Bear

The Bear represents ancient wisdom and grounding. Reflection, rest and introspection are called for with the bear, so you can work with this animal for healing and introspection, soul-searching and the acquisition of wisdom. There is a primal and earthy power associated with the bear. Creativity and artistic projects are linked here. Also, the bear is deeply instinctual and protective of loved ones, so this is energy you can adopt; fierce protectiveness and instincts. Rest and meditation are important for self-alignment and to become the best version of yourself, for your own dreams and aspirations and for friends and family members. The bear teaches you how to be a mother or father, develop these instincts (motherly/paternal) and provide grounded support and care to those you love. Nurturance can be developed. It's time to contemplate life's deeper meanings and your own path and destiny. Finally, dreams are linked to the bear spirit animal, the lessons and messages you can receive from your subconscious during dreams. You should pay attention to your dreams as they offer significant insight into your emotions, passions, personal life and relationships. Dreams can show us what we're doing right, where we're going wrong, and every aspect or theme of our lives. Rest stimulates the senses and intuition.

The overall message of the Bear: Take time out, relax, and pay attention to your dreams. Trust in your instincts and nurturing qualities too.

Mouse

The mouse reminds us of the small details in life. The mouse is an extraordinary little creature, yet is often overlooked as significant in the spirit animal world- and treated negatively and unfairly in the physical one. This animal shows us the importance of communication and remaining humble. The mouse is very humble, down-to-earth, and modest with unique skills in perception. Energetically, the message is to pay attention to the small details and attend to daily chores, duties and errands. "Take care of business," in other words. Domestic, family and practical issues should be addressed, and dreams and goals can be nurtured through being mindful of the small details. *Think small (sometimes, in moderation) to dream big*. The mouse also calls for patience, taking your time to discover what you need, what works for you, and what your best course of action is. Have you been overlooking an amazing opportunity or something extraordinary in your rush? Are you being too impulsive, or lacking grounding and patience? These are just a few questions this spirit animal brings into awareness. Self-awareness is a further association. You must become aware of all the seemingly insignificant little details to make sense of the whole. You hold more power than you give yourself credit.

The overall message of the Mouse: Tend to the small things and focus on the minor details. A practical and domestic outlook is called for.

Squirrel

The squirrel symbolizes the power of resources. Abundance and prosperity can be yours with this spirit animal's assistance. You have a sufficient accumulation of wisdom, knowledge, resources, talents and skills to see you to the next level in your career or a relationship. You should trust in your power and personal authority, as you have more than enough for success. This is the squirrel's message and meanings. The universe is abundant and benevolent, you alway have enough so you should embrace your full potential. Due to the connection to the natural world, the squirrel also represents the fertility of projects. Prosperity can be yours with perseverance and hard work, determination and effort too. Spirit is generous, surrender to the flow of giving and receiving while being open to increasing your resources.

The overall message of the Squirrel: Resources are increasing in your life right now, so stay inspired.

Stag

The stag spirit animal is a call to leadership. It's time for you to step and take control and charge of your life. Be bold. Your self-leadership skills are strong right now. Be self-assured and strong but equally compassionate. Empathy expands abundance and inspiration, you're better able to communicate and connect with others in healthy and loving ways when you're practicing compassion. Life force flows through you rather effortlessly when the stag arrives. This animal is a symbol of power, self-sovereignty and empowerment. Courage inspires devotion to your path and destiny, while standing strong in your truth- and being able to speak your truth, emotions and feelings- allows you to be your best self. There's a sense of self-mastery and personal empowerment, confidence and high esteem with the stag. Walk gracefully and with confidence. Manifestation powers are strong, and self-responsibility increases with self-leadership. Integrity and a compassionate heart are called for as well. Not everyone may be as far along their journey as you, they may not be as evolved or self-empowered either, therefore it is important that you keep your integrity and compassion levels strong. Be dignified and noble-respect and honor life and the interconnectedness of it all. Protection is offered with the stag spirit animal.

The overall message of the Stag: Take the lead, have courage, and walk in dignity and grace.

Wise and Insightful Spirit Animals

Cow

The cow encourages wisdom and sacredness. Even though we eat this animal, cows are respected by a significant number of communities and cultures. We also cherish this animal, relying heavily on their milk and flesh for strength and nutrients, life and sustainment. We may not show them the gratitude they deserve but we still unconsciously love them through our codependency and extreme reliance. Cows, therefore, provide wisdom, deep spiritual insight into our connection with nature and the planet. This spirit animal can teach you the importance of miracles and self-sufficiency. Working on the land and with the earth is included in this animal's energetic meanings. Community, kindness and generosity are core values of the cow. Questions of how you nourish your soul too; what conscious choices do you may to contribute to your life, health, and spirit? Do the decisions you make help your relationships, finances and the like, or hinder them? Miracles are all around you. Count your blessings and appreciate the beauty and abundance the planet offers.

The overall message of the Cow: See the miracles around, for life is abundant and sacred!

Coyote

The coyote asks you to trust in the divine detours and setbacks. The coyote represents embracing the parts of your life that may have not gone to plan or aren't currently going to plan. Everything happens for a reason and sometimes failure is a divine message. You must feel truly disappointed before you can realize success... You need to feel disconnection and breakup before you can experience the ecstatic bliss of divine love, true friendship, or intimate relationships that bring you deep joy.... And, you may have to experience poverty consciousness and lack before you can receive abundance, wealth and prosperity. This is the message of the coyote. A no can mean a yes. People closing doors, rejecting you, or simply endings and situations that call for letting go ultimately lead to all the "yeses" in your life. There *is* a divine plan! Divine detours. Coyote also asks you to laugh- laughter is medicine and a healer, particularly when you can laugh at your failures or setbacks. Humor births creativity and appreciation. Laughing at unexpected twists releases you from your attachments while creating space for humility and appreciation; trust in the divine plan of it all, and the cosmic joke. Furthemore, this spirit animal can help you to release control in general, such as becoming too fixated on a goal or end result and not enjoying the journey. Some things just aren't meant to be, and the things that are should be enjoyed and engaged in fully. Participate in your life with all of your senses.

The overall message of the Coyote: Divine detours lead to many yeses and open doors, so embrace the setbacks and disappointments.

Elephant

The elephant represents memory and ancient wisdom. This animal could arguably go in *Down-to-Earth and Grounding Spirit Animals*, as it brings a wonderfully grounding and nurturing energy. However it is mainly associated with wisdom, ancient knowledge, and insights linked to intuition. The elephant inspires royalty, a connection to the earth, family and friendship bonds, and a link to past lives. Memory, both short term and long term, and in this life and many is connected to this magnificent creature. The elephant is deeply instinctual, meaning that it can sense vibrations through the earth and emotions and feelings through heightened sensitivity. Elephants are capable of incredible displays of empathy- compassion on par with the more evolved humans of our species. This animal teaches us to respect our kin, elders, teachers and family. Also, to honor and cherish the sacred bonds that connect us, again- within this lifetime and past lives. Past life memories can be attained through the energy of the elephant. Sacred wisdom and ancient knowledge of our existence and the previous bonds we've shared, connecting us through time and space, on an eternal level, is accessible through the earth. Being one with nature opens pathways to self-discovery and memories that can serve our higher selves in the now. Intimate relationships, emotions, our capacity for empathy and compassion, and loving, supportive and authentic relationships are enhanced with the elephant's medicine. Community is very important too. The past provides light and wisdom into our futures.

The overall message of the Elephant: Learn from the past and then let go; wisdom and knowledge into your multidimensional self is available... Be royal and dignified and compassion will flow.

Fox

The fox represents agility and swiftness of mind. This spirit animal is all about your instincts, mental abilities, and intellect and wit. The fox symbolizes your capacity to think on your feet. All matters of reason, logic, sound judgement, discernment and wit come under the fox's domain Adaptability too. You should be adopting a flexible and quick-thinking mindset, and seeking to develop your wit, mental agility, and sharpness and brightness of mind. The fox is both intelligent and intuitive, curious and cunning. Judgements influence our lives everyday but judgements don't have to be negative; sound judgement is called for- discernment and combining logic and reason/rationality with intuition. There's no time for hesitation, be bright and communicative and you will see much success and self-development in whatever area you're hoping to affect. Relationships, career, finances, love, health, lifestyle, travel, spirituality, learning... be of an agile and open, inquisitive but self-assured mind. Commit to change and positive transformation. Swift action is the message! Further, thinking outside of the box, innovation and cleverness, inventiveness and originality are other direct associations. Don't play mind games with yourself or anyone else, and be mindful of deception and manipulation too. Keep things real.

The overall message of the Fox: Think of your feet, keep your mind bright and sharp, and use wise discernment in all of your significant relationships.

Parrot

The parrot reminds you of the power of light, color and communication. Self-talk and the way you communicate with others, including the words, phrases and slogans you use, come under the wisdom of the parrot. Of course, parrots mimic sounds and this provides insight into our own human potential. You should be mindful of the way you speak. Are you using your voice to heal, uplift, inspire or connect with others? Is your communication rooted in love, harmony, compromise and unity- kindness and integrity? Or has your communication become off point, negative, mean-spirited or birthed from lower human emotions, like envy, greed or spite? Truth and honesty are also associated with the parrot, specifically self-honesty and how honest and pure your intentions and words are with others. Speak with light and love, dignity and grace. Be honest with yourself so that you can transcend the need to manipulate or deceive others, don't give into self-deception. Emotions, feelings and vulnerability can be mastered. This in turn allows you to reflect vibrations and sounds of color, purity and the highest levels of self-expression. The universe reflects back the stories you tell, the frequencies you emit outwards, and the beauty within and around. The parrot simultaneously symbolizes the soul's many colors.

The overall message of the Parrot: Speak with integrity and honesty, and be mindful of communication.

Higher Self Connected Spirit Animals

Crow

The crow brings the qualities of magic and the co-creation you have with spirit. Magic pulses through the energetic universe, but only if you're willing to tune into the frequencies and vibrations. Everything in the physical universe exists on a basis of frequency and vibration, of sounds and subtle energy, colors and spiritual life force. Everything is interconnected. Sacred laws shape our human experience; thoughts shape reality, and emotions and feelings, philosophies and beliefs give rise to the physical world. Everything begins on a subtle and unseen level, and there's a divine order for everything. Excitement and wonder can be yours when you connect with spirit, with the sacred and divine energy that flows through every living thing, and life itself. When you trust in spirit, harmony and a feeling of unity consciousness enters your life, mind, being/body and self. The crow also works with the universal laws of Abundance, Compensation, Frequency and Praise, so spending time in contemplation and meditation to connect to your

223

higher self, and learning about the universal laws through study and wisdom acquisition, is ideal. You are a co-creator with the universe! This is the message of the crow.

The overall message of the Crow: Co-create with Spirit and trust in a higher power.

Eagle

The eagle is connected to your Higher Self, all aspects of vision and spirit. Illumination, sharp sight, courage, inner strength, the ability to see hidden truths, and rising above the material to see a spiritual reality are all direct associations of the eagle. This spirit animal is the animal to call on work with for anything related to getting to the root of spiritual truths, insight and awareness. Vision is enhanced and the sacredness of life can be seen, in addition to the "big picture." One can look past illusion, deception, and material and physical realities, and thus see in terms of a divine and spiritual reality. Wisdom can be attained. Intuition and psychic abilities can be increased including the gifts of precognition, clairvoyance, and advanced and evolved empathy. The eagle symbolizes dignity, grace, personal power and balance too. You can walk your life with integrity, high morals and grace with the eagle's assistance. Also, personal power and authority increase. Knowledge of magic, the secrets of the universe, healing and creation are accessible. You may seek the help of an elder, teacher or mentor to help you acquire wisdom and intuitive guidance. Or, your own abilities and powers naturally increase when working with the agle, which then amplifies your desire to become a teacher or mentor yourself. Spirit guides and spiritual teachers can be connected with in addition, and spiritual realms in general are more accessible. Finally, hard work and perseverance, determination, and dreams and aspirations- goals and striving towards success as well. Soaring high is the eagle's strength, combined with unique vision, foresight, spiritual awareness and mighty courage. The eagle is known as a messenger for sacred messages and spirit! Power, healing and divine knowledge can be yours.

The overall message of the Eagle: Spirit has your back, you are divinely protected.

Hawk

The hawk brings the gifts of clear sight, vision, observation and intuition. Everything associated with your higher self can be strengthened and enhanced through the bat's medicine and energy. The ability to see the bigger picture, channeling and wisdom from the universe, illumination and spirituality are all associated. The hawk is very significant in Native American culture. Native

Americans consider this spirit animal as a messenger of and from spirit, a divine guide and connector to the spirit worlds. There is therefore an element of *magic*. Universal truths can be obtained and understood and deep insight into life's hidden meanings and magic can be discovered. The hawk brings with it an astral energy, the capacity for past lives recollection and recall, ancient memory, and sacred wisdom. You can look to the hawk for healing and insight into consciousness. Air is the element associated with this spirit animal and evolved levels of 'vision' can be accessed- visionary qualities in addition to an inspired life purpose can be achieved. Creativity, inspiration and self-responsibility to fulfill your destiny are also key meanings and messages. Soul purpose is very important if the hawk shows itself to you, and you can actively call on the hawk for self-development in this area.

This bird reflects intensity of feeling, emotions, beliefs and spirit, spiritual forces are strong in your life and you are likely to possess the gifts of clairvoyance and foresight. The hawk will help you develop these if you should so choose. Finally, the hawk teaches us how to focus on prophetic and intuitive vision instead of being too preoccupied with logic, analytics and rational thought. Courage, wisdom, seeing the big picture, and the universe's magic and truths can all be attained.

The overall message of the Hawk: Spirit is your guide and source of power, trust in your intuition.

Owl

The owl is a very symbolic animal respected by spiritual seekers and shamans alike. The owl represents clear sight, vision and intuition, all at the highest levels. You're able to see in the dark, get to the root of hidden and unseen truths, and look past deception or manipulation. You can see beyond the veil of illusion. You also find comfort in the darkness, in your shadow self, with the owl. Hidden feelings, emotions, internal sensations and thoughts are all seen as something to embrace, not to deny or repress. There's no rejection of your shadow self and you are further able to alchemize the lunar "yin" energies into something healing and intuitively insightful. You find wisdom and comfort in the shadow aspects of self and in the nighttime's energies. Moon magic- lunar energy- is often connected to the owl, and Shamans are known to shapeshift into this creature (the most advanced energy workers and healers). Clear sight, precognitive dreams, psychic ability, clairvoyance, powerful intuition, and well-developed instincts too. With the owl's assistance, you can read between the lines and also never be deceived or manipulated again; all that's invisible to the nakes eye becomes crystal clear. Sensitivity is a superpower. Your senses are heightened while wisdom shines through when you detach from things that hinder your third eye and allow you to connect to your soul. Return to innocence and be one with nature, as this will increase your psychic and intuitive abilities.

The overall message of the Owl: Clear vision and sight is available to you now; embrace your shadow self and trust your intuition.

Beetle

The beetle is linked to ancient Egypt and god and goddesses energies. This spirit animal is all about magic, the divine, and your own spiritual powers. You are a sensual, creative, imaginative and majestic creature. You are one with the divine and the universe is one with you, benevolent energies are everywhere. Creativity flows through you effortlessly- you should embrace artistic and imaginative gifts now, because they can bring you incredible abundance and opportunities. The beetle symbolizes infinite potential. Creative magic, co-creation, and self-alignment associated with connecting to your inner Source are strongly available to you. Channeling and mediumship is also associated with the beetle. You may be a natural conduit and messenger of spirit, divine messages, or ancient wisdom; or you could be a channel for extraordinary creativity and new creations. There's a deeply ingrained sense of clearing the old to make space for the new with the beetle. Releasing old chapters and cycles which no longer serve you, or your higher self, enables spirit to send you new energy, new opportunities, and new connections. Vitality and a sense of fearlessness to take on the world and achieve your dreams comes with this animal's energy. Remain optimistic and work hard to see your dreams manifest; you can accomplish anything you desire.

The overall message of the Beetle: Magic flows through you for creation and spiritual illumination.

Raven

The raven is a message of magic. Believe in your power, because there is a lot of powerful energy available to you now. Raven energy teaches that nothing in the universe is random, everything is interconnected and synchronicities are everywhere. There is an intricate web of co-creation that weaves so many forces together, and has done since the beginning of time. Coincidences have meaning and apparently 'random' events are connected by a divine cord. Patterns are all around and within for those with eyes to see. The raven links to the higher self and your third eye, the seat of psychic vision and intuition, spiritual perception and the subconscious.

There's a magical plan that only spirit and the Creator knows! But, we are able to access it too if we open ourselves up as channels and do the healing work necessary. Align with good intentions and positive, proactive, and pure motivations. Inner guidance is available through self-healing and spiritual self-development; find the light within and around and self-empowerment will come. Everything is designed to work in harmony and find unity- it is only the human mind or more specifically ego that seeks to separate, or destroy and create chaos, distortion and disharmony. Trust in the magic of the conscious universe. Great spirit flows through all living things.

The overall message of the Raven: Trust in your own magic and the universe's.

Spiritually Evolved Spirit Animals

Cat

The cat represents independence. This animal is all about self-respect and self-esteem. The cat wants you to step into your fiercely independent and self-protective nature, so you can live your best life for you. This is a great spirit animal for people who suffer with codependency. Relationships are meant to serve our higher selves, spirits and souls; they're intended to nurture us and aid in our growth. They're not meant to limit us. Allowing yourself the quality of protection enables you to be protective of loved ones when the time calls, as well. Healthy boundaries and self-love leads to healthy intimate relationships, friendships and platonic & romantic bonds. Self-sovereignty is called for with the cat. Let your spirit roman free. Further, by doing so you subconsciously affect the space around you, allowing other people to be free to be themselves. There's a sense of going after your dreams and goals with courage and strength too. Affectionate, mysterious, and deeply intuitive and instinctive, the cat symbolizes powerful instincts and some unique "superpowers." Cats have extraordinary hearing and sight, psychic sixth sense, a highly attuned sense of smell, unique flexibility and muscle structure, and amazing balance and reflexes. Quite simply, cats are amazing creatures! These strengths are all attainable for anyone working towards self-mastery and spiritual/self evolution. Physically, mentally, spiritually and emotionally balanced- and rather extraordinary- the cat shows us what it's like to possess a wide range of skills and advanced abilities, while remaining their independence.

The overall message of the Cat: Claim your independence, trust your instincts, and break free from limitations & restrictions.

Chameleon

The chameleon is a unique spirit animal representing adaptability and spiritual evolution. Every aspect of adaptability and flexibility comes under the chameleon, so you can look to this animal to help in your career, relationships, finances, business, love life, or with some creative project or health regime. The outer world is a reflection of your inner world. Internal thoughts, feelings, impressions and reflections create physical reality around you. Everyone's reality is different, because everyone's reality is subjective. Sensitivities are an indicator that you're in tune with your feelings and emotions, with your true self and authentic being. You should pay attention to your sensitivities. Also, a sensitive nature leads to self-awareness, and your ability to adapt. Without sensitivity, be them psychic, emotional, intuitive, psychological or physical, you wouldn't be able to sense danger or potential disappointment and failure. The chameleon, therefore, teaches the power of self-evolution and self-development. Always be learning, changing, growing and evolving; seek to transcend to the highest heights that are possible for you. You're unique as you'll have a set of talents and strengths others don't share. Don't compare yourself either, it will hinder your growth.

The overall message of the Chameleon: Engage in self-care, honor your sensitivities, and hone your psychic and intuitive abilities.

Dog

The dog symbolizes loyalty and unconditional. There is no act too extraordinary for this wonderful and faithful creature, there is a reason why they are coined "man's best friend." Loyalty, devotion, friendship and kinship are all associated with the dog. Love and commitment stands the test of time. Regardless of our personal journeys, our own individual self-evolution, and situations we may outgrow or people gravitate away from; love will always remain. Love is unconditional and this is the message of the dog. Commitment can also be energetic, it doesn't only refer to being in someone's life physically. For example, you can choose to stay committed to love and a soulmate, romantic or friendship bond long after you've parted ways, by deciding to never have bad or negative thoughts towards them. This is the true meaning of commitment. Luck and prosperity and other meanings. This animal represents our desires and how we attract luck and good fortune, blessings and new opportunities. Gratitude should be practiced daily and self-care engaged in. It's important to keep a healthy mind, body and spirit for holistic well-being. Abundance is birthed from loyalty and integrity- to yourself and others. The other message of the dog is forgiveness. Betrayal, hurt and pain caused by others can be forgiven with unconditional love and compassion. The same is true if you need to forgive yourself.

The overall message of the Dog: Love unconditionally and learn how to forgive; loyalty births devotion.

Dragonfly

The dragonfly represents truth and illusion, the breakthroughs associated with seeing through illusion. You're being reminded that wisdom and higher truths and perspectives are available at all times. There are many dimensions existing, life is multidimensional, and you have the capacity to tune into the multidimensional nature of reality at any given time. Just look at a dragonfly and you will see a reflective body; it's body reflects light and energy through it's unique wings and body. Truth is subjective, yet there is a higher truth- a divine truth rooted in oneness and spiritual illumination. The dragonfly seeks to illuminate and help you see through hidden truths, meanings and messages. Due to its connection to water this spirit animal is also linked to emotions. If you feel comfortable in the realm of emotions and feelings, your inner world;

and if you possess psychic and spiritual sensitivity, you most likely already have the dragonfly as your ally and spiritual helper. Equally if you want to grow in these areas you should work with the dragonfly. The higher self and divine wisdom are associated here too, and this occurs when you open yourself up as a channel for Source and spiritual energy. A deep inner knowing permeates through you when you activate your intuition, your inner guiding light and omniscient voice. Wisdom can be accessed through hidden and invisible realms in addition to your subconscious mind, and shadow self (emotions, feelings, usually repressed or denied parts of self etc.). Align with the divine.

The overall message of the Dragonfly: Truth transcends ilusion... activate your intuition and trust in your power and higher self.

Frog

The frog symbolizes purification. This is purification of mind, body & spirit, your emotions and soul & psyche. Clear out the clutter. Engage in a detox or cleanse, eat healthy and make significant lifestyle choices. Internal shifts and changes in your health, well-being and daily habits will lead to long term results. Simplify your life too. Declutter excess and heavy emotions, beliefs, ideologies, patterns of thought and behaviour, and physical clutter in your life- material excess. It's time to simplify your life and your emotions, the cycles 'on repeat' everyday. Relationships may need decluttering too, perhaps you've let people treat you unfairly or there's been little balance recently, or for a while? Alternatively emotions and interactions have become messy, chaotic and argumentative- there's little harmony and cooperation left, and no kind or genuinely loving feelings at all. The frog asks you to simplify, clear, cleanse and restart. Bring in fresh energies and new chapters. Health and well-being can get a boost, diet and exercise/movement specifically, and this would be the perfect time to go on a spiritual retreat or healing break too. Replacing materialism and the accumulation of things with a new spiritual perspective and outlook could be taking priority in your life as well. Evaluate what's been weighing you down and making you feel "heavy," and make the essential changes. Psychic cleansing is included in the frog's medicine too.

The overall message of the Frog: Cleanse and declutter your life. Clear the old and take a detox if necessary.

Lizard

The lizard is a message and symbol of dreams. Everything related to the dream worlds, your subconscious mind and the messages and insights you receive from dreams, is connected to the lizard. Your subconscious mind is incredibly powerful. It shines a light into your desires, inner motivations, emotions, feelings, beliefs and philosophies, and borth your light and shadow self. The shadow self, of course, is the part we usually tend to deny, repress, reject or dismiss- the tricky or undesirable emotions and desires we don't want to embrace. It is in dreams where we are given a light into these secret and hidden parts of ourselves. And knowing these help us in waking life, contributing to our relationships, finances, creativity, inspiration, health and spirituality in some way. So, all aspects of dreaming are brought into awareness and can be enhanced with the lizard. This spirit animal also relates to the imagination, however. Inspiration flows when the imagination is strong and active. Inspiration, imagination and creativity are available to you now. Are you dreaming your world into being? You're a powerful creator. Dream big, listen to the messages in your dreams, and start to write your dreams down. Dream insights will help you learn from your past while providing knowledge into your future. Finally, visions and psychic and intuitive abilities merge into the lizard. Be mindful of any actual visions you may have, and start a meditation practice if you haven't already. Visualization is a powerful method to get in tune with your heart's true desires.

The overall message of the Lizard: Pay attention to the signs, messages and symbols in your dreams. Dream big too and connect to your visionary self.

Snake

The snake is a powerful animal representing creativity, healing, wholeness and kundalini. Life force, spiritual and psychic energy, intuition and personal power and sovereignty are all connected to the snake. The snake is very significant in many religious and spiritual texts. Ultimately, this spirit animal symbolizes wisdom, ancient knowledge, and insight into our divine nature. Universal and cosmic forces too. The snake represents rebirth and alchemy, transformation and self-evolution. You are able to connect with your higher self, higher mind, and cosmic divine self. Spiritual insight is strong and intuitive powers are amplified. Make time for self-care and to renew, repair and replenish your energy, including emotional and psychic sensitivities and vulnerabilities. This is really important for your health and capacity for strong and healthy relationships. People with this spirit animal tend to have healing hands, or a healing presence. You may be a natural healer if you resonate with the snake. Like the Owl, this is a shaman's spirit animal too. Psychic, astral, spiritual, mental, psychological, emotional, and physical healing is necessary to be your best self. Self-mastery is linked here. Shed the past, let go of old and limiting cycles, and patterns of destructive behavior, and step into self-leadership- a new you and new way of being. Healing can occur on all levels with an open mind and heart, and a willingness to release all that no longer serves.

The overall message of the Snake: Heal, engage in self-care, and open up to the spiritual Source and divine wisdom. Align with your inner healer and develop your channeling abilities.

Spider

The spider is a beautiful spirit animal of creative life force and the interconnected web of life. This mystical creature weaves its web portraying the energetic nature of the universe, how matter arises from spirit. You can learn from the spider spirit that you are fully capable of realizing your dreams, and that the Universe is here to support you. If your goal or desire is in harmony with your higher self and best path, your soulprint (unique soul's blueprint) and destiny, the universe is wise and benevolent enough to help you along the way. There is a grand design of life which is built on the foundation of harmony, unity and cooperation. The spider helps to remind you of the power of co-creation, Spirit and Source energy. Make your dreams real by taking steps to manifest them, however big or small. Creative life force flows through you when you get in tune with the universal energies available. Your vision and perception can be expanded too. Open your Crown chakra so that you can channel cosmic energies. This will help you in any project you take on- music, journaling, writing, painting, gardening, cooking, channeling, visionary art, or even academic studying. Your crown is your source of spiritual wisdom and insight, illumination and connection to divine higher energies. Subtle energy flows through you and everything in the universe. Be open to abundance and your full potential.

The overall message of the Spider: Weave your dreams into reality and remember the power of creative self-expression.

Whale

The whale symbolizes the ancient memory and mystery of life itself. This spirit animal represents the beginning of time, all memory of the planet from its history and roots to the secrets of creation. The whale embodies the energy of the Great Mystery; time and space itself, the universe and the subtle powers of the unseen and invisible realms. Sound and song is associated with this magnificent creature too. Spiritual wisdom, insight and illumination is available just as much as developed intuitive, intellectual, and inventive gifts are. This is a great spirit animal to have if you are a philosopher, poet, musician, artist or astrologer, tarot reader or numerologist, or some other metaphysical/esoteric field. There's a mystical element to the while and many believe this animal links with angels and light beings. Intuitive and psychic abilities can be developed, and one tends to be deeply sensitive and empathic with this spirit animal. Empathy, the ability to know exactly what it's like to be in another's shoes, and compassion are accessible. It's time to expand your senses and clairvoyant, spiritual and divine gifts through meditation, introspection, spiritual contemplation and soul-searching. Music, song and playing instruments, in addition to reciting poetry, can further help you access your innate gifts for self-development and conscious evolution. Trust in the process of creation and pay attention to your dreams. There is more to life than a material reality.

The overall message of the Whale: Song, sound and music will enhance wisdom and self-awareness in your life. Be mindful of the Great Spirit and mystery/mystical energy.

Creatively Gifted and Inspirational Spirit Animals

Bee

The Bee is a symbol of community and the soul. This animal shows the importance and power of community, of teamwork and working together as a collective. The bee works hard to contribute to its community and social group. Bees are hard-workers, determined, persevering and perceptive. They're in tune with their surroundings and understand the importance of self-sustainability. The bee can help you to understand your role in your community, it can teach service and stewardship, how everything is connected, and the magic of life. Just look at the miraculous honey, a sweet nectar of life, created by bees. Sustainability, self-sufficiency, and collective unity are key themes. Your mind, body, heart and soul know there is a higher truth and deeper reality at play; harmony is the design of life, and we ourselves strive for harmony and cooperation. The bee reminds us of the divine, spiritual, and interconnected universe where magic and miracles are possible. The psyche and soul are just as important as the body and emotions! Much potential for connections, abundance, joy, experience and creativity awaits. Unlimited potential and amazing opportunities are around and in store. Working consciously with nature, the universe and people who resonate with community values will see rewards and fruitful blessings for you.

The overall message of the Bee: Sweet results await, work hard and with soul, and be mindful of your place in your community.

Buffalo

The buffalo is here to remind us of our place in the universe and the abundance that comes from being true to ourselves. Abundance is the main message of the buffalo. Manifestation is available to you at great lengths. You can manifest your desires, dreams, wants and needs with positive focus and intention. You must trust that the universe has your back- trust in the power of Spirit. Adopting a mindset of abundance is essential for your well-being and success. Be mindful of poverty consciousness, victim-hood, and any self-limiting tendencies or beliefs. You are worthy of beauty, love and prosperity! Gifts will come to you when you live in tune with your higher self and soul. Follow your dreams and aspirations and stay true to your unique path, destiny is integral to your personal story; you have your own set of talents, beliefs and skills that will help you. Inspiration, money, resources, intimacy, love, new experiences and blessings are all available to you. The buffalo will help you to connect to the qualities you wish to manifest while aiding in your manifestation powers. Practice gratitude too. Gratitude allows abundance and beauty to grow. Shift your mindset away from poverty and towards fortune and financial security- you are protected and cherished.

The overall message of the Buffalo: The universe is benevolent and abundant, it will provide for all of your needs.

Butterfly

The butterfly is a symbol and spirit animal of transformation and the soul. There is joy and lightness of being in the butterfly's medicine. She teaches the struggles and alchemy of change and growth, personal transformation comes through hardship and a complete desire to be free. Freedom from limiting structures and oppression, restriction and stagnation are all possible with the butterfly. You have unlimited potential- to become the best version of yourself and achieve significant breakthroughs. Breakthrough is a key word here. Self-empowerment comes with recognizing your flaws and follies, and then committing fully to the path and light ahead. Talents, soul gifts, creative and artistic abilities, and living life with integrity and soul are all connected to the butterfly. There is a natural beauty associated with nature and the planet, the natural world and universe, too. And this is what the butterfly teaches; to honor and cherish the natural world and divine simplicity of life. See the magic and beauty everywhere, as it is all around you. Career, relationships, finances and health can all be in for a breakthrough if you make the sufficient changes. This animal is linked to commitment and self-mastery. Surrender to the journey, practice gratitude daily, and open to your soul gifts and talents.

The overall message of the Butterfly: Transformation comes with breakthroughs and acceptance of change; there is beauty all around, and within.

Giraffe

The giraffe represents being able to see the big picture, having vision and a sense of idealism. Big picture thinking allows for success, abundance, love, prosperity, and a healthy and happy life with longevity. The giraffe is all about longevity. High-flying and high-achieving tendencies are associated with this animal, so you can call on the giraffe for goals, dreams and aspirations that require hard work and expansive thinking. *Vision*. It's time to broaden your horizons too, mental, emotional, physical, philosophical and spiritual horizons. Wisdom, knowledge, higher truths, memory and inspiration can all be gained with the giraffe's energy and assistance. Stretch yourself, don't be afraid to go after your dreams or aspirations with courage. This applies to self-mastery too or any skill or talent you're aiming to fine-tune and develop. Reaching expertise status, becoming a guide, teacher or mentor in your chosen field, is also linked. New and fresh perspectives and advanced analytical, logical and observational skills are available. Look towards your future with positivity and optimism, but don't forget where you've been and all you've learned. Take the wisdom and self-mastery attained through lessons, hardships and failures- success and wins- and apply it to your future self. Forward-thinking is called for.

The overall message of the Giraffe: See your future with bright and optimistic eyes, maintain your vision and "big picture" mindset.

Moth

The moth represents your ability to surrender and open up to the light. Enlightenment, in short. This animal asks what's guiding you in your life right now, where is your energy and attention directed? Are you in alignment with spirit? Are you listening to your soul and innermost heart desires? Self-love and utmost integrity is called for with the moth. Yes, this creature can sometimes create its own destruction from getting too close to the light, but this is a beautiful message in itself. Try not destroy all that is positive and beautiful in your life in the name of self-realization. Don't go "too far," maintain balance and enjoy life's pleasures in moderation. Codependency, karmic bonds, toxic energy and relationships, and addictions are linked here. Be mindful of all of these and if they're are some outdated cycles and patterns of behavior still occurring. Transcendence is the key. Learn to let go of unhealthy attachments, all that no longer serves you- relationships or thoughts & actions that hinder your evolution. The moth also teaches the power of hard work, patience and virtue. Spiritual evolution is available to you if you can surrender to your true path and inner light, and embrace balance.

The overall message of the Moth: Let go of toxic, karmic, addictive and codependent cycles, behaviors and relationships. Surrender to your journey and true path.

Peacock

The peacock spirit animal is a symbol of light, color and your ability to shine. That's right, shine! This spirit animal is unique in that it's one of the few that really ask you to get in tune with your glamorous, spotlight-loving side. If you have talents and unique skills, you are surely being directed by the universe that now is the time to shine and show off all you have. Be beautiful, radiate confidence and self-esteem, and allow yourself to glow. Your inspirational and talented nature will allow other people to be inspired, and connect to their own talents and gifts. Radiate inner beauty. Self-expression is very important. However you feel to express yourself, it's important that you feel free and liberated. Liberate yourself from negativity, cynicism, judgements and the possible gossip or envy of others; shine in all of your glory and see your world and connections change. When you align with your true self the universe sends you friends, soulmates, and kindred spirits who match your frequency. "Showing off" to one may be warmly received as "divine inspiration" to another. Show your true colors. Come out of the shadows as they no longer suit you. You weren't created to play small or meak, and you don't need to appease or people-please; be your true self and watch the people you love come out of their shells too. The peacock is also about self-expression related to dance, song, music, art, poetry and sensual and imaginative self-expression- artistic abilities, and divine inspiration. You're a channel for the divine, creative energies, therefore celebrate the luck and good fortune you have been blessed with. Joy, pleasure and celebration will spark your soul even further.

The overall message of the Peacock: Shine… be bold, bright, colorful and self-expressive. Let beauty radiate out to inspire others and enhance yourself.

Rabbit

The rabbit is a symbol for fertility and creativity. Fertility is all around you, you are gifted with artistic and imaginative gifts, and unique psychic and sensitive abilities. Tune into your sensitivities now, for they will bring much abundance and prosperity! Good fortune and luck is in store, your future is bright. Intelligence, innovative, originality and creativity are all qualities that can be nurtured and developed with the rabbit. Make use of the Springtime too. Rabbits come alive in sprint and this is the perfect time to nurture projects and personal growth. New seeds can be planted, metaphorical and literal, so all aspects of personal growth and transformation are on the horizon. There's also a sense of vulnerability and grounding with the rabbit. Be honest with yourself, express yourself- emotions, feelings, thoughts; openness and authenticity manifest abundance and helpful partnerships in your life. Magic is all around you, especially connected to Mother Earth and Gaia. The planet is rich in benevolent, creative and fertile energies and forces, so tune into them. You have many possibilities and unlimited potential, resources too. Productivity and perseverance, determination and effort are called for. It's not a time for laziness or idleness! You must connect to your inner artist, visionary or creative genius for fruitful blessings. Co-creations with partners and colleagues, or friends and kindreds, can be lucrative at this time. Be creative, express yourself artistically and innovatively, and tap into that bright mind of yours.

The overall message of the Rabbit: Fertility, abundance and creativity are amplified in your life.

Goddess Archetypes

The divine feminine is a unique energy that flows through men and women, and spirit itself. Spiritual energy is transcendent of duality. It is both yin and yang, a unification of feminine and masculine energy. Shakti is something you may have heard of already. Shakti is the female counterpart of Shiva and together they bring wholeness and unity. Creation itself can be seen to be formed from Shiva and Shakti, with Shiva being consciousness and the 'masculine principle' and Shakti being power and energy, the 'feminine principle.' Generally speaking, Goddess energy is symbolic of shakti.

Please know there is no sexism taking place. The reason why we've chosen to focus on Goddess Archetypes as a primary focus of healing is because they can apply to both women *and* men. It can't be overlooked that there is a raw power and primal force that comes with Goddess energy. Just look at terms adopted today; we call our planet *Mother Earth* (because it relates to the feminine principle, a female energy), and it is women who give birth to new life. Men provide the seed yet it is females who carry new life in their wombs- we *physically* give birth to new life.

Thus, Goddess archetypes are insights into consciousness, the highest potential we can attain and specific 'frequencies' of being. Each brings a unique vibration reflecting our soul, psyche and self. We can learn about our emotions, desires, potential weaknesses and strengths, desires and true colors through each archetype. Linked but not directly synonymous with the topic is the reality of Tarot cards- there have been many beautiful and on point Goddess cards (like traditional Tarot but with the main Goddess energies) created to help people in their journey of self-discovery. You may want to consider purchasing your own deck from a reputable source, and using them for daily, weekly or cyclic inspiration. The Goddess archetypes cards can guide you and reflect your current state of consciousness at the time, including messages and wisdom from your subconscious.

Without further ado, let's look at the Goddess archetypes of wisdom, guidance, soul alignment, healing and inspiration. Remember how much power and beauty there is in the feminine. There are hundreds of Goddesses from Babylonian/Mesopotamian, Celtic, Greek, Indian, Hindu, Japanese, Egyptian, and basically every culture from around the world. I've chosen *36 Goddesses* to focus on, as 36 adds up to number 9;

the number of spiritual completion and the end of a cycle. With endings comes beginnings.

Aphrodite

Aphrodite is a Greek Goddess of love, romance, sensuality and personal power. This Goddess welcomes romantic love and self-love, the capacity for intimacy and sensual self-expression. She is an embodiment of Venus, the planet of love, beauty, romance and sexuality. You can call on (connect with) Aphrodite to help you express yourself, get intune with your sensuality, and learn how to play more. Sensuality and sexuality are inherently linked to creativity, so there is a strong aspect of creative freedom and artistic expression with this Goddess energy. Self-love, a sense of unconditional universal love, and romantic love are available to you. Pleasurable activities and self-empowerment can be yours... Passion, beauty, pleasure and procreation are all enhanced with Aphrodite's energy and assistance. Further, this Goddess is associated with fertility and is connected to Eros (love). Symbols include roses, doves, swans, apples and shells.

Artemis

Artemis is a Greek Goddess of focus, action and forward motion. She brings the energy of action and self-empowerment, putting plans into motion and taking *conscious action*. Focus, concentration, learning and educational, intellectual and professional pursuits can all be expanded and developed with Artemis' help. This Goddess is also known as the Goddess of 'the hunt.' She is depicted as a warrior Goddess with an arrow, which shows the level of focus and dedication that can be achieved. Commitment to a cause, vocation, path or goal will be amplified through Artemis' divine assistance. Wild nature, chastity and childbirth are also associated with her. Artemis is known as the daughter of Zeus and twin sister of Apollo; she can be called upon to help with all aspects of thriving in the wild, connecting to your own wild nature, enhancing chastity (purity) and giving birth. Love, success and opportunity can be yours with clear focus and following your highest path.

Athena

Athena is another Greek Goddess, the Goddess of wisdom, ancient knowledge, and Divine will. She represents intellect, logic, intuition and the higher self, all aspects of higher learning and a connection to the divine. Wisdom is her specialty and she can assist in writing, publishing, teaching, speaking and studies. Both the Owl and the Snake are associated with Athena. The Owl symbolizes wisdom and intuition- an ability to see beyond the surface and veil of illusion. Also, the shadow self. The snake represents kundalini energy, source energy, and wisdom; ancient memory and power connected to spiritual awakening. As both a Goddess of war and power and spiritual divinity, Athena can help you to connect to both the masculine and feminine sides of your personality for wisdom and awareness to shine through. If you resonate with Goddess Athena you're most likely destined to be a wayshower for others through your connection to the Higher Self. Again, speaking, teaching, writing (books and articles), and publishing are all fields you can excel in.

Benzai-Ten

Benzai-Ten is the Japanese Goddess of beauty. She helps to remind us of our inner and natural beauty. She can teach self-esteem, acceptance, self-love and honor. Benzai-ten reminds us of the power of cherishing our spiritual gifts and inner beauty in a way that is mentally and psychologically, emotionally, spiritually and physically nourishing. There is wonder and inspiration all around us; it can be found in the natural waters that flow through the earth, the birds and animals, and nature as a whole. Referred to as Sarasvati Devi in Sanskrit, Benzai-Ten is closely connected to the Hindu Goddess Saraswati. She, Benzai-Ten, represents flow: water, poetry, speech, words, time, music, self-expression, grace and eloquence. There is a natural rhythm and self-awareness that comes with her energy. She is also known as *Benten.*

Brigid

Brigid, a Celtic Goddess, is symbolic of creativity, energy and sparks of insight. Imagination, artistic abilities, and inspiration can all be increased and attuned to with Brigid's help. Beauty, insight and magic can be created through your ability to express yourself imaginatively and authentically. You may receive divine inspiration and insight into what you can create through art, music, poetry or theatre. Inspiration flows to you from many sources. Music can inspire and heal you on the deepest of levels, further opening your mind and inner spirit to the limitless potential and abundance of the universe. If you have a family you may want to consider introducing arts & crafts or creativity into home life. 'Creative spark' is rich with Brigid. She is also associated with Springtime, fertility, healing and poetry, specifically. If you're an artist, poet, painter, musician, or healer of any kind you can call on Brigid's assistance to expand and develop your endeavours. Finally, Brigid is linked to the element of *fire* and generally means "bright." Symbols include candles, flames, sunrise, springs and wells, and poetry.

Danu

Danu is the Celtic Goddess of the female principle. She is an earth-mother Goddess who is associated with fertility and wisdom. Her energy brings evolution and self-development in creativity, fertility, sexual union, nurturing and cycles of growth. In Irish mythology, Danu is linked to the fairy realms and therefore aids in magic and divination. Creative inspiration, magic and the occult, passion projects, the divine feminine, and sexual union can be learned and embodied through this Goddess. She represents time cycles and emotional cycles of growth. Motherhood is also linked to Danu. One can gain wisdom into their true self, desires and needs. Furthermore, Danu provides reassurance and clarity into your life purpose, power and path; she helps you to see whether you're on the right track, if you have what it takes to show up and shine. Danu gives birth to magic and fulfillment of dreams and desires- she can help you realize these within yourself too. Her message is to stay positive and in flow, be open to new opportunities.

Demeter

Greek Goddess of agriculture, harvest and motherhood, you can look to Demeter for inspiration relating to kindness, giving and generosity. This Goddess is all about caring and nurturing, the love and gifts you are happy to give to others- and your current level of self-esteem and kindness. There is a strong connection to the earth with Demeter. Mother earth energies and all aspects of fertility, abundance and prosperity are linked here. She can remind you that feeling healthy and abundant within can lead to outward displays of giving and generosity. Affection, love and devotion too. The abundance of the earth is rich and there is a written law- a divine order- in which all things flow. Demeter serves as a bridge between the divine and heaven and the earthly, physical realms, and she shows you these parts of yourself as well. Sacred law, the cyclic nature of life and death, and rebirth and personal transformation are things you can understand and integrate with her wisdom. She is a Goddess nurturing love, sharing, abundance and unity through kindness and connection. Her message is to be open to the abundance of the universe.

Elen

Elen is a Celtic Goddess. She is also known as the Green Lady, here to show us patterns and cycles that can lead to growth. She is connected to the forces of nature, specifically those associated with the forests and woodlands of the earth. Elen represents soul and creation- the paths we choose and which are laid out before us. We can learn how to follow our hearts and connect with soul for the best possible futures, letting go of past patterns of thought and behavior that no longer serve us. She shows us how to be disciplined, committed to a path, and self-aware so happiness and miracles can enter our lives. Choices are guided by intuition and wisdom combined with an awareness of our pasts. Elen also aids in self-alignment, creation, and has links to the wellbeing of the environment and planet. Guardian of sacred waters, sacred wisdom, and shamanic (Earth respecting) roots and traditions, Elen can aid in earth magic and eco-passions and endeavours. There's an aspect of mystery and fertility of the land.

Eostre

Eostre is a beautifully mystical Goddess of New Beginnings. Eostre brings hope and the promise of the Springtime, fresh energy and perspectives and fertility. She is a Germanic Goddess who is here to show us the power of nature's energy, the power of opportunity, and the power of life force. New opportunities and blessings are showering in your life right now, and there is a powerful force and energy residing within that can help you. Eostre is connected to the Spring Equinox, where harvest energies are rich. There are also opportunities for co-creation, new projects, and creative and artistic insight; the Spring Equinox represents new beginnings and a new cycle in emotions and self-leadership. She is also referred to as Ostara and has a symbol of a *white rabbit*. White is symbolic of purity whilst the rabbit signifies creativity and fertility. There's a strong sense of renewal and rebirth with Eostre, so you can look to this Goddess to assist in personal transformation and giving birth to the new, whether that be projects, relationships, mindset, beliefs, or life cycles and chapters.

Epona

Epona helps to bring out the wise leader in you. She can assist in stepping into the world with poise, grace, dignity and strength. Epona is a Celtic and Roman horse Goddess of leadership, wisdom and guidance- she is here to show us that you hold immense power through purpose and intention. Intentions serve as a compass to our highest self and to our true path and destiny. As a Goddess associated with the horse, an animal with energetic associations of movement, personal power, freedom and self-sovereignty, Espona shows you how to go after your dreams and aspirations. Accomplishment is a direct result of positive intentions and steps towards conscious action. Things you can gain through her energy: self-assury, confidence, self-esteem, wisdom, intuitive guidance, power, success, achievement and victory. Integrity and humility are key to personal growth and any future goals you hold. You're a wise leader, or at least have the potential to be!

Freya

Freya is sometimes called Freyja and is a powerful Norse Goddess. She represents sexuality, primality and power- inner drive and desires. She is linked to war and destruction that leads to creation. Her main associations are love, beauty, divination and magic. Freya teaches radical acceptance of yourself, others and situations. She can help you come to terms with your shadow self, your sexuality and need for intimacy and affection. She exerts personal power and confidence and is therefore here to remind you of these aspects within yourself. Nature, wildness and unseen realms can be discovered and understood, connected to and integrated as part of your reality. Love, fertility, romance and beauty can be embodied and learned too. Freya brings the wisdom of mistakes and lessons learned through experiences and past cycles. She projects an image of fierce sexuality and personal authority balanced with beauty and success. Prestige, fame, wealth and talent are also things that can be embodied through Freya's wisdom and energy. Inner strength comes through acceptance while self-love allows you to shine in relationships.

Gaia

Gaia is an earth Goddess, a divine representation of Mother Earth. She is the embodiment of the earth principle and female energy, intuition, sensuality, nurturance and empathy. She is both grounded and spiritual and brings the message and teaching of respect. This is respect for your body through the foods you eat, and how you treat it; respect for the environment and natural world including animals and sentient creatures, and respect for others. Spiritual wisdom and intuitive guidance can be yours with Gaia's energy and blessings. She's a Greek Goddess although is known amongst many New Age and modern spiritual communities and cultures. Sleep patterns, self-care, diet, exercise and movement routines, living sustainably and in harmony with Mother nature, and all aspects of self-love and well-being are associated with Goddess Gaia. Conscious awareness and mindful living, in addition to empathic mindful communication, are direct associations too. She can help you to expand spiritual foundations and recognize your divinity. Call on Gaia for all aspects of spiritual and divine guidance... Roots, community and culture can be understood too.

Green Tara

Green Tara is a Tibetan and Buddhist Goddess who is referred to as the Savior Goddess. She is popular in Nepal, Tibet and Mongolia and is closely linked to *White Tara*. Green Tara represents the night and lunar energies, while White Tara symbolizes the daytime. Green Tara is feminine in nature and connected to the energies of yin, nurturance, caring, empathy, sensitivity and receptivity. She is magnetic and understanding with qualities including tolerance, understanding, patience, acceptance and compassion. Green Tara allows you to connect to your inner empath and care-giver to nurture others, and provide self-love and empathy to yourself. White Tara can equally be connected with to increase serenity and grace. However, there is an aspect of salvation that is associated with Green Tara Goddess; the Divine, community, cooperation and friendship are key associations and themes. Trust can be developed and compassion cultivated for more harmonious, mutually respecting, and trusting and supportive friendships and partnerships. Green Tara will help to show you where you're out of alignment and where you've been going wrong in personal connections and spiritual bonds.

Gula

Gula is a Babylonian Sumerian Goddess of healing and medicine. She is connected to Sirius, the star system known to be linked to ancient wisdom and a high vibration of spiritual insight. People who have past life memories of Sirius, or a deep and intuitive connection to it, know they are of star seed origin; i.e. they come from the stars and have a soul, a timeless and infinite aspect to themselves. They're also aware of spiritual gifts such as advanced empathy, intuition, psychic ability, and extrasensory perception. Sirius is also known as the 'Dog-Star,' and Gula is a Goddess of dogs. There's an important link here. Gula is therefore a healing deity and can be called on to engage in self-care and healing. Medicine is available in the stars and celestial activity up above, plants, herbs, gemstones and crystals, nature, and in the level of meditation, spirituality and self-care you provide yourself. You may be drawn towards learning an ancient healing art, like Reiki or shamanic energy healing. Or you could simply feel the need to work on yourself, release yourself from self-destructive wounds, past fears or trauma, and integrate your "light" qualities more. Healing with Gula is to both yourself and others, so you might want to consider becoming a healing channel for others and integrating a cyclic healing practice.

Another Goddess you should be aware of is *Ixchel*. She is a Goddess of healing and medicine too, but is Mayan in origin. Ixchel brings a powerful energy of self-awareness and stimulates self-healing mechanisms. She also sparks the desire to be a channel for others and channel Mother Earth's and the Univere's medicine (healing energy, Source, Spirit, the divine life force).

Hecate

Hecate is a Greek Goddess of magic, movement, travel, positive/light witchcraft. She represents the "in betweens" in life, such as crosswords, chapters in between the old and new, and the shift from cycles of your old self to your future self. Transformation and positive alchemy are associated with Hecate. She mainly embodies the energies of the nightime and the Moon, but does represent the transitions of good and bad/evil as well. Hecate can teach you how to be aware of your past and the choices made, and conscious of your future. Self-responsibility and a sense of duty to self and others can be learned. Also, indecisiveness can be combated- perhaps you are stuck and at a crossroads unsure of which path to choose? Hecate shines a light on the best possible courses of action. Other associations include communication with spirits, divination, wisdom of herbs & plants, lunar magic and channelling and mediumship. You can get in tune with your inner sorceress and witch through Hecate's energy and power, further transcending the old version of you to align with a more self-empowered, wise and insightful version.

Hera

Hera is the Goddess of marriage, family and childbirth- all aspects of the 'ideal woman.' Alliances and allies are the message of Her. She can be called upon and connected with for help in the issues expressed, but also for intimate relationships and both platonic and romantic bonds. Hera is also known as *Juno* in Roman mythology, and she is a queen of the ancient Greek Gods due to being the wife of Zeus. Motherly instincts, nurturance, taking on a caring and providing role in the home and family, and all aspects of childbirth, family and marriage are where Hera's energy touches. Sacredness flows through you and you are a divine embodiment of a beautiful and loving feminine energy. You can ask for guidance on marital unions, sacred sexuality and intimate bonding. Symbols include the cow, lion and peacock which all portray her and your unique vibration. If you feel a resonance with this Goddess, be mindful of jealousy and resentment. Hera is fiercely protective, just like a mother, and with this comes the tendency towards anger, resentment, and envy- especially in matters of the heart and romantic love.

Hestia

Hestia is another Greek Goddess with a Roman counterpart (*Vesta*). Hestia is Goddess of the home and hearth. *The message*: Now is the time to look towards your domestic and living environment. Be mindful of your daily chores, duties and routines. A lot can be learned with how you spend your time at home, how clean and orderly your living environment is, and the type of items and ornaments you keep. Are you a lover of natural beauty, sacred and spiritual items, or crystals? Do you keep pictures of spiritual or religious deities and prayer by an altar everyday? Keep check of your daily habits. Hesta represents purity and sacredness too. Family, practicalities, resources and finances, security and comfort are ruled here. Domestic life can either be a curse and a burden, or a blessing that allows you to thrive and shine. Shift the way you engage with your physical and home environment; be more conscious of your surroundings, thoughts and emotions associated with material and domestic life. You can align with your true self and achieve self-realization through this Goddess' help and assistance. Focus on the small details to see the big picture.

Iris

Iris is a Greek messenger Goddess of color and communication. Communication can be improved in all of your relationships with her assistance! She symbolizes your ability to take control and own up to your inner feelings, convictions, beliefs and impressions, and then express them to improve your life. She is often associated with a "rainbow," she's the personification of the full color spectrum. And this shows how powerful honesty and being true to yourself is- we ourselves are made up of colors, the rainbow, and each vibrates a certain *frequency*. These color frequencies then influence our thoughts, emotions, feelings, philosophies, ideologies, overall health state and vibe, and mindset. Iris can help you speak your truth with kindness, integrity and grace and uplift and inspire others. Fruitful communication is called for. New and amazing opportunities and connections can manifest when our communication is up to par, and you should always be clear and open in your self-expressions. Truth and integrity is a higher vibration message. You may want to begin writing down your personal reflections, start your debut or new book you've always dreamt about, or open up to others in your community. Storytelling and using your experiences and stories to bring hope and wisdom are other associations.

Ishtar

Ishtar, the Mesopotamian and Babylonian Goddess, is also known as *Inanna* from ancient Sumeria. She reminds you of your connection to divine wisdom and Source, the purest and highest energy available to mankind. Source energy is the starting point of spiritual energy and illumination, inspiration, wisdom, psychic and intuitive sight, and all aspects of subtle communication. You can develop an intimate connection with the invisible and unseen worlds through Ishtar's energy. Communication with the universe itself, the subtle life form and subconscious energies- divinity and spirit, is available. You should pay attention to signs, messages and omens, mystical synchronicities and messages that seem to be subconscious or subliminal. Ishtar helps you to see the importance of intuition and spiritual insight over logic or reason. *Message*: connect to your higher self, and remember the power of sacredness in your life; ritual, prayer, mediation, and spiritual connection. Self-empowerment and enhanced self-awareness are accessible! Ishtar/Innana is also linked to love, beauty, sex, war, justice and power, so look at these themes and how they're showing up in your life. Symbols include Venus, the Goddess/planet of sexuality, beauty, love and romance, and the Lion- a majestic and community focused animal. Sacred sexuality too. Ishtar can help to show you the power and significance of sacred, sexual, and divine love, sexuality where the higher self and soul are present.

Isis

Isis is a respected Egyptian Goddess of magic, the moon, sacred sex, and feminine energy. She represents rebirth and resurrection in its purest, the rebirth of self, life and hidden or repressed parts of yourself. All matters of past life memories, soul retrieval, and astral influences (projection, travel, etc.) can be accessed through her assistance. Wounds and painful memories, trauma and ancestral wounds are all direct associations of Isis, as is sexuality and the pain and suffering accumulated through lifetimes. Hope, faith and self-love is the message. Engage in healing, shamanic and spiritual healing, and past life memory recall/soul retrieval. Isis helps with childbirth, womanly problems, and themes linked to the "Mother." She is a healer, priestess, divine mother and lover in one. Moon magic can be learned and you can thus connect to your feminine energies, and the lunar/yin energies around. Sacred spells, protection charms, light (positive) magic, divintation, telepathy and telekinesis- advanced spiritual gifts, are available through her frequency. She is a personification of nature and divine feminine and can help you to realize this truth too, enabling you to become one with Mother Nature and the divine feminine within.

Kali

Kali is a Hindu Goddess of liberation and positive destruction. She seeks to destroy all that no longer serves in order to create new life, new growth and new change. This may include mindsets, beliefs, behaviors, relationships, diet and lifestyle choices, limiting or destructive cycles and patterns- emotional, psychological, spiritual etc., and anything that doesn't serve your highest and best self. Kali's energy leads to rebirth by reminding you of your personal power and sovereignty, and through healing your shadow. The shadow self is intrinsically associated with this Goddess. She inspires bravery, courage and fierce liberation. There's a depth, beauty and grace about her too, but some people see this as scary or something to fear. It's only when we deny or repress, reject or seek to hide part of our shadow selves that we see this fiery depth as frightening. Her ferociousness is catalytic and cutting, powering through blocks and illusions to get to the root of both truth and self-empowerment. Kali can help you come to terms with your own shadow and find inner strength and courage in addition to devotion and self-love. Healthy boundaries as well. Past pains are released to make space for a bright and bold future. Other associations include Shakti energy, kundalini and Tantric power. She's the creator and destroyer.

Kuan Yin

Kuan Yin is a Chinese Goddess of compassion, self-love and unconditional love. She is a Bodhisattva, a divine representation of female Buddha-enlightenment and the highest points of self-realization. She promotes mercy, kindness, benevolence and grace. Purity, divinity, faith, love and ancient knowledge can all be achieved through Kuan Yin's energy. She's compassion embodied. Her message and teaching is that compassion can help you overcome a range of lower human emotions and behaviors; envy, greed, spite, anger, jealousy, judgement, jerkiness, and the need to control, dominate, overpower or suppress others. This Goddess helps you to take control of your own life in an empowering way so you don't gravitate towards "lesser" human impressions, actions and behaviors/thoughts. Kindness is an act of the Goddess! You feel less inclined to prove yourself, be right, differentiate right from wrong to undermine anyone else's beliefs or perspectives, or any other ego mind-games. There's a loss of the ego and instead selfless and universal, unconditional compassion reigns. Compassion is your guide to true light, true love, prosperity, and new experiences and opportunities that best serve your higher self.

Lakshmi

Lakshmi is a respected Hindu Goddess of fortune, wealth and prosperity. This is the Goddess of abundance, the Goddess to call on to increase your luck and success in life. Manifestation powers can be enhanced with her energy and you will find yourself becoming lighter, more full of joy, and more positive in your ability to attract and manifest fortune. Celebration, purpose, joy, positivity and optimism, and material and spiritual success can all be yours. Her message is that abundance arises from a spiritual vibration.... Being spiritual and living life with joy, peace, contentment and integrity naturally allow for greater luck and abundance. You should practice gratitude daily too. Gratitude amplifies your manifestation powers. Also, sharing your wealth with others from a pure heart space enhances your wealth. Time is multidimensional and life timeless; the more you give the more you will ultimately receive. Purity of thought is essential and Lakshmi is therefore known as someone to worship in a spiritual self-development sense. People use her image and energy for prayer, sacred ritual and meditation. She also increases love and beauty in your life through building a connection with the divine. In Hinduism Lakshmi is known as a Great Goddess, a protector of the universe, and someone associated with royalty and majesty. Her symbols include the Owl- a messenger animal who can see in the dark, and who's also linked to intuition and psychic vision; and the lotus, symbolizing purity, spiritual illumination and peace.

Lilith

Lilith is a Hebrew Goddess of liberation and holy independence. Her energy is powerful and can show you how to choose freedom over restriction and repression. She chose to rise above the conditions and domination of man and align with freedom, self-respect and self-sovereignty instead. As such, she has been called a demon and associated with darkness, something very similar to the "witch trials" and "witch hunts." Essentially, Lilith is a Goddess of beauty and individual liberty, freedom from oppression and suppression, but has been 'demonized' due to her feminine power and beauty. Self-evolution, personal authority and power, soul independence and spiritual wisdom are all direct associations. She's linked to ancient Sumeria and

Babylonia and is one of the earliest Goddesses known to mankind. She's also been linked to astrology and references to the psyche, the shadow self for example and the journey one goes through of coming out of darkness and oppression to discover the light within. Magic is your superpower with Lilith, and not being scared of being wrongly judged or accused. People will misperceive and judge, in other words. It's your job to rise above and rediscover your own power, self-worth and truth.

Ma'at

Ma'at is an Egyptian Goddess of justice. Truth, fairness, equality, harmony and balance are the key messages and meanings of Ma'at. She represents the scales of justice, truth and knowledge. Themes of morality, law, order, social justice and divine law and order are connected to this Goddess. She can help you to live life with truth, fairness and equality- for yourself and others. The ultimate message is that truth can lead you to your higher self, and spiritual awareness and ancient wisdom. Complete honesty calls for vulnerability but the truth will set you free... Power and freedom are available when you live life with full integrity, authenticity, and honesty. Ma'at's masculine counterpart is *Thoth*, the God of writing and wisdom. Other associations of Thoth include science, art, judgement, hieroglyphics and magic (solar, not lunar like Ma'at's magic). He is further linked to Hermes, the Greek God of communication. It's useful to know this as Ma'at is the Goddess archetype and energy, therefore the feminine; but if you're seeking a more balanced and holistic energy you can call on Ma'at and Thoth, or all three of them. In Egpytian mythology Ma'at is associated with weighing the heart to determine the fate of a person in the afterlife. (Her name is sometimes spelt *Maat*.)

Mary

Mary is a Christian Goddess of miracles, unconditional love and faith. She is known as a protector, Mother, Saint and Goddess; she is celebrated as an embodiment of the divine feminine. Mary is here to show us the amazing blessings, miracles and opportunities in our life. She reminds us to stay humble and thankful while practicing love and compassion on a daily basis. Love, acceptance, tolerance and compassion are the seeds of wisdom and enlightenment. Divinity can be remembered and experienced through her light, as can the power of synchronicities. You are a powerful co-creator who is capable of manifesting miracles,love and abundance. She may be symbolic of divine feminine energy, but her symbols include the Sun, yellow and gold items, the virgin (Maiden). She is a priestess, sacred seductress, divine mother and virgin, with the virgin/maiden being a symbol of purity. She brings the vibrations of hope, unconditional love, faith, kindness, humility, generosity, charity and selflessness, in addition to self-alignment and a connection with Spirit. Mary is the divine grace who can help you access your own spiritual light and Source within. This then connects you to the world around and allows you to be a powerful beacon for others, and humanity as a whole.

Mama Killa

Mama Killa, or *Mama Quilla* or *Quechua*, is a Moon Goddess. She stems back to the ancient Incas and presides over the cycles of the moon and seasons. Her energy is powerful, primordial and feminine, yet grounding and down-to-earth simultaneously. Mama Killa helps one to understand natural cycles (bodily) in addition to the cycles of the earth's seasons. She represents the growing and harvesting of food, planting, and seed, crop and herb facilitation. She is symbolic of fertility and the beauty of the earth, creativity, projects and relationships, specifically relating to any project, cycle or person that promotes growth. Intimate relationships and passion projects can be nourished and nurtured with Mama Killa's energy. You should focus your time and energy on things and connections that stimulate your mind, body, emotions or soul in any way- anything that promotes positive self-image and personal transformation. If it doesn't serve your best self in some way, or honor your or the earth's natural cycles and bodily rhythms, don't give it your attention. This is the message of this Goddess. Further, Mama Killa encourages patience in waiting for outcomes. Change happens naturally over time, so be mindful of your need to rush things. A seed grows in perfect timing the right amount of love, care and attentiveness; there's a divine order for everything...

Mama Qocha

Mama Qocha, or *Mama Quacha* or *Cocha*, is a Goddess of the Sea. She is ancient Incan and rules over the sea and aquatic animals, fish, lakes, rivers... all bodies of water. She is believed to be the mother of Mama Killa the Moon Goddess. Mama Qocha instills peace and deep respect and appreciation for the waters of this earth. Water is within and around, arguably our planet should be called "plant water." She can aid in seeing the power and importance of water in your life. Water is linked to emotions and the subconscious, the subconscious and subtle realms where deep insights and extraordinary intuition, creativity, ancient wisdom, and imaginative thought are possible. Emotions allow us to perceive the world around and within. They help us to make sense of our feelings, impressions, beliefs and philosophies- the way we "tick" is operated by emotions and water. Mana Qocha assists with all of this. Call on her or work with her energy in the way explained at the end of this topic. Water serves as a reflection, a mirror to the soul, self and psyche. Water ebbs and flows gracefully and effortlessly, just like your inner currents and world if you can keep check on your emotions. Emotional chaos can be eased with this Goddess' assistance, and replaced with calmness and clarity. The power of emotional cycles and bodily rhythms also come under her domain. You are like the sea, with your waves and currents, and blend of subconscious forces and conscious mind. Other messages include unlimited potential and self-evolution.

Maya

Maya is a Hindu Goddess of illusion and magic. You can learn life's magic by embracing the illusory nature of it all. Things appear to be real, but what is reality? We observe, rationalize, conceptualize, and create things to be 'real' through our thoughts, feelings, beliefs and personal philosophies; and of course past experiences and ideologies. Everything is arguably an illusion and this is what Maya teaches. Spirit flows through everything and is neutral. Divine energy, Source energy, is real also as this exists above and beyond the "I," ego and individual reality. These are two fundamental teachings of this Goddess of illusion. You can look to her and her energy for peace, hope, intuition, spiritual wisdom, guidance, enlightenment and self-realization. Clarity of mind too- clear and rational/logical thinking, intuitive thinking and spiritual perception. Maya can help you to see how the invisible realm, unseen forces, constantly responds to our deepest desires. Setting intentions to the universe will expand self-awareness and your ability to align with your higher self, the best version of you.

(Goddess) Maya is significant in Vedic texts but has also been adopted by many New Age and modern spiritual communities as a term to describe illusion in general. The concept and philosophy itself is the forever changing and transient nature of everything, of existence itself. This realization leads to spiritual illumination and an ability to accept life and all of it's challenges or setbacks. Maya is also an epithet for Lakshmi, the Goddess of abundance, luck and prosperity. Maya is the treasure of life.

Metis

Metis is the Greek Goddess of wisdom. She provides guidance and light, wisdom and direction so you can live your best life. Magical cunning can be realized and developed too. Metis helps one to use the power of words, language and knowledge to better your life; relationships, career, finances, creativity, spiritual connection, health, etc. You can develop wise counsel. Thus, you can look to Metis if you wish to expand your listening skills, or to hold space and support others through the power of presence. Also, of course, actual wisdom, insight and deep knowledge into the meaning of life, metaphysics, soul, the universe, spirituality, and all aspects and sources of wisdom. Not only can you become more wise, but you can also develop your sense of cunning and intuition. Cunning doesn't necessarily have to be seen as bad or negative, cunning can be crafty and artful and not just devious or sly. Meditation, introspection, and mindfulness can help you to get to the root of your source of wisdom, learn how to best apply it, and develop the discernment and skilled mastery to share it.

Oshun

Oshun is a Yoruban (West Africa) Goddess of fertility, flow, generosity, healing and prosperity. She teaches that kindness and living life in flow leads to abundance and blessings in life. Working to heal yourself, your ehealth, spirit, relationships and the energy you project out into the world results in how much happiness and fortune you can attract. As a river Goddess, she is here to remind you that abundance comes from tuning into your beautiful qualities, which involves overcoming jealousy, spite, rage, envy and greed etc. We all have a space in our psyche and human self for vanity and jealousy and the like, but it's our jobs as divine beings to transcend this, further nurturing our favorable qualities. Oshun brings the energy and awareness of water and purity, the fertility and love associated with the purity of mind, thought and spirit. She is sensual too and can therefore inspire sensuality within. She can help you to connect with our divine, femininely beautiful, fertile and loving nature. Creativity and artistic and imaginative gifts can be nurtured with her energy. Destiny and divination are able to be realized. Personal liberties and a sense of independence, freedom and self-love are available when you connect to Source, and offer your appreciation to the abundance of the earth. *Her message*: if you have food to eat, friends and family to support you and cherish, shelter and security- and a range of other "simplicity" we often take for granted, then you are living life in flow! Be open to beauty and blessings.

Parvati

Parvati is a Hindu Goddess of fertility, love, beauty, harmony, marriage and devotion. This Goddess inspires these qualities and helps you to regain inner strength and personal power. She brings a gentle, nurturing and supportive energy, although she is by no means weak or timid. She has unique power and presence which leads to living your life with integrity, and stepping into true roles of leadership and self-sovereignty. Parvati is a supreme Goddess in Hinduism and Sanskrit times. She represents Shakti- divine feminine energy- and can therefore help with kundalini activation and awakening. Spiritual wisdom, illumination and enlightenment can be yours, she inspires commitment to living wholeheartedly in mind, body & spirit connection. You should be sincere and committed to spiritual growth and divine alignment. Embodying qualities such as empathy, compassion and unconditional love nurtures light within, and this aids in meditation, prayer and devotional practices (which further increase your vibration and light). Silent meditation can be developed with Parvati's assistance. Your relationship should be with the divine, source, God/Goddess, and Spirit. She also has a link to divine love and marriage between man and woman. This includes the marriage of masculine and feminine energies within, achieving true love with yourself first before being able to reflect it out into a committed partnership. Parvati, Lakshmi and Saraswati form a trinity of powerful and respected Goddesses known as a 'Tridevi.'

Saraswati

Saraswati is another special Hindu Goddess. She symbolizes poetry, music, knowledge, art, learning and language. She is a deeply sensual, creative and spiritual Goddess who can help you greatly in any of these fields. Saraswati represents self-mastery. She is the divine representation of the highest, or best, form one can attain in a lifetime. She's mastered many outlets and channels of expressions; poetry, dance, music, language, art, speech and communication, as mentioned. She holds a vibration of divinity, personal power and self-authority- she is compassionate and kind, gentle and modest, yet she doesn't take any prisoners. No-one can question her services, skills, talents or intentions as she has committed fully to becoming the best version of herself. If someone judges, misperceives, or aims to bring her down, treating her with distaste, jealousy or spite or the like, she simply smiles and sends them love and compassion. She has a healing nature and believes fully in herself. Purity is her message. Mastery of mind, emoticons, body and spirit is what she inspires, and everything mentioned is what you can learn for yourself. Deep wisdom and spiritual insight can be attained, pleasure and joy are available when you live life to its fullest.

Shakti

Shakti is a Hindu Goddess of transformation and enlightenment. Now is the perfect time to become the best version of yourself. Her energy inspires, transforms, initiates, and brings energy, optimism and capability. She can teach effort and determination in realizing your goals, seeing your dreams or aspirations followed through, and fine-tuning your talents to the highest levels. Shakti is the primordial cosmic energy of femininity, and dynamic forces that lead to creation. She is the personification of creative, self-sustaining and source energy. But, she's also destructive, consciously; she sometimes destroys to create. Breathtaking beauty and amazing rebirth and transformation is available through Shakti's divinely feminine, empowering energy. She is pure, sensual, beautiful, sexy, seductive, wise, intuitive, multi-talented and inspiring. Shakti can help you to see your heart's desires while aligning with your soul, also accessing dreams and the subconscious and subtle realms through her ability to transform. Illusions can be broken through, so truth can be seen. If you feel Shakti coming into your path, you may be stepping into a role of self-leadership. This Goddess can be called on for help with a new path, more prosperous career, and any sort of breakthrough and self-alignment. Teaching, speaking, writing and healing with links to the divine and are often symbolic of Shakti.

Sophia

Sophia is the Greek Goddess of wisdom. She symbolizes all aspects of wisdom, intuitive insight, and divine knowledge and insight. You can see clearly with her energy, she is intuition personified and is well-known in Platonism, Gnosticism, Christian theology, and the New Age spiritual movement. Mastery of mind, subtle thought, perception and observation skills are available to you. Intelligence and intellectual abilities in addition to philosophy are key qualities to work on with Sophia. Holy wisdom too. There's an unseen mystery and invisible energy that permeates all of life. The universe is a magical and mystical thing! Yet we often focus on the mundane and therefore overlook significant details, and pieces of knowledge. Sophia allows you to rise above the plane of physical matter to see beyond the veil of illusion, where spiritual insight, wisdom and unique observations are available. New opportunities, synchronicities, connections and blessings can be realized with her influence and assistance. There's a higher purpose and power linked to the capacity you have for wisdom.

Spider Woman

Spider Woman is a Navajo Goddess linked to Native American and Hopi culture & mythology. She embodies an ancient, ancestral, and grandmother energy- a wise elder with deep and vast spiritual insight. She's gained wisdom and ancestral knowledge through the tests of time, tradition and multiple lifetimes. She represents co-creation, the richness of the earth and fertility and divinity of the land. Inspiration, dreams, subconscious messages, and creative expression are all strong areas for growth and wisdom. Spider Woman takes the shape of a timeless woman who weaves energetic, astral, webs. According to Hopi tradition, she can shapeshift into a spider, this is a gift known by Shamans. She can thus help you to realize the power of the subtle realms and spirit, how everything is interconnected and how there is more than physical (material) reality. Charms, magic, herbal and plant medicines, self-leadership, community and sacred ceremony are all additional meanings and associations. So, if you need help in any of these areas you can call on Spider Grandmother. There is a powerful network of subtle and ethereal energy connecting us all, and this can lead to positive magic and co-creation when channeled and attuned to properly, with the right intentions.

The 7 Feminine Archetypes

In addition the Goddess archetypes there are also 7 main feminine archetypes. These are typically associated with women, however for any men wishing to connect to their divine feminine energy these are fine for you too. Just note that the 7 feminine archetypes are the integral archetypes & energies of *women*. These are the: Mystic, Lover, Mother, Queen, Virgin, Wise Woman, and Wild Woman.

The Mystic

The Mystic is an old soul, someone who can transcend beyond the limits and false realities of a 3-dimensional world. She sees through the veil of illusion, is incredibly intuitive, and is wise and perceptive. She radiates peace and compassion, universal and unconditional love and acceptance. She goes a step beyond the Wise Woman (as we explore soon), as she has a timeless, magical and ethereal quality about her. She is the symbol of past life memories, extrasensory and supernatural gifts, and everything connecting the divine. Subtle energy, a link to dreams and clairvoyance, and astral projection…. The Mystic is a deeply sensual and spiritual woman with many powers. They may not be powers everyone can understand, but they are real all the same. Mystical energy flows through her; she is at one with the stars, universe, galaxies far away, and the cycles of the Moon and Sun. Lunar energy is often associated with the Mystic's role. She's able to transcend the "I" and ego, the mundane and daily grind of reality, to connect with something higher, above and beyond. The Mystic channels life force energy for the good of others. She is a healer, seer, channel and medium- a giver of wise counsel and fierce protector. She protects nature, animals, people in need, and the planet as a whole. Many people don't see her gifts as she operates in the "unseen" and "invisible," she is connected to both the light and dark parts of her soul and finds joy in the simple pleasures of life.

You can look to the energy of the Mystic for healing and for your own energy healing pursuits. She, aka 'you'- the Mystic within, can help you to re-discover lost parts of your soul and psyche, the parts man and society have tried to cover up. The Mystic is linked to witches, sorceresses, medicine women and healers, seers and clairvoyants of all kinds. Time is multidimensional and life full with unlimited potential.

Things to be mindful of: **Light integration**

The shadow side of the Mystic is that one can become severely disconnected from reality. Giving into illusion and addiction is the dark aspect of this feminine archetype. There is such a strong desire to transcend that one can go too far, becoming lost in fantasy or self-denial. Also, giving into fears, anxieties and worries when not careful. Becoming lost in the dream world, seeking to escape reality, and supersensitivity are other things.

Goddesses: You can work with *Ishtar, Maya* and *Sophia*, the two main Goddess energies/archetypes, for help integrating your inner Mystic. Other significant ones to look to are Athena, Gula (and Ixchel), Iris, Isis, Mama Killa & Mama Qocha, Shakti, and Spider Woman.

How to embody this archetype?

To embody the Mystic within, channel cosmic and universal energies. Connect to your healer self through holistic medicine, herbal healing, crystals and special gemstones. Work with the elements, with alchemy and divination. Elemental healing and nature therapy are very powerful for you while alchemy can be catalytic. It's also useful to get clear on your path and destiny, how it is best to be of service and what soul gifts you have. Journal and write down some set, concrete and grounded plans. Remember the power of the Moon in your normal life too. Yin energy is feminine, receptive, emotional and intuitive, and this is where you thrive.

The Lover

The lover is a creative, sensual and sexually empowered seductress. This is the part of your personality that is confident, self-assured and worthy. You're deeply connected to your sensuality if you're in tune with the Lover archetype, and you're playful and high-spirited. You know what you want and need and you're not ashamed of your sexuality, or your urges and desires. You enjoy sex and intimacy in a sensual and romantic way. Love for you is a beautiful act of co-creation while pleasure allows you to be free and creative, liberated and in tune with your body. The Lover is emotionally aware and intelligent, with advanced levels of personal power, self-love, and empathy. She is filled with passion, magnetism, love and desire. And knows how to channel it positively to enhance her life and personal relationships, finances and projects. When the Lover archetype is strong and integrated one can use their powers of manifestation to attract things, people, experiences and luck. Wealth flows, abundance fills one's life, and there is an overall sense of excitement and joy, inner peace and synchronicity.

Power is amplified with the Lover archetype. You can create the life you long for when love flows freely, and this makes it a type of energy healing. Healing through love and self-care, sexual empowerment and sensual freedom stimulates healing on multiple levels.

Things to be mindful of: Light integration

The shadow side of the Lover is using your power to manipulate others. Seduction and manipulation, in others words. Also, sexually exploiting or deceiving and using others, craving attention and the spotlight, infidelity and extreme promiscuity, and becoming a drama queen. One seeks to control and dominate, or suppress, others and their sensuality and sexuality when the Lover is still in the dark or shadow stage of development. Sexual play is limited, one isn't in complete control or even knows what they need. Disconnection from mind, body, emotions or spirit (or all of them) can arise. There's a lack of real depth and intimacy too.

Goddesses: You can work with *Aphrodite* and *Freya*, the two main Goddess energies/archetypes, for help integrating your inner Lover. Other ones to look to are Benzai-Ten, Brigid, Eostre, Ishtar, Isis, Kali, Lilith, Oshun, Shakti and Sophia.

How to embody this archetype?

To embody the Lover within, dance more, get in tune with your body and divine feminine wisdom, and express yourself sensually. Self-pleasure is a great way to feel connected to your body and physical needs. Creative and artistic expression too. Paint, draw, write poetry and play music. Anything that gets your creative and imaginative juices flowing is perfect for sexual empowerment. You may want to write a letter or poem to an ex, for closure and healing. You don't have to send it- just setting the intention out to the universe will have positive effects. It's a sense of completion and karmic closure. Finally, eating healthy- high vibration and indulgent but soul-nourishing foods- will amplify our inner Goddess within.

The Mother

The Mother is caring, sensual, nurturing and compassionate. If you're connected to the Mother within you are generous, kind, giving and instinctive. You have a fierce protectiveness about you and know how to attract abundance for yourself and loved ones. You are gifted in the field of caring and supportive others, and you have a motherly instinct regardless of whether someone is actually family or not. Empathy and compassion for human nature define you. You burst with zest and joy for life, fertility and vitality- passion flows through you effortlessly, and you're both practical and spiritual. You possess inner balance and harmony. There's a strong desire to provide for loved ones with the Mother archetype; you believe in the power of the planet & earth, *Mother Earth*, to sustain life. This archetype helps you to embrace motherhood, feminine cycles, the seasons and cycles of the earth, and feminine qualities. You know what it's like to create and sustain life and respect the planet, generally working towards a sustainable and prosperous future. This energy can be used to begin new projects, nurture relationships, and enhance creativity too.

Things to be mindful of: Light integration

The shadow side of the Mother is codependency and smothering love, being too molly-coddling and interfering; always feeling you need to give and thus unconsciously taking away from others' independence. You do too much, engage in destructive habits through your genuine desire to 'give' and 'do,' and control people and situations.

There is a loss of self when connected to the dark side of the Mother. One can make excessive sacrifices and be too nurturing and caring. As a result, personal needs, desires and aspirations or ambition can suffer.

Goddesses: You can work with *Gaia* and *Demeter*, the two main Goddess energies/archetypes, for help integrating your inner Mother. Other ones to look to are Green Tara, Hestia, Kuan Yin, Lakshmi, Mary, Mama Qocha, and Parvati.

How to embody this archetype?

To embody the Mother within, meditate daily and cultivate the feminine qualities of empathy, magnetism, receptivity, nurturance and kindness. Seek to increase benevolence in all you do. Practice self-care, as this essential for your own well-being- so you can give to others from a genuine space of love and generosity. Taking care of your home through creating sacred space, attending to domestic and practical affairs, and nourishing your garden are ideal routes as well. Spend time playing with children, letting your own inner child run free. And, make sure you surround yourself by nature. Feng shui your home with flowers and plants, cacti and plants like the peace lily, and create a beautiful garden. Nature is revitalizing and replenishing to your soul.

The Queen

The Queen is your divine, majestic and regal self. In the modern world, we seem to call young girls "princesses," as if it's a positive thing. But a princess tends to be spoiled, immature and self-righteous, self-entitled and always wanting and needing more (things, material possessions etc.). A queen is above the princess in terms of status. She commands respect and knows what it means to lead. She is graceful and poised, full of composure and wisdom. Surely we all want to be queens and not princesses?! There's a reason why people who hold a spiritual vibration don't like being called princesses, and call themselves queens instead. The Queen archetype is your higher self. You embrace your personal power and authority, possess evolved self-leadership and self-worth, and are full of self-esteem. You work towards a better world in some way, using your power to benefit society and environments. First and foremost, you respect yourself- you don't tolerate unhelpful, pessimistic or slanderous attitudes and words about you. You're loyal, protective, wise and responsible if you resonate with the Queen archetype. Levelling up, ascending, and reaching new heights within and around are on your priority list. You seek to better yourself through education, skillful mastery, learning and self-development; you're on a path of sovereignty, wisdom, and divinity. You're always growing and transforming through your scholarly or high-flying pursuits, and you seek mentors and elders to guide you on your way. Finally, you believe in yourself and know in your heart and soul you are destined to create change.

Things to be mindful of: Light integration

The shadow side of the Queen is judgement, arrogance and self-righteousness. There is a large focus on image and status, superficial shaddow things when connected to the shadow self. One can become tyrannical, like a dictator, overbearing and callous. Vindictiveness and the need to oppress and control others is one of the worst aspects of the dark Queen. There's a sense of being under threat too, like one's crown isn't safe. This is, of course, the energetic and ethereal crown linked to the crown chakra, the source of spiritual illumination and higher cosmic consciousness.

Goddesses: You can work with *Hera* and *Athena*, the two main Goddess energies/archetypes, for help integrating your inner Queen. Other ones to look to are Epona, Kuan Yin, Lakshmi, Ma'at, and Mary.

How to embody this archetype?

To embody the Mother within, invest in spiritual growth. Take regular classes, self-development workshops, courses and educational or self-development retreats. Commit fully to your self-mastery, wisdom and skills acquisition, and personal and professional "upgrades." Don't be afraid to take risks and be bold- don't play it safe, be daring and decisive. Treat yourself as royalty too, with self-respect and like you are your own lover, soulmate and best friend in one; spend money on yourself, seek to master your health, and align with your sense of destiny and legacy. Swans can help you connect to the Queen archetype. Swans are graceful and majestic and can teach you the power of beauty, divine simplicity, and elegance. Practice self-leadership and work on self-autonomy as much as possible, speak up and make your voice heard. Intuition should be your guide.

The Virgin (Maiden)

The Virgin is also known as the Maiden. She is youthful, naive and enthusiastic. There is a unique caref-free trust and innocence about the Maiden, she is pure in every way. She views life like a child and is very much in tune with her inner child. She is excited, zestful and filled with vitality and optimism-she hasn't yet faced life's hardships and trials, so is still naive to the challenges ahead. Positively this makes the Virgin extremely positive and opportunistic about her future; she is able to secure new connections and opportunities that will expand and brighten her horizons. There is no sense of being jaded, however real adult shortcomings and sorrows, losses and tribulations are yet to be realized. Innocent and pure are the best ways to describe the Virgin archetype. Beauty fills her life, and there's a bounce in ehr step. Authenticity is strong too, she feels comfortable in ehr skin and is open-minded and friendly to all she meets. This doesn't suggest intuition is lacking- many people with an integrated Virgin/Maiden energy are deeply instinctual and intuitive, connected to their inner voice of light and reason. It does imply, however, that the child-like naivety can lead to failures and missed lessons if not careful. Mindfulness, wisdom and the experience that comes with age is called for with the Virgin. Hopeful, youthful and optimistic, she symbolizes unlimited potential and inspiration.

Things to be mindful of: Light integration

The shadow side of the Virgin-Maiden is being too obedient, codependent and people-pleasing. There is a need to listen to the advice of everyone, appease them, and give into playing small or weak. Intuition is sacrificed for the wisdom or perspectives of elders or those with more experience. But, not everyone knows best all the time- your own voice and instinctual knowings are special. Regardless of your age, divine feminine energy is strong in people in tune with the Virgin, therefore it's important to be mindful of these shadow tendencies. Practicing discernment and healthy boundaries is a sure way to overcome the three main negative traits: obedience, codependency and people-pleasing.

Goddesses: You can work with *A* and *Persephone*, the two main Goddess energies/archetypes, for help integrating your inner Virgin/Maiden. Other ones to look to for varying reasons are Aphrodite, Brigid, Eostre, Gaia, Green Tara, Ishtar, Lilith, Ma'at, and Shakti.

How to embody this archetype?

To embody the Maiden within, make conscious plans and work on discernment. Indecisiveness should be overcome and meditation should be a part of a new daily routine. Meditation enhances healthy boundaries and aids in self-alignment. Creativity should also be integral to your life, personal and social. Play more, allow your free-spirited side to shine, and choose pathways that lead to your liberation. The Virgin is very playful and innocent, she loves nature and the beauty of the natural world. Spend time around children and animals to increase your inner child. Create a vision board too, perhaps where you want to be in 3 or 5 years and where you see yourself. Any attempts to ground your energy and love of the world into physical structures, foundations and pathways will help you tenfold.

The Wise Woman (Sage)

The Wise Woman, or the Sage, is like an ancient book and global library. She possesses the wisdom of the ages, knowledge into history, culture and our earth timelines, and sacred wisdom. She is connected to ancestral and divine knowledge while being able to pick up on everything in the present moment. You, assuming you're connected to your inner Wise Woman, are intuitive beyond belief. Your intuition is so developed and evolved that you may be clairvoyant and psychically gifted. You certainly use your instincts and fine-tuned sensitivity to get to the root of situations and people. You see beyond the veil of illusion. The Wise Woman represents sage-like advice, wisdom and guidance, both the ability to receive and give it. You're an incredible listener, support system and person to go to in times of need. You may choose to expand a topic or interest into a specialist subject area. You're peaceful and sincere, extraordinarily gifted (in a range of things!) and are a natural speaker, teacher and motivator; you're inspiring and use your wisdom and communicative powers to help others. You may choose to uplift humanity's vibration in some way, such as through teaching leading courses, or writing articles and books. You'd make an excellent Reiki teacher, astrologer and metaphysical leader too.

People attuned to this archetype are introspective and avid readers. They love to gather information and spend lots of time in study and contemplation. One doesn't compare themselves to others either, a wonderful quality when we look at the destructive nature of the human ego. One speaks truth, inspires courage and integrity, and is often happy to rise above their own needs or social status to share the truth and necessary perspectives. There's a sense of idealism and high moral fibre. Personal power and kundalini is awakened, and spiritual illumination is strong. Further, the Wise Woman has embodied and integrated her *shadow self*, something which is essential for wholeness and healing. Mistakes, flaws and follies have been learned from. Experience and hardship, in addition to setbacks and naivety, have been transformed into wisdom.

Things to be mindful of: Light integration

The shadow side of the Sage is introversion, loneliness, and feeling like you don't belong. Being so wise and perceptive can leave one feeling cut off from the world. You feel everything so deeply, and intently, that there is an unexplainable disconnect and distance. Intuitive and spiritual insight leaves you feeling disconnected from your physical body and the material world. One is attuned to the higher mind, divine, and ancient, primordial and ancestral realms- including the subconscious mind- so life can be a bit lonely. It's important to surround yourself with kindred spirits, or people who understand your vision, energy and soul. Living in a spiritual or conscious community would be ideal for you. Or, stepping into your leadership role and networking with other like-minded spirits.

Goddesses: You can work with *Athena* and *Metis*, the two main Goddess energies/archetypes, for help integrating your inner Wise Woman. Other significant ones to look to are Gaia, Gula, Iris, Ishtar, Kuan Yin, Mama Killa, Mama Qocha, Maya, Sophia, and Spider Woman.

How to embody this archetype?

To embody the Mother within, immerse yourself in wisdom, learning and mindful introspection. There's a big difference between being introverted and *introspective*. Some of the most successful, respected and looked up to people with a lot of wisdom and inspiration to share have been introspectives. Also, learn how to let go and be open to change- don't cling on to old beliefs and ideas around yourself and the way things used to be. An integral part to the Wise Woman archetype's journey is leaving behind the old cycle and closing old doors. New chapters are meant to emerge when you step into your power and purpose.

The Wild Woman

The Wild Woman is the liberated Kali and Shakti energy within. This is the free-spirit, the part of you that desires to be free from chains and oppression, restrictions and limitations. Everything this archetype does is a strive towards independence and self-sovereignty, whether that be sensually, sexually or creatively. In fct, the Wild Woman is very in tune with these three things, so much so she is often labelled and misperceived. Society doesn't understand the Wild Woman. She is beautiful and graceful, liberated and wild- she dances around flames and beats her drum to ehr own rhythm. She treats others as family, sister, brother, kindred spirit and lover; she tends to be open to alternative sexuality such as polyamory and tribal forms of love. Love and intimacy for the Wild Woman are an extension of herself, a direct expression of the soul. She's untamed, naked, transparent and wholly authentic, no-one could ever question her authenticity. She's also vulnerable, a beautiful and rare quality to possess. She bares her soul to all she meets and isn't afraid of rejection or disapproval. She knows that she will inspire someone with a word, piece of wisdom, glance or smile, maybe not in the moment but somewhere down the line. She is intuitive and wise enough to know that one moment of soul reflection will stay with the person, and reach them when they need it.

The Wise Woman seeks to challenge the status quo. She does this either consciously with intention, or naturally-through her energy and organic vibration. Self-assured and confidence are off the chain... Being in tune with this archetype cna heal on so many levels. Emotionally, psychologically, spiritually, physically and mentally, the Wild Woman within is a key to spiritual growth and self-empowerment. Furthermore, she demands respect and prosperity- not in an immature or childish type of way, but in a way only those who "see" understand. She's in tune with the universe and natural cycles and forces of nature, she's connected to the seasons and spirit, to her divinity and to the laws of the cosmos. She is nature; peaceful and forceful, instorspective and extroverted, quiet and loud, watery and fiery, emotional and witty, reflective and direct, silent and communicative; magnetic and electric.

Things to be mindful of: **Light integration**

The shadow side of the Wild Woman is chaotic, unpredictable and destructive. Also, promiscuous and prone to wanderlust, immaturity and sometimes naivety (when at your worst). You cause chaos and live in self-destruction, either through addition or obsessive behaviors and attitudes. You can be a bit like a child wandering aimlessly through life. A lack of maturity and responsibility, including practical and financial affairs and concerns, are part of the Wild Woman's shadow. It's easy to get so lost in life's bliss and flow that you forget to ground, to stop still and reflect on the other aspects of life and self. Traditional values and family can be overlooked or forgotten entirely. Sexually, you may get caught up in wanderlust and free-spirited love which causes you to ner commit or experience the beautiful and supportive embrace of a monogamous relationship. Finally, don't avoid vulnerability and push people away. One can be so fiercely independent that emotions can be tricky, intimate relationships cna suffer, and one can become a 'lone wolf' travelling through life only forming superficial, temporary, connections.

Goddesses: You can work with *Kali* and *Shakti*, the two main Goddess energies/archetypes, for help integrating your inner Wild Woman. Other important ones to look to are Aphrodite, Artemis, Brigid, Freya, Gaia, Isis, Lilith, Mama Killa, Maya, and Spider Woman.

How to embody this archetype?

To embody the Wild Woman within, set clear boundaries and spend sufficient time alone. Nature and animals are incredibly powerful for you. They help you see clearly and feel completely at home. Surround yourself with music, art, creativity and imaginative ways to express yourself. Find a musical instrument and master it. Campins, hiking, going on adventures, travel and spending time in the wilderness are ideal for you. You gain mental clarity while amplifying intuitive powers through spending quality time with yourself; you thrive in solitude and meditation, connecting to your spiritual source etc. Tantra is an amazing way for you to discover your best route to sensuality and sexual intimacy as well.

Visit eco, environmental and conscious-spiritual communities… perhaps participate in work-exchange programs, where you help with animals or live on the land contributing to a sustainable and self-sufficient community. Simultaneously, to establish your own destiny get clear in your goals. Dreams and aspirations are very important.

Chapter 6: Cord Cutting and Psychic Protection

Spirit detachment and Cord cutting

An important aspect of healing yourself and awakening to your highest potential is recognizing when you have become unconsciously attached to others. Some call this *karmic attachment*, or *karmic entanglement*. "Spirit attachment" is another known name for it. Spirits can be dark or light, but we are not referring to dark astral entities or demons here. Spirit attachment is the karmic exchange of energy one unconsciously enters through daily (waking life) interactions, communications, and energy exchanges. Perhaps you have been misperceived and wrongfully judged, or maybe you are the victim of psychic attack or abuse from someone else's projections? Projection is the key word here. People project every day- our thoughts and internal feelings ripple out to affect external reality. Psychic attack is essentially the same as spirit attachment. It is when people's negative and harmful projections enter your auric field, your astral body, through being unaware of what's occurring. This may be due to weak boundaries or moments of internal confusion, vulnerability, or sorrow. It is usually when our frequency is at our lowest, but it can also be when we're vibrating at our strongest (or highest). Negative hateful people, narcissists and energy vampires, for example, like to cling on to people's light and seek to diminish it!

So, everyday we are exposed to a multitude of energies, both positive and negative. Our health, well-being and personal vibe is affected massively by the energy we let in. Stress and anxiety are the result of harmful projections, aka psychic attack, spirit attachment, weak boundaries, but this can also develop into fear and nightmares if left unchecked. This stress and fear weakens our spirit over time and decreases our vibrations- our life force is weakened, we may suffer from unexplained depression or low moods too, night terrors and feelings of feeling unsafe or discomforted. There will be an overall sense of insecurity and unprotected-ness when we're a victim of psychic attack. But we are always protected, the universe is filled with *light forces* and benevolent energies; not to mention our spirit guides and guardian animals and light helpers to call on when we need them most. Crystals, meditation, third eye/psychic protection, nature therapy, and pure high vibrational foods/diet help greatly too.

This brings us onto how to defend ourselves from spirit attachment, or psychic attack. Remember that the human/spirit system is a complex interconnected system consisting of the mental, emotional, physical and spiritual planes, or "bodies," of existence. Imbalances in any of these can lead to problems in all of the others, and in the dreamspace, the astral planes. The auric field can become polluted if significance harm is done to any of the bodies or planes of being. For example, recurring or repeating negative mental patterns happening over a long period of time. Emotional blocks. Physical ailments minor or major. And spiritual disconnection including, but not limited to, a closed third eye and crown chakra. Disharmony in any of the subtle bodies or physical body will weaken your aura- your overall frequency and energetic vibration- which ultimately leads to further problems, and greater increase of psychic attack. If you've been suffering with low mental health or emotional blockages and imbalances, this can lead to physical and spiritual tension, which then opens your aura up to the projections of others. Simultaneously physical and spiritual imbalances lead to problems on the mental and emotional planes. Recognizing a cord of attachment or psychic attack is the first step to healing and recovery. By recovery we are referring to wholeness, self-alignment and a form of self-mastery.

The Shadow's role in Spirit Attachment

You must be familiar with the shadow self by now. This is your shadow personality, the part of self that contains the qualities and characteristics that are deemed dark or undesirable. Your shadow self personality is deeply emotional, primal, instinctive and vulnerable- it is linked to the lower chakras, the energy centers associated with sex, reproduction, security, survival instincts, emotions, and complete openness and intimacy in interpersonal relationships. The lower self relates to your root and sacral chakras and although they are not one and the same with the shadow self, there are integral links. When your shadow self has taken over (and not in a healthy way such as through creative power- as the shadow also links to "emptiness" and creative energy) you are left weak and vulnerable, your boundaries are weakened. This is what leaves you open to psychic attack. We need to feel grounded and secure in our shadow selves so we can have healthy and positive emotional connections. A 'bond' (friendship, family, platonic, or romantic bond) is a cord in itself. In *spirit detachment*, we aim to break the unhealthy cords that bind us.

It's important to recognize the significance of the shadow self as emotional currents and forces hold considerable power. If we feel too open and vulnerable there is the unfortunate chance of becoming a victim, martyr or savior. This is a symbolic trio, and although psychic attack is usually associated with being a victim, taking on the role of martyr or savior can have serious negative implications too. Being a savior, either through intentionally trying to save everyone or by unconsciously taking on that role, disrupts the natural balance of power. The universe needs duality and wholeness or oneness to sustain itself, yet if you believe you are here to 'save' everyone you ultimately deplete your energy. Also, not everyone wants to be saved, nor they need to; sometimes it truly is our own projections that make us believe we are better or above another. This makes you vulnerable to psychic attack, a type of energy attachment that is birthed through tension and resentment, frustration or any other type of harmful projection from the person you're intending to 'save.'

Playing martyr has a similar effect. Martyrdom involves taking on everyone's suffering, which is (quite literally) harmful to you. One opens themselves up to unnecessary karmic and/or energetic absorbent when they play the role of the martyr. It is like the metaphor of Jesus dying on the cross for our sins. *Is it necessary? What is "sin?" Aren't the millions-billions of people who were born after him 'sinners' anyway?* See, being a martyr doesn't serve anyone, especially not yourself. Victim is the most commonly referred to aspect of the victim-martyr-savior complex, and yes- it is a complex; it has its roots in the psyche and self. Being a victim is in itself cooperating with the persecutor or abuser, giving your power away. Even by embracing yourself as a victim you unconsciously give permission to be abused, in a sense. OK, sometimes we really are victims and no matter which way we evaluate, assess the situation, or try to find harmony and love (unconditional/universal/self-love) there is injustice and wrongdoing being done. But even in these circumstances labelling your situation as being a victim *is* giving your power away. Taking back your responsibility is the first step towards healing and self-respect.

In terms of psychic attacks, victimhood creates a blockage, imbalance or weakness in one's energy field. It is a form of allowance, allowing this harmful energy and projection in. If we learned to evaluate the situation and see how, on some subtle or more apparent level, we have created it; we will see that no-one and nothing has control over us. You are the creator of your reality! You have power and control, so take charge of yourself and your life. And this is what spirit detachment teaches, it allows us to get to the root and truth and in doing so we become the ones who create our realities. Physical circumstances or other people may not be able to change immediately, but we can change the way we respond to external events. Accepting yourself as a victim creates a weakness and broken link, if you will, in your energy field. You open yourself up to further judgements, criticism and abuse; psychic attack and harmful karmic attachments. It is essentially also taking away the abuser's responsibility and absorbing it. This isn't healthy and means you take on their negativity; but taking *self*-responsibility is a different story.

So, to heal and recover from spirit attachment you need to be completely honest with yourself. Where have you had weak boundaries and where have you been giving your power away? Are you truly a victim, or have you yourself been unconsciously projecting on that person or others, to open yourself up to that type of energy? Healing is seldom smooth sailing!

Techniques for Spirit Detachment and Cord Cutting

1. Ask for divine and spiritual assistance

Firstly, you should know that there are many unseen forces and spiritual beings ready to help you. Angels, spirit animals and light beings- benevolent entities existing on the higher and subtler planes, are here for us. You can ask for divine assistance during meditation or prayer, or in harmony with a healing practice. Sacred space is an important concept in the practice of spiritual guide connection.

You can create a sacred space prior to any technique you do by getting in a meditative position, dimming lighting, and using the right spiritual tools to assist you. Lighting really adds to the effect of a cord cutting activity, so be mindful of using candles, eco lamps and non-harmful alternatives, like a himalayan rock salt (Crystal) lamp. Alternatively sunlight and moonlight (depending on the time of day) should be used. For scents and smells, use an oil diffuser and burn essential oils such as frankincense, sandalwood, or some 'lighter' ones that lead to emotional healing. Rose, patchouli, lavender and geranium make fine options. Sage, palo santo (a unique tree wood from South America), or a cleansing smudge stick can all be used too; these cleanse the air and purify the atmosphere of a room and environment, in addition to cleansing one's aura. Sounds should be added to take your self-alignment and healing experiences to the next level. (Refer back to sound healing in Energy Healing Techniques Book 1.)

2. Raise your vibration through Crystals, Reiki, and Self-healing

Crystals, reiki healing and self-healing are all perfect ways to release yourself from karmic and spirit attachment. *Quartz crystal* is particularly effective for cord cutting, because it represents pure light and therefore kundalini energy on a metaphysical/spiritual level. Clear quartz and other forms of quartz, like Spirit quartz, aligns you with your higher self and higher chakras- the third eye and crown chakras. It can lead to spiritual insight, growth, and sparks in innovation and self-realization. *Amethyst* is powerful at enhancing intuition and connecting you to perception, foresight, psychic gifts and clairvoyance. Amethyst crystal stills the mind, aids in meditation, and opens channels into higher consciousness, subtle perception and inner calmness and peace. Other crystals you can use to aid in cord cutting and spirit detachment include *Lapis Lazuli* for your Third Eye chakra (truth, wisdom, psychic enhancement) and Throat chakra (inspiration, intuition), *Celestite* for your Crown (cosmic consciousness, channeling, divine inspiration), and *Rose Quartz* or *Rhodochrosite* for your Heart chakra (opening your heart to unconditional love and healing).

Working with the techniques in the previous book will work wonders as well. Your ability to connect to the subtle realms of spirit, where healing energy is strong and flows freely, is determined by the amount of 'work' (aka self-development) you do. Making chi balls, strengthening your aura, working with crystals, and raising your vibration through meditation and sound- like binaural beats, enables a stronger connection to source and your inner spirit; which leads to an increase in healing powers. Kundalini activation and chakra healing will further amplify your capacity for cord releasing and karmic detachment.

3. Crystal water and blessing

Crystal water is a beautiful way to raise your vibration. You can cleanse and charge a crystal and then program it with specific intentions to aid in spirit and karmic detachment. Releasing negative influences and cords naturally involves karma, hence why the two (karmic release and spirit detachment) can be seen as interchangeable. Crystal water activates certain memories held within, on a subconscious and subtle-energetic level. It also helps to raise your vibration, release blocks and internal imbalances, and open frequencies of awareness which result in the manifestation of being able to get to the root of truth. You can see more clearly into your flaws and follies, what might be creating unhealthy and destructive cords or spirit attachments, and what part you played in the harmful bond. You can further gain the wisdom, clarity and spiritual guidance on how to heal from the situation, and detach yourself while regaining your personal power and self-autonomy. Crystal water carries the vibration and healing frequency of the energetic qualities.

So, start by cleansing your crystal in cold running water. This is essential as water washes away psychic impurities and negative energy. Next, charge it in sunlight for 2- 3 hours, or closer to 12 hours if you want a potent effect. Then program it with the intentions of healing, spirit detachment, and clearing past karma and cords of attachment. The best gemstone to use is Clear Quartz. You can leave your clear quartz crystal in purified, filtered or mountain water for 3- 12 hours. If you already feel confident in your healing abilities, channeling light and healing energy (life force) through your palm chakras; add an extra dose of intention through channeling power/energy/light into the water. You can then spend a few minutes blessing your crystal water before engaging in a ceremony to cut cords and release spirit/karmic attachment.

Crystal water can also be drunk throughout the day and before bed, and be made for a general "boost" in daily life. You won't need to cleanse and charge your crystal every time for this (depending on how large a container you create), but do be mindful of the fact that crystals need to be charged in sunlight for the metaphysical healing powers to kick in. Crystal water aids in hydration, detoxification, frequency/vibration alignment, spiritual awareness, healing, and purification of mind, body & spirit.

3. Diamond portal activation ('Crystal Grid Meditation')

There is something known as a 'Diamond Portal.' We cover this in more depth in *'Aura Healing,'* (another book soon to be released!) but, for now, we will go into the basics. A diamond portal is a *crystal grid* used for meditation and healing. It is a very advanced form of energy healing yet it is ironically quite simple to perform. The advanced aspect comes from how strong your vibration is; how clean and pure your channel (body) is, and how much self-healing and self-development inner work you have done, in order to embody a strong enough light frequency. A Diamond portal Crystal grid involves a combination of: meditation, visualization, chakra healing, and spiritual/self-awareness. First, you must make sure you feel strong and centered within. Also, a 1- 3 day fast or detox is recommended to make the most of this exercise. The more cleansed your pineal gland is the more powerful your third eye operates.

To perform this energy healing technique:-

- Create your sacred space and close your eyes, taking some deep breaths. You may want to set up a crystal grid around you with (cleansed and charged) crystals and gemstones. Anything relating to the heart, throat, third eye and crown chakras will help. (You can find guidance on this in the previous *Energy Healing Techniques* book.)
- After a few minutes when your breathing begins to feel slow and steady, and potentially synchronized to your heartbeat, do the following.
- Picture a shimmering diamond in your mind's eye. To start, this visual will just be inside your mind, in your head. See the diamond glimmering in front of you, shining beautifully with a radiant healing light glowing from it. Remind yourself of the healing qualities of the diamond at this point. The diamond is known as a stone of purity, it connects you to deep spiritual insight, illumination and intuitive wisdom. It is a connector to spirit and the spiritual realms, and both your higher self and all aspects of love. Platonic love, romantic love, self-love and unconditional love are associated with the diamond. Because the purpose of spirit

detachment is to heal from karmic bonds and unhealthy harmful cords of attachment, focus on universal love and self-love in this crystal meditation.

- Once you've got a clear and strong mage of a diamond in your mind, visualize this diamond enlarging and growing around you. You are sitting inside this diamond, it is encompassing you in a massive astral embrace.... Allow the feeling of being wrapped in the shimmering glow and light of this diamond to surround you. Feel the sensations. Experience the depth of clarity, perception and spiritual wisdom. See a diamond light showering you, bathing you, in it's healing energy.

- Stay inside this mentally projected diamond for at least 5 minutes. This is enough time to feel waves of energy travelling through you.

- One you feel like you're ready for expansion, picture yourself sat inside a diamond. See yourself meditating inside a massive diamond crystal. Keep the visual strong and clear in your mind's eye.

- The feelings of energy and electromagnetic pulses should be pretty strong after a few minutes. The intention of this meditation is to expand your aura and increase your vibration. On a subtle level, you are wrapped up in an astral embrace- the diamond is surrounding you. It's sensing healing vibrations and subtle energy to your aura.

- Once you feel relaxed, calm and serene inside, ask the universe, your angels, or a higher power to *release cords of attachment.* Set your intention, repeat it a couple times over in your mind. 'I ask the universe to bless me with karmic release and healing. I am ready to let go of unhealthy attachment and bonds that no longer serve my highest purpose.' And then surrender. Say your intention and speak it to the universe then surrender to the healing and divine assistance.

Psychic Attack (Shielding Yourself + Protection)

Psychic attack can be defined as:-

- Nightmares and vivid imagery during sleep. You see 'dark forces' or 'shadows,' and feel like there is a non-benevolent energy around you, as if your spirit is trying to be harmed by someone.
- Fear and anxiety, often unexplainable and intuitively or instinctively felt. A sense of it

not coming from you due to your own usual level of happiness and contentment.

- Extreme fatigue and tiredness, again-unexplainable and illogical.
- Emotional or spiritual paralysis.
- Question your path, truth, values or sanity. Feeling like you may be a victim of gaslighting or abuse from someone (when you're strong and insightful) or quite literally questioning your sanity and mental health (when weak and suffering from attack).

Plant medicine and healing herbs like sage, palo santo, and natural herbal incenses are ideal for cleansing your space. This applies to your aura and physical space, room or home. Frankincense resin or essential oil is also advised. Plants and herbs clear unwanted energies from your energetic field. Burn the plant or herb, such as a sage stick, and 'smudge'- wave it around your body and outside environment. Use it as a fan and do so with the intention of cleansing your space. While saging yourself and your environment, concentrate on the banishing of negative or dark energy by holding *light and love* in your mind's eye. You can repeat the process with an essential oil in a diffuser, one that aids in purification (like Frankincense). This is one of the fastest ways to initiate the process of healing and spirit detachment. You can also cite some mantras to accompany. These have a positive effect on your aura and personal space and any physical environments you've been accumulating other people's energy (home, personal room, bed area….).

Some potential mantras to use include:-

- 'I release negative energies so I can be the best version of myself.'
- 'I only choose to let loving and kind people into my life, who have my best intentions at heart.'
- 'Darkness and negativity are dispelled from my life so I can serve my higher purpose.'

Cord Cutting

Try this cord cutting technique. Before you go t bed, imagine a cord between yourself and any perso or thing that comes to mind, the cord originatin from your belly. Using a pair of imaginary 'scissors cut the cord between yourself and any externa energy that you envision.

Just like the kundalini serpent spiral that flows through our own bodies, there is a spiral that connects everything on an energetic, ethereal and subtle level. If we take the DNA double helix, we see two spirals intertwining-

interweaving around each other. DNA is symbolic of a *snake*-like energy, also representative of kundalini and vital (universal) life force energy which flows through our bodies and spine. If we then look at the Story of Creation and Christian spirituality, we realize how the snake stands for wisdom, knowledge, and a connection to the higher mind, self, and divine. The snake led Adam and Eve out of the garden through temptation. Well, lust, sex, intimacy and everything related to the *shadow self* (what the Bible defines as 'unholy' in Christian scripture) is quite simply an intrinsic and inherent part of one's kundalini energy. Root to Crown... primality, reproductive organs and sexuality- sexual needs and desires, and "survival" aspect; these are part of the lower chakras and root/base of the kundalini. The Bible refers to holiness and purity as the Crown and higher self, the cord to the divine where one is 'free from sin.' The story of the snake in the Garden of Eden is really just depicting kundalini energy, and the emphasis of the higher self and mind, a link to the divine and Spirit.

Sexual repression is another key element of finding wholeness within. We've covered this in the first Energy Healing book, so remember what was said on this topic. A lot of imbalances that are seen on an individual and global collective level are due to false information and misdirection in sezuality and the shadow self. Sex and basic drives for intimacy have been labelled a 'sin' by a significant number of religions, prominent belief-systems, and cultures. This leads to repression, inner chaos and struggle, confusion and *oppression*. The Christian Story of Creation, for example, had many correct points. But teaching that lust, sexual needs and urges, and deep desires for intimacy, co-creation, and bonding is a "sin"- without showing a new or better way; i.e. how are humans supposed to channel these feelings and sensations? Well, this is wrong and misinformed! The snake (Serpent) is wisdom and inspiration- divine guidance and knowledge. The snake is linked to an ancient and primordial power. In Shamanism the snake is respected and honored, it is, in fact, seen as holy, sacred, and symbolic of divine knowledge and spiritual insight. Shamanism recognizes the snake as a powerful teacher and bringer of ancient knowledge.

The point of this little digression and going straight back to the importance of the cord, is that there is a spiritual-energetic cord connecting us. It connects us beyond and through time and space, and is multidimensional in essence. This means people can be connected on many planes, dimensions and realms. The cord, which is shaped like a spiral (just like the DNA helix and kundalini serpent power), can keep two souls bonded for eternity and throughout lifetimes. It connects us on the physical plane in any one lifetime yet exists beyond the physical realm simultaneously, so the purpose of cord cutting is to get to the root of bonds and karmic connections that are healthy, harmonious, and good for our highest selves, and those which are not. Once we've recognized an unhealthy or harmful cord of attachment we can use *cord cutting* for spirit release and karmic entanglement. Cords are frequently present in psychic attack, on an unconscious and sometimes subconscious level. Giving our power or energy away leaves us open to psychic attack, the harmful and negative projections of others. This is why the first step of recognizing how you may be under psychic or spiritual attack is *so important* in recovering and freeing yourself from the unconscious link.

Similar to the Crystal Grid meditation shared before, you can **surround yourself in white light.** **Visualization meditation** is very helpful in protecting yourself from psychic attacks. The stronger your vibration is, the better able you are to shield yourself and ward off future projections. Picture a white light radiating within you and surrounding you- this will create the same effect as described in the Diamond portal activation (*Crystal Grid meditation*). **Mantras** can be used too. "I am divinely protected... I am light and love.... I am surrounded by healing energy and spiritual protection!"

Aura, chakra and kundalini healing will assist you greatly. The human aura affects people and things (stones, crystals, plants, animals, water) closest to you in your immediate environment, and the energetic space around you on a further level. Your aura is a colorful combination of your chakras, vital life force, and spirit. It is known that the chakras you resonate with the most and most connected to will be the primary colors of your aura. For example, if you're a very 'third eye open' being with a lot of empathy, self-love and compassion for animals or humanity, your aura will be purple and green. If you identify strongly with the spiritual planes and higher, cosmic consciousness your aura will be violet or white. One's aura can be a combination of any and all colors, but the general rule is that it is mainly 2- 3 colors which are quite clear and visible (to those who can see auras). There's a *pulsing vibration* that speaks to others, plants, nature, animals, and the universe on a subtle level. In cord cutting, you should be aware that you hold responsibility for what you let into your aura. Of course, at first we may not be conscious of this; we're not taught about boundaries, chakras or subtle-spiritual energy in school, for example- or how to strengthen our auras. Yet the truth is that we are completely responsible and in control of the energy we let in.

Chakra healing with the colors and visualization is useful here. Journaling, taking wisdom and insight from your dreams, and expressing yourself creatively and poetically or musically are all perfect ways to get in touch and tune with yourself. The ability to 'know thyself' leads to wisdom and self-awareness that can help you in psychic protection and cord detachment. Working more closely- and consciously- with your dreams is another powerful technique in psychic protection. Dreams are linked to your subconscious, so paying attention to your dreams and finding ways to strengthen dream recall strengthens your subconscious mind- this can then help you in waking life because we're influenced by subconscious and unconscious forces every day.

How Psychic Attack can manifest (Various forms and expressions)

1. *Jealousy, anger and resentment*: These are some of the most common forms. People we've met, don't know, or are close to us can all send harmful energy in the form of resentful or jealous projections. Someone's intense anger or jealousy can last weeks to months if we're not careful. Depending on the intensity of the attack, it can be so extreme that it keeps us up at night, gives us anxiety in the day, and makes us feel very unsafe and uncomfortable.

2. *Fantasies and intense sexual desires*: Although it can be a compliment to be on the receiving end of someone's sexual desires and fantasies, in some cases this is a form of psychic attack- and it can be very harmful. This is an occurrence in people who are ruled by lust and the lower chakras, people who may be stuck in their root chakra or uncontrolled sacral energy. When you're vibrating high and strong,

connected to your divinity, light and truth, being the constant desire of someone's lust and attraction affects us on an energetic level. It may sound strange or crude, but there are some 'seedy' and unhealed people who lust after those kingly or queenly characters, who are majestic and passionate, pure and connected to their truth. This situation is particularly true in house-shares or shared living situations where there are multiple people co-living. Everyone has their own path, frequency, aura, unique energy and personal vibration; unfortunately, you never know who is violating your aura with their self-destructive thoughts and internal struggles.

3. *Illusion, misinformation, hearsay and gossip*: These create a lot of problems unconsciously. People gossip, pass around information based on speculation or misinformation, and create 'truths' about you that are by no means representative of your actual energy, integrity or actions. Illusion is everywhere, which leads to confusion! Someone will hate you or strongly dislike you based on the story of another. False information will be passed around and before long there will be multiple made-up stories that affect your personal frequency. Over time false stories, gossip, and negative or hate speech can actually change us

as people. We're sensitive, empathic and emotional creatures- we naturally desire friendship, companionship, community and interconnectedness (there's no escaping this universal truth). Therefore, we "pick up" on the projections and thoughts of others. It can affect our mood, emotions, mental patterns, behavior, speech, and even beliefs and self-esteem over a period of time.

The main thing to be mindful of and seek to overcome is that psychic attack is a violation of your personal energy and space. You could be the most exemplary human being with strong morals and ethics, supreme compassion for humanity (and the planet, animals and plant-life), and fully committed to a path of service, healing, spiritual growth and unconditional love and empathy…. If there are enough people projecting their wrong/false, harmful or negative intentions at you, you will be affected. This is why *boundaries* are so important. Boundaries lead to self-empowerment, self-alignment, self-respect and self-love. Psychic gifts and ability open and strengthen with healthy boundaries, so you're better able to see and sense danger or potential threats. You're stronger in your truth and in yourself which signifies being able to 'foresee' and use intuitive guidance and vision to suss out who may not be on your side, who has your best interests at heart, and who may be fake, jealous, manipulative, or a hater! On a wider scale, if you are a public figure or work in the limelight self-alignment (a direct result of healthy boundaries and a strong aura) allows you to protect yourself before any bad media or deception comes out. It can't be stressed enough how important boundaries and self-love are to your health. Psychic protection, aura strengthening, and boundaries are a form of preventative healthcare.

Your aura acts as a sponge, absorbing virtually everything (if you're not careful!).

Walking down the street can affect you just as much as the personal and interpersonal stories that influence your daily reality. This isn't meant to scare you or make you live in fear, this is solely guidance and wisdom into the world of metaphysical, subtle energy. Do you ever just feel low, tired, sad or depressed for no reason? Perhaps it could be when you should be feeling at your best or most sparkly... You may have just created a vision board, eten a really healthy and nutritious meal, come out of a deep and healing meditation, or engaged in a creative, inspirational or energizing activity that initially gave you a spurge of life force and happiness. But then your positivity and optimism is suddenly transformed into negativity and doubt. You feel low, uninspired, exhausted or nervous and anxious- life force seems to be sucked out of you in an instant, and all sorts of self-pity and low self-esteem feelings take over.

If this happens often and also at regular or recurring cycles, significant moments and chapters in your life or daily routine, you may very well be under psychic attack. People, places and exchanges of energy and communication can drain us or give us life. They can instil negativity, pessimism and doom or gloom, or help us to feel empowered, positive and loved and supported. Unconscious forces from the projections of others need to be checked. Psychic protection is ultimately setting strong energetic boundaries between your personal energy and other peoples'. It's knowing what belongs to you- what is yours, and what is not. Empaths are prone to picking up on virtually everything. You can look towards the empath nature and some of the daily struggles they face to help you get a clearer view on this topic.

Best Crystals for Psychic Protection

A quick recap from earlier books: Crystals have an *electromagnetic energy field* which interacts with our own. Science calls this electromagnetism, spiritualists call it an aura. Both are true. You should always cleanse and charge a crystal or gemstone before using it for its healing properties.

To cleanse: Rinse under cold running water for 2 to 5 minutes. Alternatively you can place it in a bowl of mineral, mountain, spring or pure filtered water for up to a couple of hours.

To charge: Once the gemstone has been cleansed in water, leave it in direct sunlight for up to 12 hours. The crystal gemstone then absorbs the healing and energizing energy of the Sun, amplifying the metaphysical properties within.

1. Amethyst

Amethyst is the perfect crystal for psychic protection, as it is a stone *for* psychic protection. Amethyst is specifically for the third eye chakra. It promotes spiritual awareness, inner peace, calmness and clarity of mind, and meditation. It enhances your ability to see, think and perceive clearly, free from illusion and mental chaos, whilst relieving stress and anxiety. It is an excellent gemstone for stilling the mind and helping with meditation, subtle perception, dream states and higher self seeing. Amethyst strengthens your mind so that you can protect yourself from any potential negativity or harm. It also increases your energy field on the mental and psychological planes. It is therefore very protective and guards against psychic attack, it's actually known as the "psychic's stone."

2. Obsidian

Obsidian is another powerful one for purification and transformation. Obsidian protects and shields, increases psychic gifts and aids in manifestation-manifestation, of course, increasing your personal powers. It is a grounding yet stimulating stone and activates your mind so that you can think more logically and rationally, and intuitively. Obsidian helps to absorb negative energy around you and from nearby environments. It promotes truth, relieves mental stress and tension, and eases confusion. Obsidian further inspires truth in order for you to achieve self-realization. When you know who you truly are, some of the tactics of psychic attack and manipulation don't work on you. Compassion and strength are qualities increased with Obsidian's metaphysical healing properties.

3. Fluorite

Fluorite is aura cleansing, truth inspiring, and consciousness expanding. It expands, stimulates and activates your mind and mental abilities, including your intuition and psychic powers. It's an extremely protecting gemstone too, allowing for the stabilization of your aura while shielding you from negativity and harm. Fluorite absorbs and neutralizes negative energy... it thus encourages inner balance and harmony. Positivity is amplified and increased and you're better able to see, think and act clearer with a stronger connection to your true self and being. You're able to see past deception and manipulation with Fluorite's energy.

Chapter 7: Angels and Higher Consciousness

"Consciousness is evolving throughout the universe in billions of forms. So even if we didn't make it, this wouldn't matter on a cosmic scale. No gain in consciousness is ever lost, so it would simply express itself through some other form. But the very fact that I am speaking here and you are listening or reading this is a clear sign that the new consciousness is gaining a foothold on the planet."

~ Eckhart Tolle

Help from the Angels (Angelic realm connection)

Angelics, angels, ascended masters and light beings on higher planes of consciousness.... Life is multidimensional. Many people who awaken to their inner divinity and a spiritual path report seeing angels, or angelic beings. Spiritual awakening ultimately leads to a cleansed and purified pineal gland and an open (and activated) third eye chakra. The third eye is, of course, the seat of consciousness, spiritual perception and higher awareness. It is a direct link to the divine and the Higher Self- the higher mind. Spirituality in itself is a form of cleansing and purification. When our pineal glands are calcified, we are closed off to 'extra-sensory' abilities, or the 'supernatural.' Advanced and evolved states of consciousness including spiritual and psychic perception, clairvoyance, telepathy, and the like, are thus available when we open our third eyes and crown chakras; the highest chakra in the 7 chakra system. Angels are beings existing on the higher dimensional planes of consciousness. *Light* is a key word here.

Angels are waiting to guide you. They're benevolent forces, and regardless of whether you believe in angels quite literally or whether you prefer to remain open to the multiple possibilities and limitless potential of this magical universe, there are some key teachings we can learn from the angels. This book is in no way dogmatic but we will approach this from what is deemed wisdom and reality in the spiritual world. Angelic light beings are here to show us a new way, a brighter way filled with love and compassion. Divine knowledge and self-awareness are just two gifts of angelic connection; there is also self-love, wisdom, insight, inspiration, creative and artistic abilities, self-alignment and the capacity to connect to our soul's purpose. Of course, healing is another main blessing of the angels. Consciously connecting with angels allows you to begin to recognise their divine messages lovingly nudging you into action. These nudges may take the form of certain books to read, or a course or conference to attend, which lead you to follow a specific path. This path may enable you to fulfil your life purpose or soul mission, develop a new skill, or self- evolve to new heights which in turn provides you with financial security. It may be that your guardian angel repeatedly presents you with opportunities to attend a social event, which further leads you to you meeting your soulmate (of course, the other person's guardian angel will be working simultaneously with your guardian angel to facilitate this meeting!).

Angels have been around since the start of mankind's journey. They are supernatural beings mentioned in all religions and mythologies and are often depicted as benevolent celestial beings acting as messengers between God (Source, Spirit and the Divine) and humanity. They exist in the planes closer to Source- to ultimate light and divinity in its purest expression- and on a higher dimension altogether. Like the spiritual deities, Ascended Masters, Guardian Angels, and being of light, angels are here to show us a new way and further help evolve us on our journey. Holistically speaking all Angels have a protecting and guiding role. Let's now look at the energy of each of the angels. You can call on them in prayer, meditation or self-healing and ask for their guidance and protection.

Gabriel

Gabriel is a divine messenger of God, source, Spirit and the divine. This angel brings inspiration and can help assist you with transition, transformation or change. Gabriel can inspire you to connect to your true self and align with your Higher Self, and inner divinity. You have a soul purpose or path and unique journey based on your spirit and Spirit's guidance, Gabriel can help provide the compassion, direction and loving guidance to see you onto this path. As the "Divine Messenger," Gabriel acts as a bridge between lower and higher levels of consciousness, and between the Lower Self and Mind, and the Divine (or your Higher Self and Higher Mind).

Gabriel is also an *Archangel*, one of the two highest ranking angels in the Judeo- Christian religion. Gabriel represents the strength of God and the Goddess, he can assist in connecting you to visions, dreams, and psychic vision, and your clairvoyant, clairsentient, and spiritual abilities; just like when Gabriel came to Joseph in a dream and told Mary would conceive a son, and his name would be Jesus. In this sense, it is clear that Archangel Gabriel is the closest link to God/ Goddess and the divine.

Hamael

Hamael is an angelic messenger of strength, willpower and determination. You can be assisted greatly through Hamael's love and guidance in all matters relating to developing and embodying the strength you need to grow. Integrity, courage, purpose and passion also come under this Angel's realm. If you need help in a business or work related matter, or if you wish to grow and self- evolve for your soulful dreams and aspirations, call on Hamael. Hamael can provide the encouragement and concrete guidance you need to help you through any life challenges, decisions or transitions. Also known as the "Sacred Warrior," Hamael brings dignity, integrity and a strong sense of practical duty and responsibility. Faith in perfect and divine time, trusting the process and connecting to your inner warrior can all be attained and embodied with Hamael's assistance.

Jophiel

Jophiel is a cosmic force to help connect you to your own inner spirit. Spiritual liberation can come through this angel's love and wisdom, and is also known as the "Holy Liberator." If you need help in meditation or in finding stillness and inner presence, call on Jophiel. Releasing limiting beliefs, overcoming destructive mental patterns or emotions, and general letting go of anything can all be attained and achieved through Jophiel's wisdom and insight. S/he inspires us towards higher awareness, open-mindedness, liberation of thought and enlightenment. Creative power can come through Jophiels energy, insight and guidance.

Metatron

Metatron is known as the "Supernal Teacher." This Angel represents divine intelligence, refined wisdom, miracles and power. The higher realms and dimensions can be accessed with the assistance of Metatron, and you can also connect better to your own Higher Self and intuition within. Metatron can help you achieve wholeness, inner balance and harmony and further connect you to your soul. Metatron is another Archangel who, religiously and historically, was said to have led children safely out of Israel while also preventing Abraham from sacrificing his son. Metatron can therefore aid in communication, healthy and divinely inspired and aligned self- talk- the conversations you have with yourself- and communications with others and the world around.

Metatron also protects and watches over the *Akashic Records*. The Akashic Records are an eternal library existing in the higher planes, responsible for all memories- past, present and future- experience, soul choices, and earth timeline realities.

Raphael

Raphael brings calmness, feelings of peace and connection, connection to yourself, to others and a higher power. This angel is known as the "Holy Healer" and can further assist you in connecting to Mother Earth. Your journey can be enriched through the knowledge and experience of interconnectivity, empathy, compassion and understanding. The concept and understanding of *oneness* comes with the energy of Raphael, as does inner harmony and alignment with your soul. This Angel is also known for their deeply divine and powerful healing energy, which can help you access your own inner healing powers and abilities, and use this as a gift for self and others, if you should so choose. Jophiel teaches that healing can be attained through joy and lightness of spirit. Being in touch with your inner child and finding ways to express yourself creatively can be as equally stimulating as sitting in prayer or meditation for an hour.

Michael

Michael is the embodiment of alchemy, cosmic consciousness, ultimate presence and universal truth. Known as the "Cosmic Leader," and also often referred to as Archangel, Archangel Michael will help you expand your horizons and attract new opportunities to you through patience. "I Am" presence, transmutational, and transformational energies also come through Michael's gifts & blessings. Negativity can be cleared and cleansed and limiting beliefs, blocks and imbalances transcended. Archangel Michael is said to be connected to Jupiter's influence, and Jupiter brings the energy of luck, expansion, optimism and prosperity. Working with the planet Jupiter, with Michael's assistance, can therefore aid in the manifestation of gifts, blessings and abundance. Furthermore, Michael's connection to the divine "I Am" presence is unconditional love in its optimum. Your consciousness can be activated in unique and profound ways in alignment with love, compassion and empathy. He can help strengthen your spirit, increase virtues, righteousness and repentance, and dispel negative energy through love and forgiveness. Michael is said to be the one who communicated with Moses during his Burning Bush spiritual experience!

Raziel

This Angel is the keeper and bringer of "Divine Mysteries." Supreme knowledge of the soul and Spirit, wisdom and universal truth all come under Raziel's realm. Raziel can help you to experience life from a deeply profound and empowering connection to the sacredness of the cosmos, all of life is sacred and there is a mystical- essence to being. Life can be an illusion, for there are multiple realities and frequencies existing simultaneously. We tend to create our own versions of "reality" based upon our beliefs, perceptions and past life experiences. So this Angel can help you see past these illusions and get to the truth of matters- to the divine mystery inherent. Thus the veil of illusion becomes obsolete and you start to come to realize that love is all there is and all there will ever be. Love is the source of creation, and the source of all wisdom, divine insight, and truth. Knowledge, new thoughts and ideas, and creative inspiration can all be brought through Raziel's help. This Angel can also be of great assistance in any school, study or learning situation and experience.

Sandalphon

Sandalphon is the "Sacred Guardian" of the planet and physical earth realm. Sandalphon can help to draw creative power and energy from the planet to assist with planetary healing and evolution. The same can be done for the power within yourself. If you need help with grounding and feel or are in tune with your earth power and presence, or simultaneously if you need to amplify your connection to the divine and higher frequencies with your physical body as a channel (for example, in all sorts of channeling and mediumship work); call on Sandalphon.

This Angel oversees the Seraphim- the highest order of angels which surround the throne of God (and the Goddess!). Hence, abundance, beauty, joy, lightness of spirit, material prosperity, spiritual knowing and awareness, and universal wisdom can all be brought with Sandalphon's energy and presence.

Shamael

Archangel Shamael is the "Divine Guide" who is here to show us how to overcome life's challenges, and appreciate life's blessings, with gratitude. Gratitude and sincerity are two of the main keys to an abundant and beautiful life. When we are thankful, truly thankful for the gifts in our life, our personal power increases. Even the most testing and difficult of times can be a blessing in disguise, or at least make us stronger for better times ahead, and this is what Shamel can help teach. He can assist in filling your heart with joy, bliss and serenity, further loving life in its fullest.

Uriel

Uriel, another Archangel, represents the union of Heaven and Earth made manifest through the great OM, the universal sound of creation. In the beauty of the human heart is a space for a potential marriage between the physical flesh and the Holy or Divine Spirit. We all embody frequencies of being and sound, just like the universe is formed from the sound "OM," therefore it is through the heart where coherence between Heaven and Earth- between Human and Divine, takes place. This can help us to be conduits for the abundance of the Cosmos and for cosmic or universal consciousness. In this respect, Uriel is often referred to as the "Eternal Companion" and can aid in attracting and magnetising your life partner, ideal lover or soulmate to you. Friendships, platonic love bonds, and business or soul mission partners can also be attracted into your life through Uriel's assistance.

Zadkiel

Known as the "Divine Comforter," Zadkiel can aid in spiritual development and help increase feelings and thoughts of gentleness, comfort and charity. This Angel radiates comfort, subtle family and friendship love, and warm feelings, and can therefore help you to do the same. If you are grieving, wounded or simply going through some testing emotions, Zadkiel can help. This Angel has a gentle healing presence and can further help with spiritual healing, self- evolution and development. Intuitive healing can be developed through Zadkiel's power and presence, and the benevolence of spirit and the divine can be learned, and the lessons integrated. He is the Divine Comforter in all its branches and connotations.

Zaphkiel

Zaphkiel inspires us to acts of sacred love, connection and bonding, also governing the second chakra. The sacral chakra relates to all feelings and associations of love, emotional and intimate bonds, and sexuality, thus sacred sex comes under Zaphkiel's realm. This Angel is called the "Sacred Lover" and can greatly assist in all matters of personal and intimate relationships. Issues of shadow and sexuality, sexual empowerment and prowess, and making sure that the people you bond with sexually are on your wavelength and evolved- not toxic and harmful to your energy- can all be addressed and steps to healing and wholeness taken. Divine romance, sacred sexuality and soulmate or twin flame love may arise with Zaphkiel's presence.

Or, you can consciously work with this Angel to attract these experiences into your life. Passion, sensual and/or sexual bliss and connection the divine further link.

The Purpose of Angelic Assistance

Connecting to your angel guides and unseen helpers can help to connect you to your source of personal power and spirit. The self and psyche are complex. Your character is unique and made up of various thoughts, beliefs, feelings, past experiences and memories, and karmic exchanges. Just like spirit animals, your ability to connect with the angels lies in your openness to the subconscious and subtle realms, spiritual and multi dimensional planes of existence. Energy healing isn't just meditation, holistic massage or reiki as some people may like to believe; there are so many ways to access spirit and heal your mind, body, spirit & soul...

Shamanism (Working with Spirit & Mystical Energy)

This has already been touched on lightly. Shamanism is literally defined as an ancient practice of indigenous people characterized by a belief in an unseen world and our connection to Spirit, and spiritual entities. A Shaman is a medicine man or woman, someone who can connect to and channel spirit. The Shaman is a healer, medium, and someone greatly respected due to their connection to the Divine, a higher power, and their spiritual source. Yet, Shamans aren't always respected, or even seen, and this is the problem. You don't have to go so far into one's potential and spiritual source to dismiss, ridicule or insult working for the good of our earth, animals and other human beings. And this is exactly what Shamans do, they connect to Spirit and inner healing abilities to be of benefit to others. The earth-nature, is the main focus and attention of a Shaman's energies and intentions. Everything Shamans and shamanic practitioners & healers do are to help the planet or others in some way. Those who take on the role of the Shaman learn how to channel spirit and healing energy to be of service, there is an immense level of caring, nurturing and stewardship present.

Caring and nurturing are primarily *feminine* qualities. The earth is a *feminine* principle. Recognizing the importance of community, custodianship and looking after our planet, and other animal species, are inherently *feminine* practices. There is a strong emphasis on family and emotional connection, and emotional and spiritual intelligence and maturity. This means that if you have been out of touch with your true self, struggle with intimacy and opening up to others, or simply would like to embody more feminine energy, looking to shamanic culture and practices may be a route. In my experience, it's a powerful route with many beautiful benefits. Being shamanically aware or inclined does not mean you have to leave your home or job and spend the rest of your days meditating on a mountain, or in a monastery. Neither does it mean that you can't enjoy some of the joys and pleasures of western society, technology or your favorite past times. It does, however, portray the importance of returning to your own inner source, inner power, spirit and soul.

Even though Shamanism primarily talks about Spirit and the importance of respecting and caring for nature, soul is another thing which almost 'comes with the package.' For me, the soul makes me think of art, nature, music, beauty, abundance, prosperity, family and friendship, children, love, and community. Soul is the foundation for life and all its wonderful gifts. Linking this to Shamanism, for Shamans- all of the motivations and intentions for their work (actions) is based on the soul, as the soul is the innermost part of our true selves. It extends beyond this lifetime, to our roots, the start of our earth journey, and encompasses all the lessons and karma we have accumulated over its journey. The soul is in essence, timeless. What do you know, to have or live with your soul you need to be in touch with your femininity and emotions. The most soulful people around today are the people who are fearless in connection, the ones who bring through some magical vibration, special frequency or unique belief or viewpoint. They do this through art, music, song, dance, invention, innovation, or any other spiritual channel. Shamans frequently love expressing themselves through song, dance, tribal gatherings round a fire, and craft activities. Although they purposefully connect to Spirit, *soul* is still very much present.

The whole point of looking at Shamanic principles is to determine the differences between masculine and feminine energies, providing a *bridge* in the process. The Shaman is a bridge to unseen worlds, subtle levels of being, and a spiritual knowing and power. As we all have shamanic roots through our connection to the earth we could say that it is time society caught up. It is time to step into our power, divine masculinity *and* divine feminity, and learn from some of the teachings that have been in play for thousands of years. We are not just hunter-gatherers, fighting for survival, fighting for mates and fighting to have our physical needs met. We are empathic, soulful and emotional beings with capabilities of higher emotional functioning, also able to adopt the values many women naturally take on, through their caring and nurturing roles. Again, Shamanic principles are not solely associated with the female principle, but they are rooted in dreamwork, a connection to subtle energy and the subconscious. These are all associated with feminine energy! Mystical energy is shamanic energy. It comes from the same source, the same Spirit, and the same benevolent universal power.

As shamanism stems back to the start of our earth journey, shamanic practices range from the practices adopted from our ancestors who learned directly from Spirit, to the teachings passed on today. Despite what many sources may say there is no right or wrong shamanism and many of the Shamanic Practitioners, Masters, Teachers and Healers have received their gifts and healing abilities directly from those aligned; those who have also trained with real Shamans. This is the basis of shamanic initiation- how people become shamans, and the basis of shamanic practices. They receive their wisdom, gifts and abilities through those trained and attuned to the correct lineage. A 'lineage' refers to any branch of shamanism originating directly from the Earth, Spirit or the Divine, rooted in community and connection to the land.

Core Shamanic Healing Techniques

Ceremony

Ceremonies involve creating a sacred space for you to connect to your own source of spiritual power. Ceremony allows you to 'go within,' connecting to your inner source, the divine, Spirit, and your true nature. The core of the self can provide insight, wisdom, guidance and life direction, or help you align with a new way of being or new life path, also releasing all which no longer serves your highest potential and greatest joy. Ceremony is intrinsic to shamanism and is often used in harmony with music, song, and dance, or with the burning of sacred herbs and plant medicine journeys.

Healing Self or Others

Being a channel for healing energy is not exclusive to shamanism, however is an intrinsic part of it. Healing energy is universal and has many names; chi, qi, life force energy, reiki, source energy, or simply spirit. Healing power comes from the energy of the earth and natural forces, just like the sun shines to provide health, vitality, passion and zest for life, and the moon's silent rays synchronize women's cycles while allowing us access to the subconscious. Healing self and others is itneral to shamanic philosophy. Advanced practitioners are so self-mastered they can heal others, or the planet as a whole, through their natural vibration and frequency alone!

Healing the Earth

Chi- the universal life force energy- can also be channeled to help heal the earth. Shamans frequently engage in planetary service and earth healing practices. The outlets are many... They may sit in meditation, prayer or ceremony to send their intentions out, or they work daily through physical chores and practices to contribute to the earth's healing. They recognize that planet earth is a living, conscious, and interconnected organism. They sense, feel, see, smell and hear with the heart. Gaia consciousness is strong and integrated for people of shamanic culture and origin. Shamanic people know that the well-being of the planet, of Gaia, affects them (us) and vice versa.

Divination

Divination is connecting to the divine in some way. It involves the seeking of wisdom, universal knowledge, becoming aware of past, present and future, and, again, connecting to your inner spirit. In terms of mindfulness divination is a powerful tool for leading a healthy, creative, productive and successful happy life. Divination involves the use of herbs and plants, crystals and gemstones, spiritual tools and channeling, meditation and mediumship.

Channeling and Mediumship

Shamans can become a channel for divine power and spirit to flow through. They can connect with dream states and subtle energy from other worlds, which presents itself as wisdom and guidance. They may channel actual spirits, deceased loved ones or elders who have passed, or channel the spirit and consciousness of something greater; such as Gaia (the spirit of Mother Earth) or the cosmos itself. Alternatively channeling can be done to enhance their own clairvoyant and seer-like powers within. This way, it becomes a way to *raise their vibration* and align with the shamanic soul and way. In terms of mediumship, many shamanic practitioners and shamans alike do have extraordinary powers; advanced psychic abilities, precognition, empathy and telepathy.

Trance/Altered States of Consciousness

Through drumming and music shamans can enter altered states of consciousness. The purpose of this is for any of the reasons shared above (divinity, spiritual alignment, healing etc.). Also, plant medicines are a traditional aspect of shamanism, specifically cannabis, peyote, san pedro, and ayahuasca, to name a few. With drumming, one enters a trance state and merges with the rhythm of the universe- the drum beat becomes a *universal heartbeat* attuned to the frequency of Gaia.

Holding Space

As we evolve we need to make difficult transitions. These transitions can be done alone, or they can be done with help. When we help each other and as we evolve through difficult transitions, we call this '*holding space.*' Holding space means keeping a safe emotional, spiritual and physical environment for everyone doing work at a specific energetic frequency. These unique frequencies are physical and energetic environments created specifically for healing, self- reflection and personal self- discovery and evolution. For example, sitting in a circle, meditation or ceremony together. Holding space means not judging, not offering advice, not making suggestions, and not talking unnecessarily except for some intuitive and heartfelt guidance. It implies *active listening*. It also means holding physical and emotional safe space, providing a nurturing and platonically loving environment for friends, family or other people in your community to align with their true nature.

To get in touch with one's true core requires patience, compassion and understanding. It also requires the wisdom and higher guidance that comes with someone who has the ability to connect to their own source of personal power, for self and for others. This is the essence of holding space. What it looks like is lots of eye contact, matching breathing, head nodding, and reassuring gestures. Body language and movement, and a general aura of understanding and compassion, are essential. The best way to visualize holding space is to see yourself or another as a channel or chalice. In this channel is pure light- we are essentially made of light. How holding space works is through the space holder being consciously mindful to commit to being in their divine light, in their highest possible potential. This is why the terms *frequency* and *vibration* are often used in holding space, and too in many spiritual practices and metaphysical topics. The space holder is choosing to commit to holding and embodying a certain frequency in order to be a catalyst for another person's healing, evolution or emotional release.

Being able to hold space is not something everyone can do, however the one common factor in everyone I know who can hold space is that they all do their own work. They all meditate, do yoga or Tai Chi, or have some other spiritual practice they do daily. There is an almost awe-inspiring sense of *devotion and dedication* to those who align with a space holding role- they are gifted with qualities of service and selflessness.

The brilliant and beautiful thing is that *everyone* has the capability to hold space. You have most likely already done it at some point in your life! Perhaps you have been intently listening to a friend in need and your deeply empathic and caring side has shone through? Or, you may have naturally found yourself shifting your posture to something upright, strong and centered, and compassionately authoritative, all the while projecting thoughts of patience and wanting to be there and listen for their benefit. This is one of the keys with holding space; *intention*. People who have mastered the art of holding space and do it consciously- either through being a regular gem in loved one's daily lives, or through actively commiting to a healing path; are aware of the power of their intentions and *subtle thoughts*. All thoughts emit frequencies, what we think, believe and perceive projects outwards affecting time and space. Holding space relies a lot on physical body language and presence, but also on your energetic vibration.

A quick recap on energy, frequency and vibration

Energetic vibration is a term used to describe the holistic nature of the human system. It may not be used in traditional science, however biology, physiology and chemical structures and not that separate from energy or vibration, in essence. Your energetic vibration is the encompassing embodiment of your thoughts, beliefs, physical health, mental health and well being, emotional health and well being, and spiritual health and well being. Health can almost be equated with frequency as everything has a frequency, the universe is fundamentally sound waves, so every living organism can be measured in the frequencies and vibrations emitted. This is why people in the modern world often say someone has a 'good vibe,' or a 'bad vibe.' We literally give off vibrations. If any one of your bodies- mental, emotional, physical or spiritual, are in a bad frequency or bad state of health, this affects your overall vibration. There are many various exchanges and interplays that can affect your vibration.

Some of these are:-

- You suffer from mental health, so your mood is affected. This in turn affects the cells in your body and your physical well being, having an overall impact on your spiritual state of health and inner harmony.

- You suffer from low moods and imbalanced or disruptive emotions. This causes stress in both your body and mind, each one perpetuating the other.
- You suffer from recurring and unhealed physical ailments, diseases or problems, which affect your mental well being, emotional health and spiritual self.
- You suffer from spiritual disconnection, feelings and thoughts of separation, and an inability to connect to your higher self. Your mind, emotions and body are affected as a result.

As you can see, the mind-body-spirit system is complex and intrinsically connected. Neglecting one area is sure to affect the others.

So in terms of *holding space* this means that working to improve any one of your systems can lead to healing, harmony and health in the others, thus positively impacting your overall vibration. Your emotional frequency can change, helping you to feel more connected to others and the world around, and your mental frequency can evolve to assist in many areas of life. Your inner spirit also becomes stronger which allows you to hold more light and be a conduit for yourself and others. "Channeling" is a term connected to space holding and being able to connect to higher, cosmic and divine energies. Channeling involves being gifted and evolved spiritually and on a psychic level, but it also links to physical reality and themes more down-to-earth. (*Refer back to the '4 Clairs' in Energy Healing Techniques Book 1.*)

Being able to hold space for others and Channel *divine knowledge, wisdom, compassion and intuitive guidance* is arguably one of the highest and most advanced forms of energy healing. It is something shamans, energy workers, spiritual masters, and reiki practitioners do, and can be developed by yourself through the variety of *psychic development, spiritual protection, and self-healing and vibration-raising energy healing techniques* shared throughout these books. ✧

BONUS Chapter: Guided Meditation

There is a magnitude of information, research, and scientific studies available on the web to support and validate the areas explored below. Experience through *feeling* and actually connecting to life-enhancing techniques and exercises is something which holds more power than self-educating yourself on the endless research available today. However, it is useful to be aware that there are numerous studies out there to support metaphysical findings. For this reason, we have included just a few studies as evidence/proof (otherwise this would read as a scientific research book!). The key to healing is about *connection and active engagement.* If you are feeling particularly left- brain and analytical, you can always research the science of meditation and mindfulness in your own time. For many people, seeing is believing; yet, for someone emotionally, mentally and spiritually open with such a heightened sense of sensitivity to the subtle world of energy (which comes with expanding your consciousness and improving yourself), and an intrinsic *knowing* (which comes with educating and "knowing thyself"), a lot of this can come naturally to you.

1. *Mindfulness*: A study demonstrated by Harvard University showed how mindfulness can lead to positive change in the brain in depressed people.[2] ("Harvard researchers study how mindfulness may change the brain in depressed patients," 2019). There has been much research conducted into mindfulness to show the range of benefits and effects in a number of different health areas. Overcoming depression and other mental health issues, of course, leads to greater empowerment and manifestation abilities!

2. *Mantras/Affirmations*: An article shared by *Psychology Today* shows how affirmations, which are similar to mantras, can change neurological activity in the brain and thus have a positive effect on mood, emotions and levels of thought and perception.[3] ("To Affirm or Not Affirm?," 2019)

---

[2] Harvard researchers study how mindfulness may change the brain in depressed patients. (2019). Retrieved from https://news.harvard.edu/gazette/story/2018/04/harvard-researchers-study-how-mindfulness-may-change-the-brain-in-depressed-patients/

[3] To Affirm or Not Affirm?. (2019). Retrieved from https://www.psychologytoday.com/gb/blog/embodied-wellness/201704/affirm-or-not-affirm

3. ***Sound***: A fascinating study shared by the *National Center for Biotechnology Information* found that sound waves and mantras increased plant growth and also had a positive effect on human beings.[4] (Karnick, 2019)

4. ***Energy/chi***: *Stanford Medicine* (Stanford University) actually conducted a study with Tai Chi Master to test the validity of chi and the results led one of the research associate's to state "it was fascinating," after finding that 'Master Li' possessed the ability to control his own body temperature. Furthermore, the effects of chi were shown directly on a thermography magnetic resonance imaging responsible for measuring biophysical changes.[5] ("Tai chi master studied for power to control body," 2019).

For this guided meditation, you may want to record yourself speaking it in a calm voice. Speak it as if you are taking someone else on a guided

[4] Karnick, C. (2019). EFFECT OF MANTRAS ON HUMAN BEINGS AND PLANTS. Retrieved from https://www.ncbi.nlm.nih.gov/pmc/articles/PMC3336746/
[5] Tai chi master studied for power to control body. (2019). Retrieved from https://med.stanford.edu/news/all-news/2008/05/tai-chi-master-studied-for-power-to-control-body.html

meditation journey, with *healing* and *helpfulness* as your intention.

Accessing Heart Power Guided Meditation

Please make sure you are in a comfortable position, either inside with a sacred space surrounding you, cushions and a warming environment, or outside in nature. If choosing to perform this meditation outside, to connect to the elemental energies, make sure you are comfortable and won't be disturbed. Feel grounded and safe in your environment and potentially burn some incense, sage or frankincense, light some candles and put on some background music. As this is deeply transformative and empowering meditation, music can really aid in your journey. Nature sounds such as gently running water- like the ocean waves or light rain- can help you connect to your source of intuition, emotional wisdom, and psychic or spiritual gifts. These all come with accessing your heart power naturally. Tibetan singing bowls, bells or chimes can also be effective and send you into a deeper journey, as can meditation music with binaural beats. 528Hz is known as the "love frequency," so this can be played in the background to assist in your meditation.

Start to take some deep breaths and become relaxed in your body. Your body is a divine vessel, it holds your emotions, thoughts, beliefs, perspectives, imaginative and creative gifts and abilities, your spirit and your soul. Life is sacred, so you are sacred. Breathe easy now and begin to feel the universal life force energy flowing through your body.... This guided meditation aims to bring deep peace and send you into a trance-like state. Don't worry- you will be fully conscious and aware. You will also be connected to your body and be able to feel your heart as the powers of the meditation increase. Your heart is strongly associated with the heart chakra, the energy portal responsible for all feelings and expressions of love, compassion, empathy, love and respect for nature, and self- love which helps you thrive in all areas of life. When you have a healthy and open-heart chakra you can succeed in all you put your mind to. Relationships can thrive, new opportunities in harmony and alignment with your best self can come to you, and your personal powers of manifestation and abundance attraction can amplify. Continue to breathe mindfully and set a brief intention to connect to your heart center.

Now, begin to visualize a warm, gently glowing and beautiful green light surrounding your heart chakra or heart center. You know this light is beautiful because it has a healing energy to it- it is healing energy. Green is the color associated with the heart chakra, as green is the color symbol of nature and the natural world. The universe and its energies are magical and almost- mystical things... we exist in a world of color, frequency and vibration, and we ourselves are also created from color, frequency and vibration. There is a reason why the term for enlightenment is called enlightenment; it is the embodiment and realization of light. You, dear child of the universe, are made of light. You are from the stars, yet you are at one with this earth, this physical realm and your sacred vessel. Your body is a channel and conduit for light, color and consciousness, so what stories do you want to fill yourself with?

Momentarily bring your awareness to the ground or earth below you. Picture Gaia's roots spiraling down into the core of the planet... see the waters from the skies washing down into the earth, merging water and air with earth... finally, visualize the pulsing heartbeat of the sun shining warmth and light into the earth and the roots of the trees. You are an ancient memory; you contain ancient memory in the core of your cells. Begin to breathe more deeply now, as if the air flowing through you is coming directly down from the skies or heavens and into the leaves and trunk of an ancient oak, or other majestic- like tree. You are strong and grounded like a tree and you are also at one with the earth; you are completely connected. Take a moment to picture a beautiful, strong, sturdy and ancient tree rooted in the earth, with air surrounding and the sun shining down on it. Perhaps see the moon and her energies glimmering faintly in the background. How do you feel right now? Do you feel strong, calm and at ease...? Perhaps you feel grounded, ancient and powerful- as if you yourself hold great power? Both are true. You are a divine channel connected to the earth and the sky, fire and water, earth and air. You are also a source of great manifestation abilities.

Take 4 deep breaths. With each breath, see the beautiful green light growing in and around your heart. This light might be a golden- green and, if it is, this is perfect too. Gold is the color of cosmic and universal consciousness; it is the color for gold in its physical representation and manifestation. Gold symbolizes abundance, money, wealth and prosperity. What does prosperity mean to you? Is it love, friendship, laughter and connection? Perhaps it's money, material bliss and comfort, financial prosperity and resources? Or, maybe prosperous abundance may be new opportunities, creative pathways and doors, and connecting to your own talents, gifts and abilities? Whatever the manifestation and intention, see this golden- green or green light emanating around and from your heart. It is energizing both the ether, the astral body surrounding you and extending beyond your physical body; and the internal energies flowing through you. Your heart is powerful- you are powerful. You are a powerful being of light, spirit, soul and divinity, and it is from this place of power where everything flows to you. Continue to see this light and feel chi, the universal life force, flowing through your veins, heart and entire body.

We are quickly nearing the end of this meditation, but your journey is just beginning. This energetic space you are in does not end when this voice does. This guidance is merely a reflection of your own inner spirit, your own soul and your own subconscious mind. The knowledge, wisdom and power residing inside of you has always been there and will always be- just like the ancient oak grounded and rooted. Your capacity to manifest anything your heart desires originates from this space. Elemental energies flow through you... the sun and moon are both always present to guide you.... The trees and plants of this earth will always be here to speak to you, and provide you the direction and wisdom you need... And, the light which flows through all living things, the universe and yourself, is always ready and available to be tuned in to. Your heart is the source; it is conscious breathing, mindful awareness, and going within to find this stillness and silence where manifestation arises. Everything starts from nothing and you are a powerful creator.

When you are ready you can begin to open your eyes. Take note of the earth and air around you, and the sun or moon shining down on you. Feel the physical body that gives you life and do a little shake. Say thank you- to yourself, the universe and whichever higher power you believe in. You are divine, you are powerful, and you have an extraordinary ability to manifest anything your heart, soul, mind and spirit desire.

(You can now turn off this audio.)

Afterword

If you've enjoyed reading this book, be sure to check out the other books in our Spiritual, Metaphysical & Healing series.

Amazon Page (link)

✪

"Holding on to anything is like holding on to your breath. You will suffocate. The only way to get anything in the physical universe is by letting go of it. Let go & it will be yours forever."

~Deepak Chopra